FRIENDS IN SCHOOL
Patterns of Selection and Influence in Secondary Schools

Contributors

Jere Cohen
Elizabeth Douvan
Joyce Levy Epstein
Maureen T. Hallinan
Stephen Hansell
Nancy Karweit
Norman Miller
Robert E. Slavin

FRIENDS IN SCHOOL

Patterns of Selection and
Influence in Secondary Schools

Edited by

JOYCE LEVY EPSTEIN
NANCY KARWEIT

The Johns Hopkins University
Center for Social Organization of Schools
Baltimore, Maryland

 1983

ACADEMIC PRESS
A Subsidiary of Harcourt Brace Jovanovich, Publishers
New York   London
Paris   San Diego   San Francisco   São Paulo   Sydney   Tokyo   Toronto

ACADEMIC PRESS, INC.
111 Fifth Avenue, New York, New York 10003

United Kingdom Edition published by
ACADEMIC PRESS, INC. (LONDON) LTD.
24/28 Oval Road, London NW1   7DX

Library of Congress Cataloging in Publication Data
Main entry under title:

Friends in school.

   Includes bibliographical references and index.
   1. High school students--United States--Attitudes--
Addresses, essays, lectures.   2. Friendship--
Addresses, essays, lectures.   3. Interpersonal
attraction--Addresses, essays, lectures.   4. Cohort
analysis--Addresses, essays, lectures.
5. Interaction analysis in education--Addresses,
essays, lectures.   6. Academic achievement--
Addresses, essays, lectures.   I. Epstein, Joyce Levy.
II. Karweit, Nancy L.   [DNLM: 1. Child development.
2. Interpersonal relations.   3. Students--Psychology.
4. Schools--Organization and administration.
5. Psychology, Social--In infancy and childhood.
WS 105.5.15   F905]
LB1117.F728   1983   373.18'1   82−22822
ISBN 0−12−240540−4

PRINTED IN THE UNITED STATES OF AMERICA

83 84 85 86   9 8 7 6 5 4 3 2 1

Contents

INTRODUCTION AND OVERVIEW

1   JOYCE LEVY EPSTEIN
Friends among Students in Schools:
Environmental and Developmental Factors   **3**

                                                                            v

□□

THEORETICAL PERSPECTIVES

□□□

CLASSROOM AND SCHOOL ORGANIZATION
AND THE SELECTION PROCESS

$$\boxed{\text{IV}}$$

SCHOOL ORGANIZATION AND THE INFLUENCE PROCESS

$$\boxed{\text{V}}$$

CONCLUSION

Contributors

Numbers in parentheses indicate the pages on which the authors' contributions begin.

Jere Cohen (163), Department of Sociology, University of Maryland, Baltimore, Maryland 21201

Elizabeth Douvan (63), Institute for Social Research, Survey Research Center, University of Michigan, Ann Arbor, Michigan 48104

Joyce Levy Epstein (3, 39, 73, 177, 235), The Johns Hopkins University Center for Social Organization of Schools, and Department of Social Relations, The Johns Hopkins University, Baltimore, Maryland 21218

Maureen T. Hallinan (219), Department of Sociology, University of Wisconsin—Madison, Madison, Wisconsin 53706

Stephen Hansell (29, 93, 115, 141), Department of Sociology, Rutgers University, New Brunswick, New Jersey 08903

Nancy Karweit (29, 115, 131, 141), The Johns Hopkins University Center for Social Organization of Schools, Baltimore, Maryland 21218

Norman Miller (201), Department of Psychology, University of Southern California, Los Angeles, California 90089

Robert E. Slavin (93), The Johns Hopkins University Center for Social Organization of Schools, and Department of Social Relations, The Johns Hopkins University, Baltimore, Maryland 21218

Preface

This collection of research and commentaries emphasizes the connections between the *social organization* of schools and classrooms, the *social processes* of peer association and friendship selection and influence, and the *social development* of students. The unique feature of this volume is its emphasis on the simultaneous influence of developmental and environmental factors on adolescent friendships. The contributing sociologists and psychologists recognize the importance of the structural characteristics of the social contexts in which interactions take place, as well as the importance of the ages and characteristics of the students who interact.

Combining developmental and environmental perspectives in the examination of youngsters' friendship is, we think, a useful approach that can profitably be extended to other research in socialization, adolescence, and school effects. Clearly, sociologists interested in the structural effects of schools on students will benefit from a better appreciation of developmental differences. Just as clearly, psychologists interested in developmental changes will benefit from a better appreciation of how environmental and contextual influences impinge on student development.

The main sections of the book are devoted to three topics of traditional interest in peer group research—theory, selection, and influence. Following an introduction and overview in Part I, the chapters in Part II discuss sociological, social psychological, and psychological theories of school organization and of interpersonal attraction and selection that may be useful in studies of youngsters' friendships. The next two sections present empirical studies and commentaries about the selection of friends in schools and classrooms and their influence on each other. Because most prior research focused primarily on individual characteristics of students and their friends, there has been little systematic information on how the organization of schools and settings within schools affect the selection and influence processes. The chapters in each section focus on three aspects of school organization—school offerings, classroom instruction, and the demographic characteristics of the student population—and how they influence the nature and frequency of student contact and the selection and influence of friends.

The book should be useful to sociologists and psychologists who conduct research on socialization, adolescence, school and classroom environmental effects, internal processes in desegregated schools, and, of course, friendship formation and peer group processes. The book should be useful also to educators who need to understand how specific, manipulable features of schools and classrooms affect the formation and use of student peer and friendship groups in school.

This volume is one response to a recent challenge to researchers to focus on developmental issues in children's friendships. We offer new information on selection and influence processes across the years from preadolescence to adolescence, when strong peer group ties are developed and when friends are assumed to be gaining in influence. We hope this volume will be a genuine impetus to new research on developmental *and* environmental effects on patterns of peer association.

ACKNOWLEDGMENTS

Many of the empirical studies reported here originated as part of the work of the School Organization Program at the Johns Hopkins University Research and Development Center for Social Organization of Schools (COS), with programmatic support from the Teaching and Learning Division of the National Institute of Education (NIE). We appreciate the encouragement and guidance we received from the monitors of our NIE grants over several years, but no official endorsement by the NIE of the authors' perspectives or conclusions should be inferred.

The authors of many chapters are indebted to the individuals who provided information on themselves, their families, their schools, and their friends. Without the cooperation of students, teachers, and administrators, research in the schools would not be possible.

We are very grateful to James M. McPartland and Edward L. McDill for their participation in the research that provided the data used in many of these chapters and for their continued support and suggestions to our program of research. We appreciate our colleagues at CSOS who critiqued early presentations of this research at several Center seminars, and especially John H. Hollified—the editors' editor—for his patient and perceptive reading of the manuscript. We wish to thank Barbara Hucksoll, Hazel Kennedy, Mary R. Butler, Janet Guest, and Karen Swasey for their invaluable assistance in the preparation of the manuscript.

FRIENDS IN SCHOOL

Patterns of Selection and
Influence in Secondary Schools

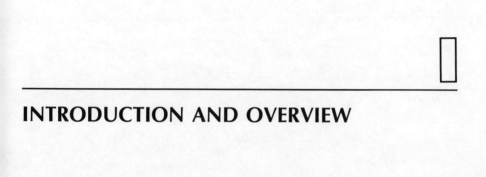

INTRODUCTION AND OVERVIEW

JOYCE LEVY EPSTEIN 1

Friends among Students in Schools: Environmental and Developmental Factors

SCHOOL ORGANIZATION AND FRIENDS IN SCHOOL

There is a difference between studying schoolchildren's friendships and studying friends in school. The former has been a topic of research for about half a century, the latter for about half a decade. In studies of schoolchildren's friendships, researchers have examined youngsters' concepts of friendship, the functions of friendship, the number and characteristics of friends, the similarities and differences among friends, and the influence of friends on each other. In studies of friends in school, researchers focus on how the school environment affects the concepts and functions of friendship, friendship choices, and the influence of friends. Studies of children's friendships examine how friends aid the development of the individuals' social skills; studies of friends in school examine the kinds of social competencies that are required by the school environment and the organized opportunities that schools provide for students to develop social skills.

At the same time that youngsters are developing a sense of self from their own reactions to events and from the reactions they receive from others, they also are learning about the demands for social behavior from the settings in which they work and play. In school they learn what behaviors are valued and what kinds of social interactions are rewarded by their teachers and by their peers. For example, in different schools and classrooms, cross-sex friendships may be required, re-

3

FRIENDS IN SCHOOL
Patterns of Selection and Influence in Secondary Schools

warded, or ridiculed by teachers or peers by the ways that activities, assignments, and projects are organized. Schools and classrooms within schools differ also in their emphasis on cooperative behaviors. Students may be praised or punished for helping each other. Cross-race interactions and multiability friendships are encouraged, discouraged, or ignored by the ways that groups of students are distributed in classrooms and by the ways that learning and social activities are organized. Thus, there are many ways that schools determine which students come into contact with each other. When the organization arranges and rearranges student contacts, it structures students' social relations and affects students' opportunities to make friends.

This book adds information to the literature on schoolchildren's friendships, but its major aim is to introduce new ideas and to stimulate more research on friends in school. Across chapters, sociologists and social psychologists elaborate the theme that the opportunities, demands, and restrictions of school environments can alter patterns of association among students. The ways schools and classrooms are organized affect who makes friends and how friends influence each other.

We can imagine dramatically different classroom organizations that could influence the acquaintance process and the friends that students make in school. For example, think of one junior high school where students are assigned to classrooms on the basis of achievement test scores. The teachers use the lecture method and prevent students from working together to think about or to complete their academic assignments. Social relations are left up to the students, but the school's organization of tracking students by ability affects patterns of interaction and friendship choice. In contrast, there is another junior high school where students are assigned to heterogeneous classrooms in which the emphasis is on learning in pairs, small groups, or teams. The teachers expect the students to work on projects together. The composition of the work groups changes with some frequency, so students have opportunities to interact with and learn from most of the students in the class over the course of the term. The teacher and the students in each class find many ways to recognize and reward the different skills and talents of all of the students as they contribute to projects. Social relations are left up to the students, but the organization of the curricular tasks, rewards, and decisions about schoolwork affect patterns of interaction and friendship choice by arranging interactions for academic purposes.

In these two hypothetical classrooms (and there are many variations on the theme), students' social contacts and the rewards for interactions in class are very different. In both classrooms, the teachers may state the same academic goals (to improve students' academic skills) and the same social goals (to improve students' social competence, communication skills, leadership and decision-making skills). In each classroom, the educational program has been purposely organized to advance students' academic abilities, even though the teachers use very different methods of instruction. However, in only one of the examples has the educational program been purposely organized to provide opportunities for advancing students social skills.

All schools have expectations for students' academic and social behavior (Dreeben, 1968; Magnusson, Duner, & Zetterblom, 1975). Social skills that often are specified as goals of schooling include respect for the rights of others, listening well, participating in group activities, and showing leadership. These skills—often graded on report cards—are observed by teachers, but they are rarely the result of the design of the academic program. Yet, as our examples suggest, the social organization of schools and classrooms could assist the development of acceptance, tolerance, leadership, and friendship among students who might not ordinarily work together in school.

Social relations are what sociology is about. We study groups in social contexts to learn about the effects of the environment on group behavior, and we study the effects of the environment and the group on individuals' attitudes and achievements. When it comes to students' friends in school, however, we have very few studies that clarify how the characteristics of individuals, groups, and school and classroom environments affect the development and changes in students' social relations. How do school environments help students develop satisfying social relations? What organizational features create the greatest appreciation of others' skills and talents? What environmental characteristics create the least tolerance and most restricted acceptance of other students? Can schools (and should schools) widen and deepen the basis on which friends are chosen?

It is not true that a school is a school is a school. The organization of school programs, of student placement in programs, and of methods of instruction differ across schools in ways that may be particularly important for patterns of peer association and friendship selection. In this volume, research focuses on three important aspects of organizations that differ in schools: the organization of curricular and extracurricular programs; the organization of classroom teaching and learning; and the distribution of students to settings from identifiable subgroups. Each of these is a manipulable or alterable organizational feature that is under the control of administrators and teachers. Each may be important for the attainment of the academic and social goals that educators set for their students. Differences in the organization of school offerings, classroom instruction, and distribution of students are examined for their effects on patterns of peer association, friendship selection, or influence of friends on students' achievements, attitudes, and behaviors.

ORGANIZATION OF SCHOOL OFFERINGS

The organization of school offerings includes whether and how the academic program is divided into curricular or ability tracks, and whether and how extracurricular activities are available.

Curricular Offerings

Tracking and grouping practices affect patterns of peer association by extending or restricting boundaries that give more or fewer students access to each other in academic classes (J. S. Coleman, 1959; Parsons, 1959). For example, some schools have *fixed* track placements based on ability. Once a student is in a particular track (college preparatory, vocational, business, general, or some other), it is not always easy or possible to change tracks. Preliminary courses may have been missed or prerequisite skills may have been incompletely covered, putting students who change tracks at a disadvantage in competing with other students for passing grades. Some schools have *permeable* track assignments. In this type of organization, courses are offered to assist students to work their way into more appropriate tracks on the basis of improved abilities or newly developed goals.

Track placements within schools affect the types of peer associations that occur during schooltime. Schools may organize tracking or grouping procedures for educational purposes—to make teaching and learning less stressful, for example—but these features of the school organization also establish physical and philosophical boundaries within which students conduct social relations. The organization of curricular offerings can set real limits on peer association, attitudes toward students in different tracks, and likely choices of friends in school.

Extracurricular Offerings

Outside of the regular academic program, some schools offer many extracurricular activities and other schools offer only a few. The extracurricular activities may have few or many prerequisites for participation, and these may be more or less based on academic ability, success in school, or other student characteristics. Extracurricular offerings that build upon already well-established skills (such as writing, intermural sports, or singing) will create different groups of participants from those that introduce new skills to students without previous training in similar skills. The composition of the groups created by different kinds of extracurricular activities will affect the status and reward systems that guide the groups' activities and the kinds of interactions among peers that lead to more or fewer friendships, and similar or dissimilar friends.

Other aspects of the school organization can affect the participants in extracurricular activities. For example, the school may offer extracurricular activities during the schoolday (as an activity or club period), before school, or after school, and may or may not provide transportation for students who live far from the school. These coincident features of the school's organization will affect who participates in extracurricular activities and, thereby, the contacts students make and the friends they select from the extracurricular settings.

In effect, the organization of both the curricular and extracurricular programs lock students in or out of opportunities for peer association during most of the schoolday.

ORGANIZATION OF CLASSROOMS

In this volume, classroom organization refers to manipulable structures that directly affect teaching, learning, and student social relations. These include the teachers' organization of the authority, task, and reward structures. These characteristics of instructional programs in classrooms determine the students' roles in decision making, the rewards for behavior and academic progress, and the activities they are expected to complete. The structural variables influence patterns and purposes of student contact and interactions.

For example, some schools and some teachers within schools give students many opportunities to make academic decisions about their courses and about many other aspects of conducting and completing their work in class. Other schools place all authority for academic decisions in the hands of administrators and teachers; all courses are required, and teachers direct all aspects of class work. If a teacher assigns seats to students and does not permit them to walk around or ask each other for help, the students have little control over whom they interact with during class time. Bossert (1979) suggests that seating arrangements affect elementary school students' playtime friends, and Byrne (1961b) reports that seating arrangements affect college students' choices of friends. Similarly, if a teacher gives students authority over which activities they will work on during class, where they will sit, and with whom they will work, then the students' interests and not the teacher's demands are likely to determine the peers with whom students interact and the friends they select.

Decision-making structures are central in studies of school organization (Bidwell & Kasarda, 1980; Corwin, 1965), and student decision making is an important part of the process (Blau, 1979; De Charms, 1968; Eckstein & Gurr, 1975; Epstein, 1981; McPartland & Epstein, 1977; Schonfeld, 1971; Tjosvold, 1978; Wang & Stiles, 1976). In this volume, we examine student participation in classroom decisions for its effects on patterns of peer association and selection of friends. If students share responsibility for their own efforts, progress, and success—if they are required to make decisions about when to work alone, when to work with a friend or with a group on projects or assignments, or when to discuss work with others—they must use different social skills than students who must always follow teachers' directions and may talk only with teachers about their work. The level of student decision making should affect how often students interact with each other, how well they get to know other students, how leadership is expressed, and what competencies students recognize and value in each other.

The task and reward structures that teachers use to organize their classrooms determine the kinds of assignments and activities on which children can interact, how students treat each other as workers and sources of knowledge, and how teachers reward few or many students for individual or group efforts. Some schools stress competition among students for admission to tracks, courses, and classes; in their daily work; and in the grades they receive. Other schools stress cooperation among students in group projects, study and learning teams, helping behaviors, and social activities. Most schools are organized around some mixture of competition and cooperation, but the emphasis on one or the other is reflected in the task and reward structures in classrooms. The task structure (Bidwell, 1972; Bossert, 1979; Slavin & Karweit, 1982) and the reward structure (Aronson, 1978; Berndt, forthcoming; DeVries & Edwards, 1973; D. W. Johnson & Johnson, 1975; Slavin, 1980a) will influence patterns of peer association and exchange.

Different reward systems may have disadvantages as well as advantages. French, Brownell, Graziano, and Hartup (1977) and La Gaipa (1981) suggest that one can push cooperative activities beyond the point that encourages cooperative behavior and actually discourage potential friendships among students who help each other. A tutoring program, for example, can result in greater dependence and subordination of the student who receives help. A competitive situation can increase the respect of students with closely related skills, make the rewards that are offered more valued, and increase friendships among competing students. Students of different statuses on an important criterion may find it difficult to cooperate unless other classroom structures are altered by the teacher to make cross-status cooperation safe from ridicule by others or self-criticism because of obvious differences among high- and low-status students (E. Cohen, 1980a).

In general, the school environment will be more responsive to students if there are many reasons for which students can receive rewards in school, if the rewards are distributed fairly, and if the rewards are based on real progress that students make rather than on relative standings. The kinds of assignments on which students are asked to compete or cooperate affect how peers interact. A student may consider: Whom should I ask for help in math? Whom should I help or not help? If I help someone, will I be hurting my own chances for academic success? If I help someone, will that person like me or resent me? The answers to these questions will differ depending on whether the students are rivals for a few valued rewards, equal in their receipt of earned rewards, or required by the teacher to cooperate with others to gain recognition and rewards. The ways that schools or classrooms organize students' tasks and the distribution of rewards will affect the kinds of exchanges that occur among peers and the friendships that are made in school.

DISTRIBUTION OF STUDENTS

The organization of student subgroups determines how students are distributed by age, race, ethnicity, or sex in curricular and extracurricular programs and in groups within classrooms. For example, some schools stress the separation of males and females for particular types of courses, classroom assignments and projects, seating arrangements, or extracurricular offerings. Other schools stress the coeducational character of these offerings and placements. Some schools resegregate students in a desegregated school, creating mostly white and mostly black populations in subject classes. Most schools separate students by chronological age into grades and educational levels. A few schools create classes or levels of mixed ages on the basis of the achievement, ability, other developmental characteristics of the students, or students' interests. The demographic features of school organization determine how heterogeneous or homogeneous groups of students are and directly affect which students come into contact, whom they select as friends, and who can be influenced directly by which other students in school.

Schools and classrooms may be organized to encourage or discourage contact of students who are similar or different from each other—to draw students together or to keep them apart. How students perceive, meet, and treat each other and how they choose, refuse, and influence each other may be affected in important ways by how teachers and administrators organize their classrooms and schools. The school organization of academic and extracurricular programs; the classroom organization of authority, task, and reward structures; and the school and classroom demographics are among the important variables that create structures of opportunities for students (Bidwell, 1972). These organizational features not only characterize the individual's academic opportunities for learning and for interacting with the teacher but also structure the social opportunities for peer association and the selection and influence of friends.

REVIEW OF SELECTED STUDIES

A few important, early studies recognized that peer relations and friendship choices are affected by the environment in which they occur. Moreno (1934/1953) hypothesized that choices and rejections of friends will depend on the tasks that group members are required to do. This assumption is related to our expectations that the school tracking and grouping procedures and classroom organization will affect patterns of friendship selection. Students who are leaders at one time, conducting one task in one setting under one system of rewards for behavior, will not necessarily be leaders of new activities when the time, setting, task, rewards, or group members change. Lewin (1931, 1935) influentially drew attention to the importance of the organization of the socializing environments on peer relations. His work is the basis for later attention to decision-making styles (Lewin, Lippitt, & White, 1939) and to our expectation that the classroom authority structure will influence the purpose of peer interaction. Hollingshead (1949) was another early observer of the importance for adolescent development of the way society treats maturing youngsters. Outside the school, the expectations and opportunities in the community for participation in social activities, community service, and occupational training will affect the groups of peers that associate for different purposes.

Despite the early astuteness of Moreno, Lewin, and Hollingshead, few empirical studies have examined how contrasting school and classroom environments affect student friendship choices and patterns of influence. Most early studies of student friendships were conducted in schools and studied school-aged students, but they ignored the school environment.

There was a time when all schools were considered to be about the same in their organization and goals, and researchers did not think it pertinent to study differences in school environments. Research on friends and peers focused mainly on the differences that existed in the sex, race, ability, age, and values of the youngsters and the friends they chose, or on youngsters with different levels of popularity. As the fields of sociology of education, educational psychology, social psychology, and community psychology matured, however, differences between and within schools have been clarified (Bar-Tal, 1978; Brookover, Beady, Hood, Schweitzer, & Wisenbaker, 1979; Epstein & McPartland, 1979; Hurn, 1978; McDill & Rigsby, 1973; McPartland & Epstein, 1977; Minuchin, Biber, Shapiro, & Zimiles, 1969; Rutter, Maughan, Mortimore, & Ouston, 1979; Summers & Wolfe, 1977). The effects of contrasting school and classroom environments on social exchange, patterns of association, selection, and influence are now topics of importance.

In previous research on student friendships, the context of social relations meant the context of the friendship group (cf. for different educational levels, McDill & Rigsby, 1973; Schmuck, 1970; Selman & Jacquette, 1978). Others discuss the situation in which friends find themselves in terms of short exchanges, episodes, and activities that engage youngsters (see examples in Mueller & Cooper, forthcoming). In this book, we extend the definition of *context* to the organization of the environments in which the students and their peers and friends are working. Here, the friendship group is considered one social context within the social organization of the school and classroom environments.

Because our focus is on secondary school environments and students' social relations, we will not review the early studies of young children's friendships that flourished since the 1930s. This literature is reviewed completely in other readily available sources (Berndt, 1982; Clausen, 1968; Glidewell, Kantor, Smith, & Stringer, 1966; Hartup, 1970; Renshaw, 1981), as is the literature on developmental studies of concepts of friendship and stages of friendship (Bigelow & La Gaipa, 1980; La Gaipa, 1981; Mannarino, 1980; Selman, 1976, 1981; Selman & Jacquette, 1978). These two sets of literature have influenced the thinking of the researchers in this volume and are referenced accordingly in the separate chapters.

Three collections illustrate the remarkable increase in research on children's friendship groups between 1975 and 1981. M. Lewis and Rosenblum (1975) included studies of animal and human social relations, and renewed attention to social behavior of infants and the social relations of young children. The research presented in that collection on infant and toddler friendships and the origins of friendships in young children prompted pertinent research in the late 1970s. Their volume raised an important question: What is the impact of specific social and physical contexts on the form and the consequences of peer relations?

Foot, Chapman, and Smith (1980) edited a useful book of reviews on friendship values, acquaintance processes, dynamics of friendship, and friendship cliques. The reflective reviews by researchers in several disciplines can be read profitably for suggestions for new research on social relations of children from infancy to adolescence.

Asher and Gottman's (1981) collection illustrates the importance of cross-disciplinary attention to key theoretical, methodological, and applied questions about friendships at all educational levels. Their chapters present important discussions about group and social–cognitive processes and describe a variety of methods—sociometric, observational, and field experimental—for conducting research on children's friendships and peer relations.

Even in these works, however, there are few new, empirical data. Little attention is given to developmental patterns of selection and influence in friendships from early to late adolescence, and few researchers study the importance of particular organizational characteristics of schools or other socializing settings in which adolescent social relations occur.

Several studies should be mentioned for their pertinent observations or contributions to measuring effects of school or classroom environments on peer relations. The studies were conducted at different educational levels—preschool to college—though rarely across levels and rarely with developmental perspectives. These articles and books are described briefly in terms of the observations, results, and assumptions about environments and social relations that are related to the research reported in this volume.

Nursery School

Clausen (1968) described the heavy emphasis of early peer group research on nursery-school-aged children, but little attention was paid to the nursery school environment or to the organization of the preschool educational programs (see also Renshaw, 1981). Rubin (1980) described two different nursery school environments, one based on structured play activities and one on free play groups. He observed that the structured, teacher-directed activities resulted in a tight-knit single group of peers. The students were, however, in competition for the teacher's attention. The less structured nursery program resulted in many small groups of students, fluid movement of members to new groups, little competition for the teacher's attention, but some competition for membership in different groups. Rubin observed differences in the physical facilities, size of the student population, and teachers' expectations for social behavior in the two settings, but these features were totally confounded at the two sites. All or any combination of these organizational characteristics could have affected the patterns of association that were observed. Asher, Oden, and Gottman (1977), Bianchi and Bakeman, (1977), Charlesworth and Hartup (1967), and Corsaro (1981) also reported different patterns of peer interaction in differently organized nursery school activities. Because nursery school environments often are based on distinct philosophies of education, the range of natural variation in the organization of environments at that educational level should be useful in new studies of environmental effects on friendship choices and influence. Studies in nursery school should provide important initial time frames for developmental studies of peer relations over the years students spend in school.

Elementary School

The most important earlier work on effects of school and classroom organizations on peer relations has been conducted by researchers studying elementary schools and students. In an observational study of four elementary school classrooms, Bossert (1979) followed about 50 students from third grade to fourth grade. The students had teachers each year who organized instruction differently. He observed that teachers who emphasized teacher-centered (lecture) and child-centered (group project) methods of instruction had different definitions of acceptable peer interactions. Among many observations, Bossert reported that homogeneous grouping in highly structured classrooms produced more stable friendships, perhaps because of the similarity among friends in their ability groups. When they changed teachers, the children seemed to accommodate their peer relations, selections, and exclusions to fit the new teacher's ideas on how to select work partners in the classroom. Thus, the teachers' organized activities encouraged the broad or narrow acceptance of other students as friends.

Bossert did not identify the measurable effects on students of the different types of peer groups that formed in the contrasting classrooms he studied. However, his perceptive observations of elementary school students and classrooms raise interesting questions for research in secondary schools. How long are students responsive and malleable in their peer relations when they change teachers? Is there some point from childhood to adolescence that an established friendship group resists changes prompted by classroom organization? Do departmentalized programs in which students change teachers for each academic subject strengthen or weaken friendship group structures? How are peer groups and friendship choices affected if, within the school, the teachers all have different classroom organizations or if the teachers all follow the same school-wide organization that fosters particular types of peer associations?

A very important study of elementary school children's friendships was conducted by Hallinan (1976a). She studied how differently organized upper elementary school classrooms (Grades 4–6) influenced friendship selection, mutuality, asymmetry, and stability of friendship choices. In this early, empirical study, she concluded that, in more open elementary classes, fewer students were isolated from friendship groups and fewer students were stars. Thus, friendships were more equally distributed. In more traditional classrooms, more mutual choices were made. Despite some limitations of the measures in this study, Hallinan made a unique contribution by questioning the generalizability of all previous studies of children's friendships that did not identify the organization of the students' educational environments.

Other studies pointed to important links between school environments and students' social relations (e.g., Guttentag & Longfellow, 1977). In a study of primary grades in elementary schools, Minuchin (1975) reported increases in helpful, cooperative behavior when students were encouraged by the teacher to be helpful and cooperative in class. The logical connections between what a teacher requests, how individual students respond, and how group behavior is affected are not necessarily automatic, however. Hartup, Brady, and Newcomb (1982) found that young children did not expect cooperative behavior from other young children, even when they were told that cooperative efforts of students would be rewarded. Students must be able to understand the conditions for rewards in order to work toward them. There is a critical link between the students' cognitive development, school organization, instructional techniques, and students' social behavior.

In the early 1970s, K. J. Edwards, DeVries, and Snyder (1972) and DeVries and Edwards (1973, 1974) initiated research on the effect of learning teams on peer relations in elementary and secondary school classrooms. They found that cross-race friendships increased when integrated teams that were heterogeneous in ability were organized to conduct academic activities and when each member of a group could contribute equally to the rewards received by the group for improved learning. The use of cooperative and competitive structures has become an important framework for research on peer association, acceptance, helping behavior, and influence on academic and social outcomes.

Secondary School

Three types of studies have influenced new research in the peer relations of secondary school students. These include studies of adolescents, observational and survey studies of school and classroom environments, and studies of selection and influence of friends and peers. Reviews of this literature are presented in other chapters in this volume (Douvan, in Chapter 4; Cohen, in Chapter 10; and Hallinan in Chapter 13). We highlight here the particular studies of adolescents, environments, and association that influenced the questions addressed by the research in this collection.

Adolescents. J. S. Coleman's *The Adolescent Society* (1961) and Douvan and Adelson's *The Adolescent Experience* (1966) were pioneering empirical studies of adolescent values and behaviors. Coleman's research focused attention on the fact that the peer groups of different youngsters emphasize distinct norms and that the social contexts of groups affect individuals' school-related behaviors. The book sparked still active debates over the nature of adolescent subgroups, the reality of adolescent subcultures, and the use of contextual measures of school climates based on aggregated student characteristics.

In 1966, research on adolescents was still in its infancy. Douvan and Adelson presented a psychological interpretation of patterns of peer association that extended Coleman's sociological perspectives on peer groups and subcultures. One

14   Joyce L. Epstein

important contribution of their work was its serious attention to developmental
patterns in students' peer relations, attitudes, values, and family relations across
the high school years, and its detailed analyses of sex differences in these developmental patterns. Neither Coleman's nor Douvan and Adelson's early research
measured the formal organization of the school or the formal or informal organization of teachers' classrooms, but these books made adolescence, peer groups, and
students' friendships respectable and important topics for sociological research
and debate.

Environments.   The early work of Gordon (1957) and later Cusick (1973)
influenced empirical and observational studies of students, peers, and friends in
schools. These researchers used different methods to study a single school, but
they each showed that the peer group is a prominent force in all aspects of high
school life.

McDill, Meyers, and Rigsby (1967) extended interest in school environments
by studying high schools that differed significantly in their academic climate. The
academic climate or press for achievement is one proximal measure of school
programs that should directly affect student behavior and achievement. The initial study, and the extended attention to peer groups by McDill and Rigsby (1973),
showed that models of peer influence could be improved when the actual characteristics of the school environment were measured along with the characteristics
of peers and friends. In their study, data were collected directly from the students'
and their friends. In much previous research, data about friends were summarized by the students, not reported directly by the members of the students'
friendship groups. However, this early research did not make connections between the variations in school climates and patterns of selection of friends, nor did
it address the developmental patterns of selection and influence of peers and
friends across the high school years.

Peer Relations.   C. N. Alexander and Campbell (1964) and E. Campbell and
Alexander (1965) reported convincingly that close friends were stronger influences than peer groups or aggregate school populations. Because conclusions were
based on cross-sectional data, however, the study illustrated why longitudinal data
were needed to examine peer and friendship influences more accurately. The
results continue to be a topic of debate in studies of peers versus friends or the
influence of strong versus weak ties.

The work of J. Cohen (1977) and Kandel (1978) improves Campbell's, Alexander's, and others' earlier research on students in groups by using longitudinal
data to estimate friends' and peers' influence on student behavior. Cohen and
Kandel each showed that the separation of selection and infuence processes was
necessary and possible, and each demonstrated and discussed how cross-sectional
data overestimated friends' or peer influence by confounding prior similarities
with real influence among friends. These two articles are important also for
including outcome measures (e.g., drug and alcohol use and dating behavior) that

may be particularly important in studies of adolescent friendships, in addition to measures of achievement and college plans. However, neither the early Campbell and Alexander research nor the more recent studies by Cohen or by Kandel measured aspects of the school environments in which the students' friendships were made and in which influence occurred, and none presented developmental patterns of selection or influence across the high school years.

College

Early studies of peer relations of college students have had more influence on studies of secondary school peers and friends than have the psychological studies of the social behavior of young children. Most prominent among the early influences was Newcomb's (1961) study of the acquaintance process. His research took into account the sequence of selection and influence of friends in a college residence hall. Changes in students' attitudes over time were charted and related to earlier selections, rejections, and new selections of friends. The similarities among friends and the strength of liking were also found to be important variables for later influence. Newcomb's concerns about the effects of the opportunities, demands, and constraints of college environments continue to influence researchers to ask questions about environmental effects on peer relations at all educational levels.

IDENTIFYING PEERS AND FRIENDS

The literature on the social relationships of secondary school students makes a distinction between *friends* and *peers*. Friends are voluntary associates who form a *primary group* or clique. Peers are the larger, often involuntary population or *secondary group* from which friends are chosen. The number of interactors, the voluntary nature of the association, and the frequency and intensity of the association distinguish friends from peers.

Unfortunately, the initial simplicity of these distinctions is quickly lost when differences in types of friends are enumerated: acquaintances, just friends, good friends, best or true friends (Foot *et al.,* 1980; Kurth, 1970; La Gaipa, 1979). Types of friends may be further differentiated by the patterns of selections that students make. The choices may be reciprocated or unreciprocated, stable or unstable over time. An additional distinction is made between symmetric, asymmetric, or complementary friendships, which signifies the equal or unequal statuses of friends on some criteria. Indeed, a peer may be anyone of equal status on some criterion, and the term applies to nonfriends as well as friends of all types. This overlap in terms is important because researchers select measures that more or less separate friends from the general peer group. The measures used in any study determine the conclusions that can be drawn about selection and influence.

Another major distinction is made between *popularity, friendliness,* and *friend-*

ship (Hallinan, 1981; Hartup, 1978; Mannarino, 1980). Hallinan suggests that popularity is measured by choices received, friendliness by choices made, and friendship by mutual choices. Most would agree that popularity is based on the choices a student receives from others whether or not the choices are returned. However, popularity can be measured in ways other than the average number of times selected, because popularity can be a recognized characteristic in others without the chooser feeling friendship for the popular person. There is little agreement about the best measures of friendship, because different types of friends have been identified, not all friends need be mutual, and not all measures are easily administered, cost-effective, or easily analyzed. (For a discussion of this topic, see Hallinan, 1981.) In this volume, the measures of friends or peers are identified in each chapter.

Developmental studies show that the concepts and acts of friendship change dramatically over the years from childhood to adulthood (Allan, 1979; Damon, 1977; Gottman & Parkhurst, 1980; Selman, 1976; L. Weiss & Lowenthal, 1975). A sixth-grader may call a classmate a "friend" because of the activities they experience in school, but a tenth-grader may require that a "friend" share feelings, beliefs, and goals or show commitment and support in a variety of activities or situations in and out of school. The definitions and expectations of friendship change with age and, we suggest, under different environmental and organizational emphases.

FEATURES OF THIS COLLECTION

The chapters in this volume contain several new emphases that substantially enrich and advance the previous work on the effects of school organizations on friendship formation, peer relations, and patterns of influence.

First, the chapters emphasize the importance of school and classroom environments and the age and developmental characteristics of the students in studies of friendship selection and influence. The studies illustrate how sociological research can benefit from developmental theories and psychological variables, and how psychological studies can benefit from attention to the social organization of environments that affect the formation of groups and the social relations among students.

Second, the studies focus mainly on students at the secondary school level, including middle, junior high, and high schools. Although the complexities of secondary schools make organizational effects difficult to measure, it is especially important to study peer relations in adolescence, when the peer group is expected to increase in importance in the socialization process (Douvan & Adelson, 1966; Elder, 1971, 1980; La Gaipa, 1979; Minuchin, 1975). The chapters emphasize the changes in patterns of selection and influence that occur across the years of early adolescence and adolescence and the effects of characteristics of secondary school and classroom environments.

Third, the theoretical perspectives and empirical research raise questions about previous assumptions and conclusions about peer relations in studies that did not take environmental and developmental characteristics into account. Patterns of selection and influence are presented from data collected in differently organized schools. These data are needed for the development of more adequate theories of friendship formation from childhood to adolescence. We stress the importance of causal models that link the organization of the environment to the structure of peer and friendship groups and that link the process of selection to the process of influence.

Fourth, the chapters focus on the meaning for educators of research on students and their friends. Teachers are already aware that they can influence students' academic skills. What these studies indicate is that teachers and administrators have the power, by the way they organize instructional environments, to affect students' social skills, the selection of friends', and students' influence on each other.

The message across chapters is that it is not enough to study friends of school-aged children without paying attention to the contexts in which the friends interact daily. The nature of the interactions can be affected by the organization of school offerings, classroom instruction, and the distribution of students in schools and classrooms. It is not enough to study the effects of schools on friendships and peer relations without paying attention to the age or stage of development that is guiding the behavior of the students. Their social exchanges and patterns of selection and influence can be affected by their levels of understanding of social concepts.

The chapters have been arranged to focus on three key areas of research on friends in school: theory, selection, and influence. The first section presents perspectives on theories of selection that recognize the importance of the environment of the school and social-psychological theories of friendship formation. These perspectives are the bases for the empirical research in the chapters that follow.

The next two sections present empirical research and commentaries on students' selection and influence processes. Research is presented on environmental characteristics of secondary schools that influence the *selection* of friends, including the classroom organizational features of authority, task, and reward structures; the demographic features of sex, race, and ethnic characteristics; and the school organizational features of tracking and extracurricular programs. A commentary linking the selection and influence processes connects these studies of selection with the studies of influence in the next section.

Longitudinal data are used to study the *influence* of friends that follows their selection. Attention is given to developmental patterns of influence across the grades and to theories of influence on minority and majority students' behaviors in classroom and play settings. New information is presented about the difference between selecting similar friends and friends becoming similar. A commentary on peer influence theories and research discusses new directions for future research.

The final section summarizes important issues for research and discusses the practical implications of the empirical findings. Current strategies of interventions are discussed to help educators understand that school and classroom organizations can be altered in ways that use peer relations to better advantage.

OVERVIEW OF THE CHAPTERS

Although most friendships and significant peer relationships take place in school, our knowledge about specific ways that schools influence the friendship process is limited. Chapter 2, by Karweit and Hansell, focuses on the settings provided by schools for peer relationships and the conditions for interaction in those settings. Schools provide two basic types of settings—curricular and extracurricular—within which students interact. Specific grouping practices, such as the division of students into grade levels and curricular tracks, determine to a large degree the opportunities for student interaction within academic classrooms. Similarly, schools provide a range of extracurricular activities in which students make acquaintances and friends.

Karweit and Hansell's model shows that such program characteristics as school size and differentiation practices of age grades, curricular tracks, and extracurricular offerings affect other more proximate conditions of schooling. These include the organization of classroom activities, the visibility of students' skills and abilities, and the social and academic status systems in which students are classified. These proximate features in turn affect patterns of contact, interaction, and selection of friends. Karweit and Hansell's review of previous research on each component in the model effectively shows why the complete model should be useful for studying school organizational effects on friendship selection.

Epstein, in Chapter 3, suggests that theories of adult friendship selection have been used inappropriately to explain patterns of results from studies of youngsters' friendships. The theories—including balance, social exchange, and status-based, initiation–response theories—fail to take into account the degree of change associated with children's school and classroom groups, and they assume an inappropriate degree of consistency in youngsters' choices of friends. Psychological theories of cognitive and social development account for change in children's friendships, but these theories omit attention to the social organization of friendship groups and the settings in which selection occurs.

In this chapter, longitudinal data on students and their friends are used to raise questions about selected concepts from theories of attraction. The data show that patterns of friendships and peer relations change across the junior high and senior high years because of age, experience, environmental opportunities and restraints, and developing cognitive structures. Patterns of selection based on proximity, cross-sex and cross-race characteristics, and student status, reciprocity, and stability are presented. The empirical analyses suggest that a theory of childrens' friendship selection must integrate sociological and psychological theories in order to accommodate cognitive and social development through adolescence and the changing character of school contexts through high school.

In Chapter 4, Douvan offers a perceptive commentary on the importance of developing useful theories for studies of adolescent friendships. She presents a traditional, psychological perspective on the adolescent's search for identity, reminding readers of the importance of the psychological fact that the *students* are in school. This perspective complements the emphasis in other chapters on the importance of the sociological fact that the students are *in school*.

The adolescent's search for identity, which includes attachment to friends and detachment from parents, is Douvan's primary concern. Friendship during this period of student development is a critical component of the student's search for a definition of the self. She describes theories that should assist researchers in creating, extending, and revising hypotheses about friendship choice, rejection, and influence. Her discussion adds Erikson's (1950) critical-stage theory to those explored by Epstein in Chapter 3 and stresses the contributions that Piagetian and social learning theories can make to our understanding of adolescent friendships.

Douvan agrees that psychological, sociological, anthropological, and social history perspectives must be integrated in theories of adolescent friendships. She emphasizes the importance of developmental research to explain differences across early and late adolescence. Finally, she suggests some new questions about adolescent friendships that could benefit from small-scale observational studies as well as from large-scale surveys to advance our knowledge about patterns of friendship.

Many researchers have recognized that structural factors alter the opportunities for social contact and define the population from which friends are selected. However, most studies have lacked the necessary data on the organization of significantly different schools and classrooms and on students' families and friends to show *how* the organization of contrasting secondary school environments affects the selection of adolescent friends. Chapter 5, by Epstein, presents the results of a longitudinal study of students in secondary schools that differ in the extent of student participation in decision making in academic classrooms. The results suggest that, in high-participatory secondary schools, friendship structures are less hierarchical and fewer students are isolated or excluded from friendship choice. Also, in the more participatory schools, more friendships are reciprocated, friends are selected from a wider set of contacts, and students who score low on several academic and nonacademic outcome measures are more often included in friendship groups and more often have high-scoring students as friends than in low-participatory schools.

The chapter extends earlier research on elementary school students by showing that, for secondary school students, too, unreciprocated friends are less stable than reciprocated friends and friendships become more stable with age. Younger students select more friends, but older students are more selective in the friends they choose.

Research on cooperation and competition is among the oldest traditions in social psychology. One of the earliest and most consistent findings of this research is that, when individuals work in small, cooperative groups, they come to like one another and to value the group itself. Social psychologists have begun to study practical classroom techniques that use cooperative, multiracial, multiethnic, or multiability learning teams to improve relationships among students of different backgrounds. In most studies, the experience of working in heterogeneous classroom learning teams over several weeks resulted in increased intergroup acceptance.

In Chapter 6, Slavin and Hansell integrate evidence from social-psychological laboratory research on interpersonal attraction and intergroup relations with evidence from field research. They review results of research on the effects of cooperative learning techniques on friendship selection and intergroup relations. Their review is organized around the major components of Allport's (1954) contact theory: contact, cooperation, equal status, similarity, and institutional norms.

Slavin and Hansell take a hard look at the conclusions that can be drawn from the research completed to date and raise some provocative questions. For example, they suggest that high-quality, nonsuperficial contact created by any reorganization of classroom instruction may be more important for altering patterns of student association than particular cooperative, competitive, or individual components. They favor cooperative tasks, however, for long-term interactions among minority and majority students.

Slavin and Hansell's suggestions about research on contact and the *selection* of friends should be read along with Miller's (Chapter 12) suggestions for research on cooperation versus competition for friends' and peers' *influence* on each other. The two chapters—one on selection, the other on influence—call attention to the importance of the organization of classroom environments when the student populations include minority and majority students or any groups of identifiably different youngsters who may be drawn together or kept apart in a school.

Chapter 7, by Karweit and Hansell, reviews and studies sex differences in friendship choices—a topic of continued interest among researchers. Most researchers have concluded that socialization and environmental factors, not biological ones, are responsible for the differences in friendship patterns of males and females (Eder & Hallinan, 1978). However, few studies have examined the influence of the characteristics of high school environments on the friendships of male and female students.

Karweit and Hansell review research on differences for males and females of same-sex choices, size of friendship groups, reciprocity of friendship choices, and basis of friendship choices. Then they present new research on the importance of status in the selections of male and female high school students. Their measures of status include curricular track and other school-related indicators of prestige to illustrate how school organizational characteristics can influence friendship selections. They find that students who are similar in status tend to reciprocate friendships more than dissimilar students, but intriguing sex differences are noted. For example, males are more likely than females to direct unreciprocated choices to friends of higher school status. The results and discussion should direct new longitudinal studies of male and female friendship networks.

In Chapter 8, Karweit explores the role of participation in extracurricular activities in the selection of friends. Schools structure opportunities for friendship selection by sorting students into grades and curricular tracks. The organization of extracurricular activities enables students from different grades and tracks to meet others who may not be assigned to their academic classrooms.

Analyses are presented of patterns of friendship within different extracurricular offerings, of the relationship of track placement to extracurricular participation, of cross-curricular choosing, and of school size and participation. Karweit points to the visibility of diverse traits, the voluntary commitment of students to the activities, and the status gained through recognition of accomplishments as features of extracurricular offerings that alter patterns of selection of friends.

Longitudinal studies must be undertaken on this important topic to pursue the issues introduced in this chapter. Also, researchers will want to look beyond the school for extracurricular, out-of-school activities that affect adolescents' friendship choices.

In Chapter 9, curricular tracking and friendship networks are studied by Hansell and Karweit. In most high schools in the United States, and in many middle and junior high schools, students are tracked or grouped by ability. This basic organizational feature may be of major importance for the selection and influence of friends, because the grouping in academic courses determines the populations in which the students work for most of the schoolday.

Research suggests that high school students in college and noncollege tracks learn different ways of relating to peers (Oakes, 1982) and to authority figures (Bowles & Gintis, 1976). These experiences in high school may prepare students for adult roles in white- and blue-collar occupations and for patterns of social exchange as adults. Research on adults suggests that individuals in white-collar occupations tend to have relatively large but loosely connected networks of acquaintances, whereas individuals in blue-collar occupations are organized into cohesive, tightly knit networks. This chapter explores whether corresponding differences in the structure of friendship networks are found among students in the school tracks that prepare white- and blue-collar workers.

Hansell and Karweit document the "reachability" of students in different curricular tracks, by grade level and by sex. They present analyses of the effects of track placement and extracurricular participation on the reachability of males and females in the high school grades. Students in college tracks reach more students than do youngsters who are not in the college track. Differences are reported in the independent effects of tracking and extracurricular participation on the reachability of males and of females. Grade-level differences are noted in the number of other students that are in student friendship networks; these differences confirm developmental patterns of selection that are reported in other research chapters. The results should initiate new research and discussions on how the school organization of curricular tracking affects patterns of association and how the early patterns prepare youngsters for different social roles as adults.

Cohen's commentary in Chapter 10 links the selection and influence processes. He discusses elements of the selection process, including the setting in which selection occurs, the characteristics on which selection is based, and the results of the selection process, including the number and types of friends selected and the types of relationships established. These components of selection affect the nature and extent of influence that occurs among friends.

Cohen distinguishes between the kinds of influence that result from friends, who are selected, and from peers, who are not selected as friends but who are part of the student's environment. Nonselected peers may be part of an interpersonal environment, members of an elite group, or part of a general school context. The influence of the nonselected students on most attitudes and behaviors will be weaker, less consistent, and less important than the influence of selected friends.

A useful distinction is made between influence that *changes* and influence that *maintains* (or *anchors*) students' attitudes and behaviors. Change or maintenance depends on whether friends are similar or different from each other on an outcome that is important to at least one of them. Similar friends maintain, or cause less change in, each other's attitudes and behaviors; dissimiliar friends cause more change in attitudes and behaviors. Cohen points out that previous research has not consistently documented a connection between the type of relationship (i.e., stable, reciprocated) and degree of influence.

The bottom line of peer group research is not how many friends are selected, how many choices are received, or how the friendship group is structured, but whether and how the choices that are made influence the individual's behavior. This has been the missing feature of many studies, in part because of the lack of adequate longitudinal measures of students' friends and behaviors. In cross-sectional studies, the selection and influence processes are confounded. The similarity of friends may be due to the fact that friends select others who are most like themselves, or it may be due to the actual influence of friends on each other during the period of association. Indeed, if we are to understand the potential of friends and peer groups as socializing agents, we must go beyond the examination of the formation of groups to address the issue of influence.

In Chapter 11, Epstein uses longitudinal data from students and their friends on a variety of educational outcomes to examine the influence of friends. The longitudinal data make it possible to account for early patterns of selection and then to chart the patterns of influence of differently structured friendship groups on students' later achievement and nonachievement outcomes. Outcomes for students and friends who are initially similar are compared with those for students and friends who are initially different on each outcome.

In the chapter, Epstein examines students in four differently structured friendship groups and introduces information on how reciprocated and stable friends influence different outcomes. The results document the positive influence, after 1 year, of initially high-scoring friends on students who initially scored low in achievement and on other measures of attitudes and behaviors. The relative influences of family socioeconomic status (SES) and friends on academic and nonacademic measures are compared and discussed. The results suggest that adolescent friendship groups are not necessarily antagonistic to adult or school goals of achievement and academic success.

Since the 1960s, the lateral transmission of values has been a major hypothesis for explaining the process by which desegregation improves the academic performance of minority children. It is assumed that in predominantly white, middle-class desegregated classrooms or schools, the values of minority students shift so that, in time, more minority students adopt the academic achievement values of the majority. In this model, students' social relations and a particular influence process are responsible for academic gains by minority students in desegregated schools.

In Chapter 12, Miller examines the social-psychological bases of the lateral transmission of values hypothesis. Besides offering a conceptual perspective, he presents data on the relationship between popularity, personality, and scholastic performance of subsamples of students whose popularity was unusually high or low. Children's social interactions in classroom and nonclassroom settings in desegregated schools are examined for evidence of patterns of acceptance or hostility among black and white males and females. These initial patterns of acceptance and hostility are intriguing additions to the discussion of the problems with the lateral transmission of values model, since acceptance is a critical factor in the applicability of that model.

Miller casts doubt on previously accepted ideas about the influence process. He draws a distinction between *normative* influence, which emphasizes learning what the values and expected behaviors are, and *informational* or *locomotion* influence, which emphasizes the resources and actions needed to turn norms into behavior. Miller rejects the lateral transmission of values theory because patterns of effects in longitudinal data show that peer acceptance of minority students by white students is a consequence, not an antecedent, of improved academic performance of minority students. His rejection of the hypothesis is based on measures of popularity of students new to a school, which change rapidly over time, and measures of achievement, which change slowly over time. Other researchers will want to follow Miller's tests of the usefulness of the lateral transmission hypothesis with studies that measure the specific conditions required by the theory.

Studies are needed to explain how the organizational features of the environments in which blacks and whites interact affect the acceptance of cross-race friends and their influence on each other. Carter, DeTine-Carter, and Benson (1980) suggest that the *type* of contact to stimulate interracial acceptance is more important than the *frequency* of contact. The type of contact is a function of the opportunities within the school organization for positive task-oriented interaction, equal participation, and rewards for accomplishments in classrooms—all alterable variables in instructional design. Patchen, Hoffman, and Brown (1980) suggest that school characteristics, including teachers' rewards for higher effort and the demographics of the classrooms in which whites are predominant, are more critical for progress in black achievement than is contact or friendship with whites. Tracking and grouping policies, emphasis on student cooperation, and recognition and rewards for few or many skills and talents are among the organizational features that can influence how equal students are in status; how accepting students are of each other's values, attitudes, and talents; and whether and how improved achievement will be rewarded.

Hallinan's commentary, Chapter 13, reviews the literature on contextual and proximate peer influence and presents a potentially useful theory for explaining and predicting peer effects. She bases her perspective on Parsons's theory of intended influence—a theory that emphasizes the need for information as a prerequisite for change in behavior. Information theory as it was defined and used by Woelfel and Haller (1971) in their study of peer influence has been of limited use because of its purposeful omission of assumptions about affective and emotional ties. Hallinan has corrected this weakness by introducing Parsons's emphasis on the importance of trust in seeking, receiving, and using information from others and in developing mutual friendships.

Hallinan suggests that attitudinal or behavioral change may be better explained by intended influence theory combined with reference group and role theory, in which the individual is a gatherer and user of information, than by comparative and normative influence theories, in which the individual is an observer and judge of the self in comparison to others. Intended influence may be especially useful for explaining influence that occurs in early adolescence, when students are especially interested in information about themselves. Early adolescence is also a time when students are developing a sense of the meaning of *trust* in developing relations with others. Longitudinal studies of intended influence (informational) and normative and comparative influence should show important developmental patterns from early to late adolescence because the cognitive concepts central to these processes are changing.

Hallinan's commentary (and other discussions across the chapters) on student development and school environments suggests new questions that should be considered in longitudinal studies of selection and influence. Must influence be intentional? Is influence only a transference of information? Is trust equally important in the influence process for children, adolescents, and adults? Is trust differently defined in differently organized schools and classrooms and other socializing settings? Is seeking information a state of vulnerability or a state of active learning? Do fear of deception and evaluation of deception guide the social exchanges and friendly relations of youngsters? Does the importance of these negative motivations change in differently structured educational environments? In some settings, students can influence their friends more than in other settings. The kinds of actions required and, therefore, the kinds of information requested and shared will differ in varied settings. Hallinan's discussion of *intended influence, trust,* and *fear of deception* dovetails with Miller's emphasis on *informational* (*or locomotion*) *influence, acceptance,* and *social threat* as affective dimensions that guide students to seek, obtain, and use information. These concepts can be contrasted usefully in future studies of influence.

Chapter 14, by Epstein, is a discussion of issues that are raised by the research and commentaries in this volume. The positive and negative effects of friends and peers, the importance of changing friends, the multiple groups to which students belong, and the multiple settings in which the groups interact are topics that must be addressed in new theoretical and empirical research on peer and friendship groups.

The implications of the research for classroom practice and educational interventions based on the reorganization of instructional programs are also discussed in the final chapter. Students and their friends associate *in* school, but research has not made clear what this means *to* the school. Currently, most educators do not take seriously the potential of peer relations as a positive force for attaining the academic and social goals they set for their students. Most education is conducted as if the teacher–student dyad were the only important relationship in the academic classroom (D. W. Johnson, 1981; Schlecty, 1976). Teachers ask the students to work on their own and interact only with the teacher on academic issues. The power of peer and friendship groups is unutilized, underutilized, or feared by many educators.

The chapters that follow stress the effects of the organization of school and classroom environments on student contact, interaction, selection and influence of friends, and the application of the research to practice.

THEORETICAL PERSPECTIVES

NANCY KARWEIT
STEPHEN HANSELL
2

School Organization
and Friendship Selection

How adolescent peer groups affect the educational values and orientations of their members has been the topic of many peer group studies, but few studies have considered how characteristics of schools affect student friendship patterns. For example, no study has examined how school size and differentiation practices influence the friendship relationships among adolescents. This lack of interest in school-level variables reflects an individualistic orientation to the study of peer relationships that affects what variables are studied and how the results are interpreted. Also, the omission of school-level variables conflicts with a major substantive focus that guides peer group research—the examination of how students influence one another's educational aspirations and behavior. Access to highly motivated, talented, or able sets of students is important for the socialization of desirable values and aspirations.

Most research on peer effects views the school simply as a convenient location for data collection on peer relationships, not as an important element that directly affects student interaction. The effects of school-to-school differences in size and grade organization on friendships, for example, has not been systematically considered. However, because socialization affects the adolescent's future and because one goal of schooling is to provide equal learning opportunities, the impact of school organization on peer interactions is important to understand. Although personal preferences determine the selection of actual friends from among the pool of potential friends, specific school practices constrain the possibilities for contact to particular types of students in particular activity settings.

29

FRIENDS IN SCHOOL
Patterns of Selection and Influence in Secondary Schools

School organization provides what Feld (1981) calls "foci" for the development of social ties. Organizational foci, such as physical settings, individuals, activities, or groups, shape the social interactions of individuals. In a general way, the purpose of this book is to investigate the sociological nature of organizational foci in schools, to chart the distribution of social relationships in important school foci, and to assess the impact of school foci on peer relations.

This chapter introduces important features of school organization and begins to explain how they affect the selection of friends in schools. We develop a heuristic model of the specific ways school features limit, expand, and condition opportunities for peer interaction. The model includes only the two organizational features of school size and differentiation practices as examples of the linkages among organizational variables and peer relationships.

In this model, presented in Figure 2.1, school size and differentiation practices, which include the system of age grading and curricular tracking, affect peer interaction directly by determining the number of school settings available for interaction and the distribution of students across those settings. The effects of school organization on peer interaction are also mediated by the nature of school activities, the visibility of student traits in each setting, and the salience of these traits in the student status system. Each component of this model will be discussed in the remainder of the chapter.

SCHOOL SIZE

Schools contain many different physical settings in which students and adults interact. Complex schedules keep different sets of students flowing through these locations at relatively frequent intervals. Schools differ not only in the number of such settings available but in the manner students are distributed across these settings. School size determines both the number of behavior settings and the distribution of specific students across settings.

Barker and his associates (Barker & Gump, 1964; Barker & Associates, 1978; Wicker, 1971) found that participation in school life decreases as school size increases. The theoretical perspective used to explain these results is that of "manning" in behavior settings. Schools have two major types of behavior set-

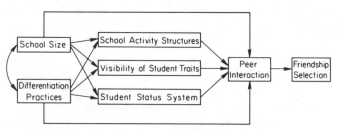

FIGURE 2.1. School organization and friendship selection.

tings—those associated with the instructional program and those outside the instructional program. Although Barker's theory of participation in behavior settings applies to a wide range of situations, it has been used most often to explain why participation in extracurricular activities is greater in smaller schools than it is in larger schools.

Barker and Gump (1964) found that, although the types of activities offered within schools do not depend on school size, the number of positions in these activities does. Thus, students in smaller schools have the same kinds of activities available to them as students in larger schools, but there are relatively fewer students available to participate in each activity. Consequently, to keep the same number of activities alive, smaller schools must have a greater proportion of students participate than do larger schools. Using the analogy of "manning the boat," Barker typified small schools as "undermanned," because the participation of a larger proportion of the student body is required than in larger schools. This manning phenomenon is thus used to explain higher rates of participation in extracurricular activities in smaller schools.

D. Morgan and Alwin (1980) document that both the magnitude and the direction of the manning effect vary with the nature of the activity. They suggest that the *centrality*, or status, of the activity and its *elasticity*, or capacity to expand, account for the observed differences in manning. Activities that are high in centrality and relatively inelastic (e.g., journalism activities) are most likely to exhibit manning. Activities that are low in centrality and high in elasticity, such as hobby clubs, show a reverse form of manning, in which rates of participation increase with school size.

Systematic differences in other student behaviors, such as truancy and acts of vandalism, have also been related to differences in school size. Several researchers have documented that school size is associated with a greater sense of anonymity and lower evaluations of self and other students. Student morale has been found to be lower in larger schools (Abramowitz, 1977; Gottfredson & Daiger, 1979; Mayhew & Levinger, 1976; McPartland & McDill, 1977). These studies, in combination with the manning research, present an image of small schools as places where participation is important, where each person is visible and valued, and consequently, where attachments to school and to other students are positive and strong. Alternatively, large schools are characterized as faceless, anonymous places where participation is not necessary and meaningful attachments to school life are not easily made.

These views suggest how school size may affect friendship selection within schools. Higher student participation can provide greater opportunities for interaction with schoolmates in noninstructional settings than in classrooms. Shared participation in extracurricular activities may thus provide students with a source of common interests and activities that may form the bases of friendships. If the reciprocation and strength of friendships are based on the sharing of multiple activities and interests, then school size may also affect these dimensions of friendships. In a large school, only those students who have special talents, abilities, and skills will become identified with those interests, particularly in inelastic, central activities. Consequently, in large schools, relatively fewer individuals are visible for their interests and participation in activities, and of those who are, a restricted set of attributes are visible. Smaller schools may permit the exposure of a wider range of each student's talents and interests, around which friendships may be based.

DIFFERENTIATION PRACTICES

Schools divide their student population into groups for instructional purposes. This differentiation process affects the likelihood of meeting particular other students in classrooms and produces a distinct social system that influences interaction among students in other, noncurricular settings. Schools use several assignment variables to create instructional groups. Age grading and grouping by ability are two common practices in most schools. The intention of these differentiation practices is to make instruction more effective by reducing student diversity for the classroom teacher, who must simultaneously teach 20–40 students. The actual results of such differentiation practices may, however, extend appreciably beyond this stated organizational purpose.

Age Grading

Age usually determines when schooling begins and how long it must continue. It is also a common measure of progress through school. Most schools are divided by age into grade levels. Although it may be educationally sensible to allow passage from one level to the next on the basis of competence alone, this practice is not widespread in the United States.[1]

Courses in high schools are often structured by grade—sophomore English and freshman math, for example, are subjects geared specifically to the year in school. Other courses, such as biology and geometry, are not specifically defined as a freshman or sophomore course, but they are usually taken by students in those grades. Elective courses, such as some social studies, science, or math courses, exhibit a greater variation in the age range of students, but often only for upperclassmen and within rather narrow limits of one or two grade levels. Consequently, the distribution of students across specific classroom settings is strongly determined by their grade levels, so that most secondary students never take a course with a schoolmate of a different grade.

Obviously, sorting students by age into instructional periods for the major part

---

[1]Victorian Britain provides one example of a system organized by academic achievement rather than by age. Classes were age heterogeneous, whereas achievement levels were homogeneous. Sorensen (1978) notes (citing Dent) that teachers were paid according to the number of students they were able to pass from one grade level to the next.

of the day has important implications for their choice of friends and acquaintances. Most friendship choices within schools are confined to the same grade. The existence of greater age heterogeneity in naturally occurring friendship groups, such as in neighborhoods, suggests the strong age restriction on friendship formation imposed by school organization.

Older students usually have special rights and privileges in their school and higher status in the peer social system. Most positions of prestige within the school are either explicitly reserved for older students, such as the prom queen, or are earned by them, such as editor of the yearbook or quarterback of the football team. The status accorded to upperclassmen makes them attractive foci for the attention of younger students.

Although extracurricular activities seem to provide one arena for possible cross-grade friendships, they actually provide few opportunities to form friendships between age groups. First, many activities—such as junior softball, sophomore bowling, or junior varsity basketball—are specifically geared to a certain grade level. Second, because age is such an important status characteristic, leadership positions in extracurricular activities are usually held by upperclassmen, and it is unlikely that associations across age groups actually form given the social rank associated with age. Because age-graded instructional settings prescribe the opportunities for interaction among students for almost the entire schoolday, most friendships occur within age groups.

Other settings in the school, such as lunchrooms and corridors, may provide limited opportunities for peer interaction across age. However, the cafeteria is scheduled to be occupied by a specific class. Even when it is not, there are strong tendencies for students to segregate themselves by age within these settings for casual contacts. Age grading provides one example of how differentiation practices segregate students into subgroups with differential status, and how such groupings affect interaction patterns within and among student peer groups.

Curricular Tracking

Another differentiation practice that affects student relationships is curricular tracking. Specialized programs for academic and vocational students of varying ability are designed to facilitate teaching, but they may actually serve quite different purposes. By labeling some students as more academically competent than others, tracking creates different teacher expectations for the performance of various groups. These expectations tend to become self-fulfilling prophecies, so that the academic achievement of students in the various tracks reflects and legitimizes their original track assignment. However, the assignment to tracks is somewhat arbitrary and not based on consistent or well-understood criteria. Indeed, tracking is often said to be based more on students' social class origins than on their aptitude or ability. Tracking is viewed as a means for perpetuating social class position in society, and some researchers warn of the potential stigma of being assigned to low-achievement tracks (Bowles & Gintis, 1976; Rehberg & Rosenthal, 1978; Rosenbaum, 1976).

Regardless of the intended function of tracking, it is clear that it is a major segregating device within secondary schools, with important consequences for peer associations. Tracking ensures that students will form friendships with other students having similar backgrounds and origins. Tracking limits contact with diverse students. In particular, tracking reduces contact between educationally advantaged students and disadvantaged students. This fact is readily acknowledged and accepted in secondary schools as if it reflected voluntary preferences of the students themselves rather than the restriction of friendship formation by school organization.

However, it is erroneous to interpret curricular tracking as an individual attribute rather than as a structural feature of the school. First, student placement in a college preparatory track depends on the number of slots available in each program and the student's relative positioning in the pool of applicants for these slots (Sorensen, 1978). The number of slots in each track also depends on the number of qualified teachers in specific subjects and community pressures to create specialized programs. Schools rarely have absolute entrance criteria for track assignment but instead allocate students to a fixed number of slots. Consequently, the same student could be placed in a college preparatory track in one school and in a general education track in another.

Also, there are school-to-school variations in tracking practices. Sorensen (1970, 1978) describes the scope of a tracking system as the extent to which students take classes with the same students. The scope of a tracking system is particularly important for understanding the effects of tracking on opportunities for peer associations. Curricular tracks with high scope limit opportunities to form friendships to the same 20–40 students who regularly flow through classes together. An alternative tracking arrangement might place individuals into courses by their ability levels in each subject. This would allow greater mixing of different students but would be difficult to implement. Another arrangement lower in scope would track students in such core subjects as math and English but randomly assign students to other courses. This arrangement would also provide greater opportunities in classrooms for student interaction with a wider set of peers. Scope, then, is an important way in which tracking differs from school to school and is more variable than is commonly recognized.

Tracking, as an organizational feature of schools, largely determines the opportunities for peer association and the nature of peer relationships within the school. Tracking affects peer relations in a manner similar to age grading. Tracks segregate students into differentiated pools of students and cause greater within-track interaction and less cross-track interaction than would occur under conditions of random friendship formation. The status differentiation provided by curricular tracking also affects the structure of contacts across curricular tracks. Following Homans (1974), we expect more contacts will be initiated from lower status students in noncollege tracks to relatively higher status students in college tracks.

Thus, tracking encourages the formation of reciprocated friendships among peers with similar status within tracks and unreciprocated choices between students in different curricular tracks, usually made from lower status general education students to higher status students in the college preparatory track.

The opportunities for interaction with different peers are determined largely by the scope of the tracking system, and the opportunities for interaction across curricular tracks are also affected by this variable. However, actual interaction also depends on how important students judge such interaction to be in the context of student value systems. Furthermore, if several different value systems coexist in the school, it is important to consider the extent to which these value systems conflict or are compatible. For example, if the students in noncollege tracks do not wish contact with college track students because they view these students as alien and unattractive, then little mixing across tracks will occur regardless of the opportunities provided by school organization. Instead, these peer groups will evolve into tightly knit and separate networks between which interaction is mostly negative. Rejection of higher status students may occur by lower status students in spite of, or even because of, their relatively disadvantaged social position.

If the barriers to interaction across status groups are not too great, participation in the same extracurricular activities may provide the opportunity for friendship formation among dissimilar students. However, many extracurricular activities replicate the status structure of curricular settings. Subject matter clubs, such as the math club or French club, are extensions of classroom environments and probably mirror the classroom dominance of college preparatory students. Such clubs as the Beta Club or National Honor Society are explicitly limited to college preparatory students. Perhaps even more important, students in the noncollege track participate less often and in fewer extracurricular activities, thus limiting the possibilities of cross-track interaction (Schaefer & Olexa, 1971).

Track placement may also physically segregate students, further discouraging informal interaction between students in college and noncollege tracks. Shop courses and electronics courses, which require specialized facilities, may be physically located in a completely separate wing of the school. Students may have most of their classes in this relatively isolated area, so that interaction with other students is drastically reduced. Students in noncollege tracks may also work part of the schoolday or take courses away from the school, so that opportunities for contact are further reduced. Scheduling requirements may keep these students from congregating on school grounds before or after school with other class mates.

Curricular tracking, then, creates segregated groupings of students with high rates of internal interaction and low rates of external interaction, and it appreciably alters the opportunities for peer interaction within schools by constraining student interaction. Differentiation by curricular track also confers different statuses on students and thereby curtails interaction across tracks even when opportunities for relationships between heterogeneous students are present.

SCHOOL ACTIVITY STRUCTURES

Schools provide settings for peer interaction and distribute students with various attributes to those settings. Once students are located in a setting, the development of friendships between particular students is influenced by their personal attributes but also by the characteristics of the setting.

The work of Bossert (1979) and Rosenholtz and Wilson (1980) describes how activity structures affect peer relationships. Bossert considers how the task structure, or activity structure, of the classroom affects the nature of friendship ties that emerge. He argues that when the entire class is engaged in the same activity, such as in teacher-led discussion, the teacher controls the choice of activities, the pace of instruction, and the sequence of the lesson. As a result of the use of public question-and-answer sessions, the class is able to evaluate the relative performance of its members. To be fair, teachers must use a reward system based on relative academic ranking of class members. This ranking becomes very important for friendship choices because the tight teacher control of activities does not let other characteristics of students become visible.

Bidwell and Kasarda (1980) and Bossert (1979) examined the effect that teacher rankings have on peer group structure. In classrooms dominated by whole-group instruction, interpersonal friendships are more likely to be based on students' task performances and their relative rankings by teachers. The best students receive the most friendship choices and are sociometric stars. The worst students are likely to be unpopular or sociometric isolates.

In contrast, when all students are not engaged in a common task, interpersonal ties are less likely to be based on task performances or relative ranks within the class. Bossert argues that in multiple-task classrooms, children are more likely to establish affiliations based on criteria other than academic performance.

This argument is also supported by evidence that students are highly aware of ability differences in single-task classrooms. Rosenholtz and Wilson (1980) suggest that the extent of shared understandings about ability differences depends on the classroom practices of task differentiation, grouping practices, teacher evaluation, and student autonomy. "High resolution" classrooms, which use single tasks, whole-class groupings, standard evaluation, and low student autonomy, produce much greater agreement among students, and between teachers and students, on the ability differences in the classroom than do "low-resolution" classrooms.

Thus far, studies of the consequences of task structures for peer relationships have been based on elementary school classrooms. Because many elementary schools involve the same students in a single classroom over an extended period, these effects are likely to be particularly strong. Moreover, elementary school students have few in-school opportunities outside of the classroom to interact with other students.

In junior and senior high schools, activity structures of classrooms may not have strong effects on peer relationships because students change classes and teachers several times a day, thus diluting the effects of any one learning environment. Also, the student status system more frequently conflicts with the goals of teachers, thus diminishing the impact of teacher evaluations.

For example, noncollege track classrooms have been characterized as similar (E. P. Morgan, 1977) to the high-resolution classrooms described by Rosenholtz and Wilson (1980). However, it is unlikely that the sociometric stars in noncollege track junior high school classrooms are the best students as ranked by the teacher. Instead, popular students may be the most disruptive students, precisely because their behavior conforms to nonacademic norms of the other students.

VISIBILITY OF STUDENT TRAITS

Interactions and activities within certain school settings can make specific traits of students visible in the context of the student status system. For example, classroom settings generally make the academic competence of students visible, but this can be modified by the social organization of the classroom (Bossert, 1979). In contrast, such settings as the cafeteria and hallways may make social abilities of students most visible. Some activities, such as music or sports, foster the visibility of specialized talents. Some settings may allow multiple student traits and abilities to become visible. Athletics, for example, not only provides for the display of physical strength, stamina, and coordination but also allows the student to show teamwork and team support. Settings comprise locations within time and space for student interaction. Interaction inevitably changes the visibility of certain traits of individual student participants.

STUDENT STATUS SYSTEM

The visibility of traits is significant for friendship selection because students are likely to form friendships with students who are similar to them on important attributes. But not all traits that are made visible are equally important as the basis for friendship selection. The salience of a trait depends on the preferences of the individual students and on the value attached to this trait in the student status system. The salience of athletic skills is usually high because athletics is of central importance in the student status system. Athletic achievement may thus be more consequential for friendship formation among a wider pool of potential friends than, for example, photographic talent, which may only be salient to members of the camera club.

The salience of certain traits may differ across peer groups. For example, academic ability may be required for membership in some peer groups, but it may be of little value in others. The effect of the visibility of academic competence on friendship formation depends on the value placed on such abilities by specific subgroups of students. For students in an advanced college placement course, excelling academically may contribute to their status in the group. In a general or vocational education track, academic excellence may not be rewarded and could result in active rejection. Thus, traits do not have stable, intrinsic values for friendship formation but assume various values depending on the status systems of specific student cliques.

SUMMARY

This chapter suggests how organizational features of schools affect friendship selection. School size and differentiation practices are particular features that influence the number of settings available within the school for student interaction; they also affect the distribution of students with various attributes to those settings. The nature of the activity within a setting determines which attributes of students will be made visible. The salience of visible traits for friendship selection is shaped by the values and norms of student reference groups. Because multiple and conflicting status systems may exist simultaneously, the importance of a particular trait for friendship formation can vary greatly within the same school.

The importance of school organizational features for the selection of friends has been typically overlooked in most studies of adolescent friendships. Indeed, friendships have been treated as if they were exclusively the result of individual preferences and idiosyncracies. Although friendships are usually made between students who are similar in certain traits, characteristics of the individual are not the only factors guiding the selection of friends. This chapter points out how the social environment, resulting from differing organizational arrangements, may heighten, sharpen, or lessen the visibility and importance of specific individual attributes. Although friendships are formed between individuals, the social context in which the friendships take place helps shape both what students have opportunities for interaction and the nature of their interaction. Future research in adolescent socialization could profitably be more attentive to contextual and environmental influences.

JOYCE LEVY EPSTEIN

3

Examining Theories of Adolescent Friendships

Theories of attraction, formation, maintenance, disruption, and dissolution of friendships that were developed in research on adult social relations have been uncritically applied to research on youngsters. Although there may be some similarities in the determinants of interpersonal attraction and friendship choices of adults and children, there are also important differences (J. Reisman & Shorr, 1978). In order to understand which theory or which assumptions of several theories explain children's selections of friends, we need information about patterns of selection across the years of childhood and adolescence. In this chapter, we use data from youngsters to cast a spotlight on several key concepts in theories of adult selection of friends. Two additions to these theories may be especially important to explain youngsters' selections of friends in school. First, recent psychological studies of children's concepts of friendship suggest that a developmental perspective will be required in a theory of selection (Bigelow & La Gaipa, 1980; Gottman & Parkhurst, 1980; Selman, 1976)—the growth and change in social and cognitive skills from childhood to adolescence must be incorporated. Second, recent sociological studies of peer association suggest that an environmental effects model may be required in a theory of friendship selection (Bidwell, 1972; Hallinan, 1976a). The environmental opportunities and constraints of school organizations (or other educating and socializing settings) affect how youngsters contact and interact with each other, how they interpret each other's behavior, how they select friends, and what others they select as friends.

39

FRIENDS IN SCHOOL
Patterns of Selection and Influence in Secondary Schools

QUESTIONS ABOUT THEORETICAL CONCEPTS

Longitudinal data collected from 4163 students in Grades 5, 6, 8, and 11, and again in Grades 6, 7, 9, and 12 provide information on youngsters' friendship choices among preadolescents and adolescents, across the grades of middle school and high school and in differently organized schools. They permit the examination of developmental and environmental factors in the selection process in ways that cannot be accomplished with cross-sectional data, data from a single grade level, or data from a single type of school environment. The empirical exercises and discussions in this chapter are not formal tests of theories. Full tests would require data collected on all the critical concepts in contrasting theories. Here we discuss how the patterns of friendship choice in our data raise questions about some of the basic aspects of friendship selection theories—proximity, balance, status, and exchange. These examples (and others throughout this volume) should set new tasks for future theoretical and empirical research on the selection of friends in school.

Proximity

Proximity is a basic element in all theories of attraction. In most cases, persons will not become close friends unless they are in close contact, but it is equally true that many persons in close and frequent contact do not become friends. Heider (1958) discusses proximity as a condition for balanced adult relationships, but developmental and environmental effects on the definition of and importance of proximity as the basis for friendship selection have not been elaborated. In this chapter, three patterns of association are examined that suggest that the concept of proximity changes across the school years and as a result of the organization of school environments.

Balance

Balance theory posits that associations will be more satisfying and beneficial if friends select each other and make similar selections of other friends. Feelings of distress are assumed to result from asymmetric (unreciprocated) adult friendships. Hallinan (1976a) surmises that students experience the same kind of distress if they are members of intransitive triads or unreciprocated dyads. However, several studies suggest that an emphasis on reciprocity may not be appropriate for understanding youngsters' friendships because of the continuous reshuffling of students in school and classroom environments (Douvan & Adelson, 1966; Parsons, 1959). Students change grades, teachers, schools, neighborhoods, school programs, elective courses, and after-school and summer activities with unusual frequency. Hallinan and Tuma (1978) report that mutual friendships of elementary students last an average of 90 days. Epstein (in Chapters 5 and 11) reports patterns of changing friends through high school.

Changing friends and unreciprocated or unbalanced friendships may not produce the stressful effects in children that are assumed to occur in adults. Asymmetric and unstable choices are normal conditions of students' associations and may be necessary rather than detrimental for personal and social development. Indeed, it may be the lack of stability and reciprocity in friendships that moves youngsters to new levels of social skills and social cognition. This chapter explores patterns of reciprocity and stability in friendships for different age groups and in different school organizations and discusses effects of these conditions of friendship on measures of stress.

Status

The concept of status is also basic to theories of friendship selection. The status-based initiation–response model asserts that one individual reaches out for friendship to another of higher status. The other may respond with acceptance or rejection (Hallinan, 1976b, based on the work of Waller, 1938; Goffman, 1963; Karweit & Hansell, Chapter 7, this volume, based on the Davis & Leinhardt, 1972, ranked-cluster model). It is assumed that individuals are aware of particular desirable qualities in others and need to associate with those of higher status to enhance their own positions. However, status—as something to desire, reach for, and be granted through association with friends—is a flexible concept. For students, status may be situation specific, age specific, a function of the organizational emphases of different schools or classrooms, or a function of how peers, family, teachers, or other adults define *desirable*.

The status-based initiation–response model explains friendship choice as the selection of *unequals,* with the individual evaluating others' attitudes and abilities in terms of presumed benefits to the self. Other theories explain friendship choice as the selection of *equals* (such as social comparison theory, Festinger, 1954; and personal construct theory, Duck, 1973; Kelly, 1955), with individuals evaluating personal attitudes, beliefs, and abilities in order to select others who will confirm or support their own current perspectives. It is likely that students pick friends who are equal on some criteria and unequal on others. For example, people may "pick up" in status on some criteria to improve a social position or to anticipate an expected social position. They may "pick equal" in status because of the expected cohesiveness in relationships with others similar to themselves. Or they may "pick down" on other status characteristics to obtain recognition of superiority or to accept a friend who may be low on one quality but high on others. Students will have different reasons for basing selection on one status criterion or another. Basic questions for new research are how the basis for choice changes over the years from childhood to adolescence and how different educational environments promote different choices based on equal and unequal statuses.

Status characteristics may affect the *dissolution* of friendships more than the *selection* of friends (Duck & Miell, 1982; Tuma & Hallinan, 1979). Classmates' disdain and ridicule about a friend could cause students to reject another student as a best friend. In a class where high achievement is valued, for example, a high-achieving student may find that association with a low achiever decreases the student's own status with others. The student would have to consider the costs of association in that situation. Similarly, analyses reported in Chapter 5 suggest that teachers' rewards for certain behaviors can influence what students value in their peers and could affect the initiation, continuation, or dissolution of friendships. The organization of classroom activities—such as peer tutoring or working in groups, teams, or pairs—may create common, equal statuses that minimize other differences that typically stratify students.

Verbrugge (1979) notes that adult friendship choices are based on eight social positions—occupation, employment status, educational attainment, political preference, age, marital status, sex, and length of residence in an area. Children share only three of these characteristics—age, sex, and length of residence in a neighborhood or school. We know very little about the critical and changing dimensions of status in children's friendships. In this chapter, patterns of initiation and response in differently organized school environments are examined.

Exchange

The concept of exchange is a fourth basic aspect of friendship selection theories. Social exchange theory explains adult selections and rejections of friends on the basis of the rewards and costs that result from their association (Blau, 1964, 1974; Homans, 1974; Thibaut & Kelley, 1959). Certainly, youngsters can identify the costs of painful or conflict-ridden friendships and the rewards of pleasurable activities and experiences. It is unlikely, however, that they are cognizant of the give-and-take that is assumed to propel adult interactions. For example, it is suggested that the rewards of adult friendships are proportionate to the costs of time, energy, and financial and psychological commitments, but these are not likely to be the costs and rewards that children consider.

Costs and rewards are abstract concepts that gain meaning from social experiences. School and classroom environments may impose rewards and costs on particular types of associations, despite the students' personal preferences or decisions. Students can afford to discard investments in relationships and are often encouraged or required by outside sources to start new friendships. The replaceability of students' friends in school settings and the forced associations that result when students are assigned to work together may change how youngsters interpret investments in friendships from childhood through adolescence. Among youngsters, even when exchanges with friends are "unfair" or when some rewards are inequitable, associations or friendships may persist. What is considered unfair at one time may change over time as one or both friends improve their concepts of fairness or learn how to resolve disagreements about fairness. These developmental conditions suggest that the usefulness of concepts of exchange should change from childhood to adolescence as youngsters' evaluations of costs and rewards become more comprehensive.

Adults may invest in friendships by making commitments of time, energy, and service to friends in return for commitments from them (Blau, 1964). Youngsters' commitments are often more shallow, less well defined, and more easily revised. Youngsters' time and energy may be invested more in activities than in relationships.

The meanings of rewards and costs to students may be quite different from their meanings to adults. To fully consider the rewards or costs of association requires the ability to synthesize the results of previous social exchanges and to anticipate expected consequences of friendship. Theories of cognitive development suggest that synthesis and prediction skills may not develop until late adolescence, when youngsters learn to manipulate simultaneously past, present, and future orientations (Inhelder & Piaget, 1958; Piaget, 1932, 1959). In this chapter, we examine how different friendship group structures are related to the rewards of reciprocation of friendship and the costs of feelings of stress about school.

ADDING DEVELOPMENTAL PERSPECTIVES TO THEORIES OF SELECTION

Student cognitive and affective development proceed at different rates. As a child advances in cognitive or social skills, new activities are experienced, new groups of students are encountered, and earlier friends may be discarded or devalued. Theoretical and empirical studies suggest that, over time, students increasingly choose friends who are similar to themselves in characteristics, interests, or abilities. Students also may choose friends who are dissimilar to themselves for reasons of admiration, expected prestige from association, or mutual benefits from symbiotic or synergistic relations. Selections become more complex as youngsters obtain and use more advanced logic, interact more in their environments, use more information about the self and others to make their choices of friends, and test their ideals against the realities of social relations.

Theories of cognitive development recognize change as a critical aspect until such time (if ever) that development is complete. Change is the constant whether development is conceived of as proceeding in invariant stages (Inhelder & Piaget, 1958; Piaget, 1932, 1959; Kohlberg, 1969; Selman, 1976), in hierarchical or spiraled accumulations (Bigelow, 1977; Duck, 1973; La Gaipa, 1981; Werner, 1957), or in unstaged, generative accumulations (as suggested by Bandura, 1969; Brody, 1977; and Maccoby, 1968, in their interpretations of social learning theory). Some connections between cognitive and social development have been examined, such as changes in friends due to growth in linguistic skills (Hartup, 1975, 1978; Peevers & Secord, 1973), communication skills (Flavell, Botkin, Fry,

Wright, & Jarns, 1968; Gottman & Parkhurst, 1980; Mannarino, 1980; Youniss, 1980); concepts of friendship (Damon, 1977; Hartup, 1978; La Gaipa, 1979; Selman, 1976; Selman & Byrne, 1974; Selman & Jacquette, 1978), and acts of friendship (Carter, DeTine-Carter and Benson, 1980; Levinger, 1974; Peevers & Secord, 1973; Rubin, 1980). Contradictions abound in this literature because the linguistic skills that students use to describe friends and friendship may be more or less advanced than the actual social behaviors that students perform as friends. Theories based on invariant stages in development are contradicted by evidence that young children display advanced social skills or that adults continue casual one-way friendships or retain immature moral and social concepts and behaviors. Nevertheless, behind the debate about how the development of social skills proceeds, there is agreement that, in general, social relations develop from shallow surface contacts to deep mutual associations characterized by more accurate perceptions of self and others, more awareness of one's own and others' errors in judgment, more intense emotional involvement, and more ability to resolve conflicts (Berndt, 1981; Flavell, 1977; Lipsitz, 1980; Selman & Byrne, 1974; Selman & Jacquette, 1978; Weiss & Lowenthal, 1975).

One key developmental characteristic that has implications for friendship selection is the increasing ability of youngsters to consider many simultaneous pieces of information in making decisions and to hold constant one characteristic in order to think specifically about the importance of another characteristic (Inhelder & Piaget, 1958). This skill may be the result of a combination of neurological maturation and the accumulation of experiences in social environments. Older children can consider simultaneously all available information about the self, the friend, the friendship, the implications of friendship for the future, and the demands of the environment in which the friendship will occur. These skills should result in greater selectivity in older students' choices. The data from most empirical studies show that older students select fewer friends and increasingly similar friends (as shown in Chapter 5). Younger children's less well-developed cognitive operations leave more room for surprise or unpredictability in students' social relations, less selectivity, and more frequent occasions to test relationships and change friends.

A related developmental concept is the increased ability of older children to take the perspective of others in the course of social exchange (Gottman & Parkhurst, 1980; Peevers & Secord, 1973; Selman, 1976). This other-perspective-taking is closely linked to Mead's (1934, 1947) symbolic interaction theory that has been useful in describing adult friendships. The psychological studies, however, recognize the developmental quality of this skill from early childhood. Other-perspective-taking stresses the growth of social skills that results from using advanced cognitive skills to put oneself in another's place and to perceive the self as perceived by others. These perceptual skills help students develop realistic expectations of their friends, of themselves as friends, and of friendship as a social relationship.

In this chapter, we examine patterns of development in concepts of proximity,

3. Examining Theories of Adolescent Friendships 45

balance, status, exchange, and other-perspective-taking across the middle and high school grades.

ADDING ENVIRONMENTAL FACTORS TO THEORIES OF SELECTION

Recent research on developmental issues has not considered that the environments in which youngsters interact influence whether, how early, and how deeply children develop abilities to consider many pieces of information simultaneously and take the perspective of others in social situations.

Inhelder and Piaget (1958) maintain that the social milieu and the physical environment interact with neurological development to produce new levels of cognition. To the extent that the environment affects thought processes, it should also affect how friends are perceived, understood, selected, or rejected. How one perceives and interprets others' thoughts and feelings, and how important it is to do so, may be influenced directly by what social behaviors and abilities are valued and rewarded in the environments in which children are grouped and friends are made.

School environments may influence person-perception and other-perspective-taking in direct ways. In differently organized classrooms, rewards are offered for different social behaviors—for example, whether cooperative or competitive behavior is rewarded may depend on how tasks are designed and how grades are distributed. Conflicts among peers may be ignored or resolved in different classes; activities may be included or excluded in the school program that help students anticipate reactions of others and consequences of their actions; and decisions can be made to include or exclude identifiably different students in work groups. Thus, the developmental perspective on social relations is not the only important aspect of childhood that must be added to adult theories of selection of friends; the environmental conditions of social relations must also be considered.

EXAMINING SELECTED THEORETICAL CONCEPTS

Longitudinal data were collected from 4163 students in Grades 5, 6, 8, and 11 in 1973, and again in Grades 6, 7, 9, and 12 in 1974 (Epstein, 1980; Epstein & McPartland, 1979; McPartland & Epstein, 1977). The two surveys obtained information from the students and up to three of their close friends in school on their personal characteristics, family and school environments, and achievement and affective outcomes. These data are described more fully in Chapter 5, which presents analyses of patterns of selection, and in Chapter 11, which presents analyses of patterns of influence. We use these data in this chapter to examine how the concepts of proximity, balance, status, and exchange work for youngsters, and how developmental and environmental perspectives add to an understanding of the selection process.

Proximity

Proximity and Changes in Cross-Sex and Cross-Race Selections. The panel on the left side of Table 3.1 shows that the correlations between a student's sex and the sex composition of the school population is small and consistent across the years. In this sample, as in most schools, there are about equal numbers of males and females. In contrast, the correlation of a student's sex with the sex of best friends is always strongly positive. Students tend to select same-sex friends. However, the correlation coefficient changes markedly in Grade 12, when a greater number of cross-sex choices are made. Other analyses show that this increase is mainly due to an increase in girls selecting boys as best friends, although cross-sex choices in Grade 12 increase for both sexes.

This pattern, due in part to increased dating in the high school years, illustrates a developmental change in social awareness and acceptance. Males and females are in proximity from first grade on, but they begin to associate as best friends only when it becomes sufficiently rewarding for them to do so.

Proximity also affects students' cross-race choices of friends. The panel on the right side of Table 3.1 shows that the correlation between a student's race and the racial composition of the school remains comparable across the grades. The slightly lower correlations in Grades 9 and 12 reflect the more equal representation of blacks and whites in high schools. At the middle school level, students are more likely to attend schools where, on the average, their own racial group may be more predominant than at the high school level. The percentage of same-race choices of best friends increases markedly in Grades 9 and 12, even though there is greater opportunity for cross-race contacts in high schools. The increase in same-race choices may be linked to the increase in students' cross-sex friendships, if earlier cross-race, same-sex best friend choices are replaced by cross-sex, same-race choices. Or the patterns of fewer cross-race friends may result from greater segregation in high school tracks, courses, and extracurricular activities.

TABLE 3.1
Correlation of Student Sex and Race with Average Sex and Race in School and Friendship Group, by Grade

	Sex		Race	
	Correlation of students' own and		Correlation of students' own and	
Grade	Average in school	Average in friendship group	Average in school	Average in friendship group
6	.101	.902	.268	.757
7	.083	.920	.318	.628
9	.070	.895	.209	.823
12	.085	.690	.225	.886

If we looked only at the selections made by the total high school population, gender and race would appear to be the only important characteristics for the selection of close friends. By looking at developmental patterns across the grades, we can see that maturation and social development alter how students who are in proximity change in their cross-sex and cross-race selections of friends in school. Males and females increasingly acknowledge their proximity where they previously ignored each other; blacks and whites increasingly ignore their proximity where they previously acknowledged it (see also Asher, Singleton, & Taylor, 1982; Singleton & Asher, 1979). The varied ad hoc explanations for the patterns we report can be clarified in future research with measures of the cross-race, cross-sex choices of all friends (not only best friends) and with measures of the racial composition of the various proximate school and classroom environments that students experience during the schoolday.

If race becomes a characteristic on which balanced associations are built, then there should be an increase in reciprocated relationships in the more balanced choices of same-race friends. Longitudinal data across grades for several years are needed to detect this development. In terms of exchange, increased selections of cross-sex friends may result from increased rewards for association; fewer selections of cross-race friends may result from decreased rewards for association by other students, family, or the formal organization of the school. Research on perceived rewards and costs across grades in coeducational and desegregated settings will clarify these issues.

Change in the Meaning of Proximity by Expanding Boundaries.   Other developmental and environmental patterns related to proximity are reported in Chapter 5. These analyses indicate that younger students in middle school grades select more of their friends from their own academic classes, whereas students in high school grades select more friends from outside their own teachers' rooms. Moreover, in differently organized middle schools, students select friends from different vicinities—students in high-participatory instructional programs choose more students from outside their own teachers' classrooms; students in low-participatory programs choose more students from their own classrooms. Students select friends from expanded or limited boundaries based on how the school organizes student contacts.

Balance

Balance theory emphasizes the importance of reciprocated and stable friendships. This emphasis raises important questions for student friendships. In our sample, almost half the students do not have one reciprocated best friend at school, and over two-thirds do not have a stable best friend over 1 year. Future studies need to obtain better data on reciprocity and stability based on more complete measures of friends in and out of school, but we can use our data to explore whether there is movement *toward* reciprocation and stability in longitudi-

TABLE 3.2
Standardized Scores of Reciprocations among Students, Best Friends, and Friends of Friends at Time 1 and Time 2, by Grade and Sex[a]

	Reciprocation student and friends		Reciprocation student and friends—female		Reciprocation student and friends—male		Reciprocation friend of each other		Reciprocation student, friends, and their friends	
	Time 1	Time 2	Time 1	Time 2	Time 1	Time 2	Time 1	Time 2	Time 1	Time 2
Grades										
5–6	.094	.097	.105	.117	.082	.077	.208	.179	.279	.244
6–7	.084	.104	.096	.115	.073	.092	.184	.186	.241	.262
8–9	.101	.108	.123	.134	.076	.079	.187	.165	.233	.222
11–12	.075	.087	.103	.109	.045	.063	.122	.135	.149	.175
Female	.107	.120					.217	.205	.285	.281
Male	.073	.080					.150	.136	.190	.185

[a]Friendship selections were standardized for number of choices made.

nal data on best friends—the friendships most likely to be reciprocated and stable. Table 3.2 shows changes in reciprocation for each grade from one year to the next for students, their best friends, and extended social networks that include relationships among a student's best friends and among the friends of the best friends.

At each grade level, and for males and females, there are small but consistent indications of increased reciprocation between students and their three best friends. From one year to the next, more friendships were reciprocated among best friends. The increases in reciprocations are greater for females and for students progressing from Grade 6 to Grade 7 and from Grade 11 to Grade 12.

When broader networks of friends are considered among best friends and among the friends of best friends, the pattern is mixed. Students in Grades 6 and 9 *decrease* in reciprocations, and students in Grades 7 and 12 *increase*. These mixed patterns may be related to the school organization of grade levels. In this sample, students moved from elementary to middle school after Grade 5 and from middle to high school after Grade 8. These natural upheavals place students and their friends in larger, more diverse populations. The transitions to new schools do not affect the reciprocations among best friends, but they do affect the patterns of relations in the extended social networks.

Both for close friends and in the broader network of friends, males in Grade 6 have fewer reciprocated friends than they had 1 year earlier. This may be because the major transition years—Grades 6 and 9 for this sample—are more disruptive for male than for female friendship networks, or it may be that males make friends in new and larger schools in different ways and at different rates than females, with males' best friends making wider choices among students in new schools. Eder and Hallinan (1978) suggest that boys may have less difficulty than girls making new friends. It would be informative to compare these patterns for males and females to the patterns in schools that have different transition grades (i.e., beginning junior high school in Grade 7 and high school in Grade 10). Also, these patterns could be compared to the patterns of males and females who change schools at various grade levels.

TABLE 3.3

Range of Percentages of Stable Friends from Grade 6 to Grade 12, for Time 1 Reciprocated or Unreciprocated Friends, for First, Second, and Third Best Friends[a]

	Percentage reciprocated and stable	Percentage unreciprocated and stable
Friend 1	32–56	7–10
Friend 2	25–42	6–8
Friend 3	20–44	2–5

[a] In all cases Grade 6 is the low and Grade 12 is the high percentage in the range.

Table 3.3 shows the range of percentages from Grade 6 to Grade 12 of students whose first, second, and third best friends are stable. First-named friends are more likely to be stable friends whether or not they are reciprocated. Reciprocated friends are more likely than unreciprocated friends to be stable. Tests of differences in proportions of stable friends across the grades showed that first-named, reciprocated friends are significantly more stable than second-named, reciprocated friends for students in Grade 12 only—another indication that older students exercise greater selectivity in choosing friends.

In other tests not tabulated here, we examined whether youngsters reported more stress under different conditions of friendship. Measures of five types of stressful behaviors or attitudes were used: high anxiety about school life, poor classroom behavior, eagerness to change schools, feelings of low control over the environment, and low self-esteem. Students had significantly higher stress (less positive adjustment) if they made no friendship choices themselves or if they had *neither* reciprocated nor stable friends. For example, with initial Time 1 classroom behavior taken into account, students continued to have poor classroom behavior if they made no choices of best friends or if their choices were neither reciprocated nor stable. The same continuing effects were present for feelings of control over the environment. With Time 1 scores statistically controlled, students who selected no friends in school or who had neither reciprocated nor stable friendships had significantly lower feelings of control over the environment than did other students.

Other research also notes the uncertain importance of reciprocity on influence. Kandel and Lesser (1970), for example, point out the greater importance of the person selected "best friend overall" or "school best friend," regardless of the reciprocity of the selection. Leinhardt (1972), Hallinan (1976a), Hallinan and Tuma (1978), J. Cohen (1977), and Rubin (1980) note the short-term, unstable nature of student alliances.

We have some evidence that there are developmental and environmental conditions that affect reciprocation and stability in student friendships. Tables 3.2 and 3.3 suggest that reciprocity increases slightly in students' friendships, especially in years when students remain in the same school. Older students have more stable friends. In order for friendships to be reciprocated and stable, students must respond accurately to cues given by others about their needs for support, understanding, or company (Leinhardt, 1972). But if the skills needed to take the other's perspective or to perceive the self through the eyes of others are not yet developed, or if the environment does not permit the expression of these mutual awarenesses, then mutuality and stability will not develop between friends.

Status

Status in students' friendships may be defined in terms of what a child *has* (e.g., video equipment, a new type of pen, a collection of records) or *does* (e.g., play a sport or game well, dance well, do magic tricks). There may be great diversity in the particular status-enhancing conditions at different ages, for males and females, for students from different socioeconomic backgrounds (Pope, 1953), and in differently organized schools or classrooms.

Developmental and Environmental Patterns of Initiation and Response. *Initiation* refers to the *selection* by low-status students of high-status friends; *response* refers to the *acceptance or rejection* by high-status students of low-status friends. Table 3.4 shows the percentage of reciprocated and unreciprocated first-chosen best friends according to their family social class. About the same proportion of low- and high-SES friends are reciprocated and unreciprocated. It is no more likely that a low-SES student and low-SES friend will reciprocate their choices than will a low-SES student and high-SES friend. Similar nonsignificant patterns are found for students' second and third choices of best friends. Social class does not appear to be an important status characteristic for reciprocation of friends in school.

A different interpretation is needed, however, when we take environmental conditions into account. An examination of high- and low-participatory schools shows how school environments affect the initiation–response processes. In high-participatory schools (with greater opportunity for meeting and working with diverse students), low-scoring students make more selections of high-scoring friends. In Table 3.5, three status criteria are used: SES, college plans, and self-reliant behavior. In high-participatory environments, students who are low in self-reliance, college plans, and SES more often select at least one friend who is higher than themselves on each criterion. The reciprocations or responses to low-status students by high-status friends also vary in contrasting school environments. In high-participatory schools, about 54% of high-status students reciprocate the friendships of lower-status students on these measures. In contrast, in low-participatory schools, about 36% of high-status students reciprocate low-status choices.

School environments can affect the number of high- and low-status students who select each other as friends. The programs and experiences in high-participatory schools, which put more students in contact with each other on important activities and make students more aware of the varied strengths and weaknesses of others, may increase the likelihood that low- and high-status students will accept

TABLE 3.4
Percentages of High- and Low-SES Students with Reciprocated High- and Low-SES Friends[a]

| | Low-SES friend | | High-SES friend | | |
Own score	Reciprocated	Unreciprocated	Reciprocated	Unreciprocated	χ^2
Low SES	56	44	57	43	0.045 (NS)[b]
High SES	55	45	60	40	2.367 (NS)

[a]N's for the table are low SES: 370, 282, 272, 202; high SES: 272, 220, 466, 314.
[b]NS = nonsignificant.

TABLE 3.5
Percentages of Low-scoring Students Who Select at Least One Friend Higher Than Themselves, in Low-, Mid-, and High-Participatory Schools

Student's own score	Low-participatory	Mid-level participatory	High-participatory	χ^2
Low in self-reliance	72	73	83	13.43
Low in college plans	55	66	80	43.73
Low in SES	75	80	93	22.25

each other. The students may place less emphasis on any single criterion of status if the school emphasizes the importance of what students *do* rather than what they *have* or what they *are*. Low-participatory programs based on fixed group memberships, restricted interaction on schoolwork, and close supervision by teachers may emphasize the traditional meanings of *status*.

J. Cohen (1979b) points out that socioeconomic class becomes less important as a criterion for choice of friends when the visible material possessions of students are similar, despite other real differences in family status. Our data suggest that school organizations can blur traditional status criteria by reducing the emphasis on differences among students and by making particular behaviors more visible and important than standard status criteria.

Table 3.6 examines the selection of high-scoring students as friends across the grade levels. About 85% of the sixth-grade students have at least one friend who is high in SES, compared to 63% of the twelfth-graders. The older students restrict the number of their best friends and increasingly select students more like themselves.

These explorations suggest that SES is not a criterion on which students base reciprocation of best friends. However, the process of selection and reciprocity of high- and low-scoring students was influenced by the age of the student and by organization of the instructional program. When the invitation for friendship is

TABLE 3.6
Percentages of Students Who Select at Least One Friend Higher Than Themselves, by Grade Level

Grade	High SES	High self-reliance	High college plans
6	85	80	87
7	79	75	83
9	70	72	82
12	63	68	83
χ^2	131.63*	33.88*	6.95 (NS)[a]

*χ^2 significant beyond the .001 level.
[a]NS = nonsignificant.

extended in a high-participatory environment, a positive response may be returned more readily because students have come to know about a variety of traits and characteristics of other students through their frequent interactions.

Exchange

Similarity as a Reward or Cost in Relationships. All interaction is a system of exchange, but exchange theory requires explicit attention to the rewards and costs of relationships and to the equivalence of rewards and costs in social exchanges. We can investigate the costs or rewards that are associated with whether students and their friends are similar or different on particular attitudes a ıd behaviors.

Table 3.7 shows rates of reciprocation and stability among friends in differently structured groups when college plans is the criterion of equal or unequal standing. Students are categorized as belonging to four differently structured friendship groups—LL, LH, HL, and HH. The first letter in each category indicates the students' own scores (L = low; H = high) on measures of college plans on the Time 1 survey. The second letter of each category indicates the average Time 1 scores of the students' friends on the same measures. Two of the assumed rewards of social exchange are reciprocation and stability of friends.

There is no difference in the percentage of students with reciprocated friendships in each type of friendship group. And only the high-scoring students with high-scoring friends have significantly more stable friendships than students in other groups. There is no indication that reciprocity of friendships is a reward that is more likely to occur when friends are similar on this measure. Nor is there support for the assumption that high-scoring students typically reject each other to reduce the stress of competing among themselves. We know very little about whether, how, or when students begin to think in terms of costs and benefits of association, or about the ratio of payoffs to expenditures in their friendships (Hamblin & Pitcher, 1979), or about the criteria on which these questions are decided. Other analyses in Chapter 11 of this volume suggest that these differently structured friendship groups have different influence patterns that could be considered rewards or costs to development.

TABLE 3.7
Percentage of Students with Reciprocated and Stable Choices in Differently Structured Friendship Groups

	Friendship group structures at Time 1[a]				
	LL	LH	HL	HH	χ^2
Percentage reciprocated	64	63	65	65	0.554
Percentage stable	38	38	36	42	6.873

[a]Based on college plans: LL = low student, low friends; LH = low student, high friends; HL = high student, low friends; HH = high student, high friends.

Stress as a Cost in Associations.   Some would equate stress with costs in relationships. For example, when we classify students and their friends on achievement test scores, we find that students in LL groups (initially low-achieving
students with initially low-achieving friends) are more eager to change schools
than are students in LH groups ($\chi^2 = 3.927$, $p < .05$). Low-scoring friends may
carry a cost for other students. Students may feel that if they went to a different
school they would have different and more positive friends or have better attitudes
about school.

In studies of adults, the costs and rewards of friendships may be determined by
the likelihood that friends will contribute to the individual's aims and goals. These
goals may be social (companionship), economic (advancement in business), interest oriented (improvement of personal skills), and so on. Youngsters' goals are
in the process of definition and development. For example, students report an
increasing awareness of their own interests:

	Grade			
	6	7	9	12
"I really can't say what my interests are" (% false)	68	76	77	84

The increased awareness of personal interests may help to explain why older
students' friends tend to be more similar in characteristics and more stable. If they
can better identify their own goals and more accurately compare their friends'
attitudes and goals with their own, then they can select and keep friends with
whom they can exchange support for goals.

Future research on the use of exchange theory for explaining student friendships should combine longitudinal survey data and intensive interviews across age
groups to study the emergence and development of student awareness of rewards
and costs of friendships in differently structured friendship groups and differently
structured environments.

COGNITIVE DEVELOPMENT AND THE PERCEPTION
OF THE SELF AND OTHERS

Youngsters may be as incorrect about their self-assessments as they are in their
assessments of others (Elkind, 1971, 1974; Flavell, 1977; Flavell *et al.*, 1968).
These inaccuracies contribute to the testing and changing of friends. In this
section, we illustrate how evidence on students' cognitive development can enhance the other explanations of adolescents' friendships.

TABLE 3.8
Percentages of Students Who Say They Would Not
Want to Sit Next to Some Other Students, by Sex

Grade	Females	Males
6	86	79
7	78	77
9	70	75
12	57	63

Restructuring Perspectives

One of the tenets of cognitive theory is that older students are better able to take the perspective of others, which is said to be the prerequisite for true mutuality in friendship. Early adolescents show a unique and important egocentrism in their interactions with others—they focus most of their attention on themselves (Elkind, 1971; Flavell, 1977; Inhelder & Piaget, 1958). Adolescents do become increasingly aware of others and are able to act in others' interests, even to a point of sacrificing self-interest (Carter *et al.*, 1980; Levinger, 1974; Schofield, 1981; Selman, 1976). In our data, two items—one concerning choice of seating arrangements and the other concerning laws and rules—offer clues about the restructuring of perspectives about the self and others. Table 3.8 shows clear differences by grade level in students' responses to an item that asked if there were students they would not want to sit next to—a question that deals partly with consideration of the feelings of other students. There is a significant decrease in exclusionary responses across the grades ($F = 38.71$) and especially in Grade 12 for males and females.

The reasons for the differences in students' responses must be sorted out in future research. Younger students may be expressing same-sex preferences in seating patterns. Students may be exhibiting a tolerance of others, or students may be grouped more homogeneously in later grades. Older students may have

TABLE 3.9
Percentage of Students Answering "True" to Questions about Laws and Rules

	Grade				
	5	6	8	11	F statistic
Laws are necessary	89	88	92	96	5.16
School rules are necessary	86	81	95	89	3.35
Students should never question school rules	41	37	17	8	54.55

more control over whom they sit next to in class, or they may be able to separate sitting next to from befriending or be more alert to giving socially accepted answers. Whatever the reason, however, the pattern shows that older students react differently from younger students when they are asked to think about themselves in relation to others.

Students also change their perceptions of the world and their place in it. For example, across the grades, students agree that laws and rules are necessary, but older students clearly perceive their right to question school rules (see Table 3.9).

Comparing Self and Others

Another set of survey questions asked students to report perceptions of themselves and others on a variety of attitudes and behaviors. Table 3.10 shows differences across the adolescent years of perceptions of self and others on several measures: classroom motivation, self-reliance, values of good grades and popularity, and admission of anger. To questions about the self ("I"), students' responses about their motivations in class (e.g., that they would *not* work their hardest if they were not given grades) become increasingly realistic. They report increasingly that they become more self-reliant, value good grades less, say popularity is *not* the most important value, and admit that they get angry.

Students consistently report themselves in a more positive light than others, but they change their perceptions of self more than they change their perceptions of others. The more realistic personal assessments result in generally less difference in reports about the self and others on some measures. For example, differences between the self and others all but disappear on importance of good grades in school and the acknowledgment of feeling angry at times. However, reported differences between the self and others increase on the measures of self-reliance and the importance of popularity. Students raise their estimates of their own self-reliance, while estimates of others' self-reliance remain relatively stable. The importance of popularity decreases for the self, while it is viewed as continuously important to other students. Other-perspective-taking may mean that students perceive similarities *and* differences of self and others more accurately with age. Measures that define particular groups of others (e.g., best friends, all students in a school or grade, nonschool friends, other males or other females, etc.) should be part of future studies that compare students' perceptions of themselves and other students.

Males report that they have lower motivation in school, have lower self-reliance, are more in search of popularity, are less in search of good grades, and are less likely to get angry than females. Although the differences between males and females are small, the patterns are consistent across most grade levels. On most measures, in all grades, males report less difference between themselves and others than do females.

Other analyses indicate that the students' self-perceptions may be related to patterns of friendships. For example, students who admit they get angry have a

TABLE 3.10

Mean Scores of Students' Reports of Self and Others on Realistic Classroom Behaviors, Self-reliance, Importance of Good Grades and Popularity, and Getting Angry, by Grade and Sex

	Sex	Grade level			
		6	7	9	12
Realistic classroom behaviors[a]					
"I"	F	1.32	1.53	2.00	1.94
	M	1.62	1.93	2.22	2.33
"Other"	F	3.43	3.51	3.71	3.79
	M	3.01	3.23	3.26	3.53
Difference (I − 0)[b]	F	−2.10	−2.02	−1.76	−1.93
	M	−1.48	−1.29	−1.04	−1.19
Self-reliance[c]					
I"	F	7.75	8.33	9.03	9.98
	M	7.77	8.08	8.78	9.67
	F	5.83	5.82	5.62	5.95
"Other"	M	6.06	5.96	6.98	6.08
Difference (I − 0)	F	2.43	3.09	3.73	4.13
	M	2.38	2.79	3.17	3.94
Importance of grades (% true)					
"I"	F	86	79	66	59
	M	85	78	72	48
"Other"	F	63	52	47	52
	M	58	56	54	56
Difference (I − 0)	F	24	25	20	05
	M	27	20	17	−04
Importance of popularity					
"I"	F	15	15	15	06
	M	21	23	19	13
"Other"	F	61	62	66	62
	M	56	61	62	58
Difference (I − 0)	F	−45	−49	−49	−56
	M	−35	−39	−42	−44
Sometimes get angry (% true)					
"I"	F	57	55	69	69
	M	56	56	60	63
"Other"	F	78	70	77	71
	M	63	68	72	67
Difference (I − 0)	F	−22	−17	−09	−04
	M	−07	−10	−10	−03

[a]This scale of 5 items includes: If there were no report cards, I/other students would still work just as hard in school; if I/other students knew the teacher was not going to collect my/their homework, I/they would not do my/their best. Internal reliability is .63. The scale is scored so that a higher score indicates a more realistic (or less prosocial) response.

[b]Difference (I − 0) scores are the average of individual differences, not the simple subtraction of averaged Other from averaged I.

[c]This scale of 13 items includes: I just cannot say "no" when my friends call me to do something with them; I like the kind of teacher who tells me how to do my work. Internal reliability is .70.

greater number of reciprocated friendships than do students who do not; those who say popularity is most important tend to be those without reciprocated or stable friends. Much more must be done with longitudinal data to explicate the connection between the awareness of others and patterns of friendship across the grades and in differently organized environments.

DISCUSSION

There are important differences between theories *applied to* and theories *generated from* the experiences of different age groups. For example, Kohlberg's (1969) theory of moral development generated from research on males was applied uncritically to females and discussed as a general theory. Work by Gilligan (1977) shows that the moral development of females requires a different model and cannot be usefully examined only by using males as the standard for comparison. In research on friendship selection, it is important for known differences between adults and children to guide the theoretical model and the interpretation of data on children's selections of friends. Theories of adult attraction and friendship selection must be combined with theories of cognitive and social development and environmental effects to explain children's friendships.

Even theories of adult friendships are not very clear about how basic concepts work in actual friendships. Heider (1958) was uneasy about the contradictions in and exceptions to balanced relationships. He recognized the need to consider the cognitive matrix that underlies the interpretation of others' behavior and the misperceptions of others' behavior due to adults' cognitive dissonance, illusions, and misunderstandings. These concerns are even more important when considering youngsters' choices of friends. If a young person cannot perceive or judge accurately the behavior of another or the importance of a behavior, then it is unlikely that a balanced, stable relation can be formed. As perceptual skills of self and others improve in adolescence, reciprocated and stable choices should increase.

Blau (1964) reviews problems with exchange theory by discussing other relationships—love, obedience, gratitude, and greed—that are not based on equivalent rewards or costs, justice, fairness, or equity. He and Gouldner (1960) recognized that multiple forces cause adjustments and reassessments in adult relationships from the point of attraction, to the point of estimating rewards and costs, to the point of mutual acceptance and intimacy. Even more adjustments may occur in youngsters' relationships because of concurrent cognitive, social, and moral development; requirements imposed by socializing environments; and the vagaries of daily social exchange.

The important concepts in favored theories—proximity, balance, status, exchange—each have some importance for students' friendship choices, but developmental and environmental effects change the way the concepts apply and how they are interpreted.

Proximity. Proximity can be narrowly defined for younger children and broadly defined for older students. Curricular, extracurricular, and out-of-school activities extend the geographic and motivational bases for older students' friendship choices. School organizations can restrict or expand the boundaries that determine which students are in proximity. Social and biological development affect how youngsters who are in proximity interact. Thus, the boundaries within which friends are selected expand with age and change with the structure of the school environment.

Balance. The important feature of balanced friendships for adults is their relative predictability and stability. We know that youngsters' friendships are neither predictable nor stable over 1 year. The cognitive, social, and environmental conditions that are prerequisites for balanced relationships do not exist for children in the same way as for adults. Two students may have different perceptions of a third friend; one member of a friendship group may move away or change schools or classes; two students may not agree for long about the importance of an object or an attitude. The emergence in older students of more accurate estimates of their own and others' attitudes, behaviors, and goals may help to move students toward reciprocated and stable friendships.

Our data suggest that academic and social stress in school may be associated more with isolation (not making or receiving any choices) than with imbalanced, unreciprocated, or unstable friendship choices. We need much more information on whether certain school environments make isolation, nonreciprocation, or instability more important and more stressful to students than do other environments.

Status. The definition and distribution of status is shown in our data to be altered by the age and cognitive structures of the students and by the social organization of the school and class. Little is known about students' definitions or concepts of status. Our data suggest that socioeconomic status is not an important variable for reciprocation of friendships, that different demographic characteristics of students in schools and classes determine whether students' friends will be more or less heterogeneous on varied characteristics, and that educational environments can emphasize the importance of particular status characteristics and affect the selection or rejection of certain students as friends.

Exchange. To anticipate the rewards or costs of friendship choices, one must be able to predict the benefits or problems that would occur in a relationship and how problems among friends will be resolved. This requires a synthesis of knowledge about people and past events and an evaluation of the likely consequences of association. Piagetian theory predicts that these skills are unlikely to develop in most students before mid- to late adolescence. Some school environments hasten or retard the development and use of these cognitive skills in ways that affect students' social relations.

Real mutuality in friendships requires that both parties have the ability and the inclination to forgo self-interests when necessary (accept the costs of friendship) and express genuine concern for the other (give rewards for friendship). Until mutual relations are considered worth their costs, friendships are guided by the kind of egocentrism described by Elkind (1971), which serves mainly the individual's own social, emotional, and informational needs.

These observations can be integrated to relate friendship selection to developmental and environmental characteristics:

> In terms of the student's cognitive development, the more *complex* the individual's cognitive structure, the more *exclusive* the individual's selection of friends. Conversely, the *less complex* the individual's cognitive structure, the more *inclusive* the selection of friends.

> In terms of the school environments in which friends are made, the more *associative* the environment, the more familiarity and *acceptance* in the population, and the greater *diversity* in the characteristics of the individual's friends. The more *dissociative* the environment, the more unfamiliarity and *isolation* in the population, and the more *similarity* in the characteristics of the individual and his or her friends.

These principles, derived from the current exploration in selected theoretical concepts, must be examined in future research on the selection of friends and best friends. In this chapter, and in others in this volume, results are reported that younger students select more best friends and change best friends more frequently than do older students, who tend to be more selective in school, make more out-of-school selections, and make more stable choices over 1 year. The development of more complex cognitive structures permits greater differentiation and selectivity of friends. Students in more associative (participatory) environments find at least one friend more readily, reciprocate their friendships more often, and make more diverse friends from wider contacts in schools. More complex cognitive and environmental factors may increase the changing of friends as more opportunities for interacting and testing friendships occur. Students who continue to learn about themselves and others have the chance to be right *and* to be wrong in their judgments of self, friends, and the values on which they base their selections of friends.

Negative features in an environment—ridicule, discrimination, low expectations, stereotypes, repressions, punishment, isolation—may increase the dissociative quality of the setting and affect the thought processes and social behaviors of students. Positive characteristics of an environment—rewards, equity, high expectations, appreciation, esteem, opportunities for participation—may increase the associative quality of the setting and affect cognitive and social behavior. Students' selections of friends may be influenced by positive and negative features of the environment at any age in ways that affect expected stages of social development.

No single theory, but a sequence of theories and combination of concepts, may be needed to adequately explain youngsters' friendships. For example, being directly rewarded for taking turns—a cost to the individual in an exchange—could help 3 year olds learn social skills and improve their social relations. However, being directly rewarded for personal sacrifice—another type of cost in an exchange—would not be understood by preschool children. For another example, young children do not typically make long-term plans, nor do they understand or prepare for delayed consequences of their own and others' behaviors (Maccoby, 1968). Selections of friends are first based on immediate consequences of shared games and activities, candy, or company, and these interactions are destined to be short lived. Thus, young children can internalize basic but not advanced elements of exchange.

It is suggested that balance and status are concepts about attraction and friendship choice that may be too static to adequately represent students' selection processes. *Social exchange* implies a rational determination of real and abstract benefits and losses of associations, and actions based on the estimates of rewards or costs. These elements of exchange may not fit youngsters' patterns of thought or the demands of school environments for seemingly high-cost, low-reward interactions. When developmental and environmental perspectives are used to interpret patterns of association, we get a better understanding of how the selection process changes across the years of childhood and adolescence. The illustrations offered in this chapter should generate new hypotheses and more pertinent theories of youngsters' friendships.

ACKNOWLEDGMENTS

The author is grateful for helpful suggestions from Denise Kandel and John Gottman, who served at professional meetings as discussants on earlier drafts of sections of this chapter.

ELIZABETH DOUVAN   4

Commentary:
Theoretical Perspectives
on Peer Association

Adolescence is a period in life when friendship and peer relations move to center stage in the developmental drama. Both psychological and social structural forces contribute to the young person's need and aptitude for friendship. The biopsychological changes of puberty disrupt childhood adaptation and defenses, stirring and opening the personality and launching the child on the search for a workable, acceptable identity.

The impulsiveness of adolescence is decried by parents, but it is also an aspect of the loosened personality structure that provides the youngster both motivation and talent for friendship. Interpersonal attraction and the mutual exploration of selves that define close friendship are stimulated by the lively, colorful, intense, and open quality of the adolescent self. When, as adults, we settle securely into roles and an identity, we close options and aspects of the self. We slip into routine performance of roles that express our selves, but the self is, in a real sense, distanced from social interactions. In adolescence, the self overflows its tentative boundaries and engages others directly. Friendship at this stage is rich, intense, vivid, and volatile, and it absorbs and centers much of the young person's energy.

Peer interaction and peer norms have particular force at this time because the young person is in the process of detaching from parents and seeking new principles by which to guide behavior and to define and structure the forming identity. The fact that friendship and the role of friends are in the process of formation in this period may expose aspects of the process that are obscured in the more settled

63

FRIENDS IN SCHOOL
Patterns of Selection and Influence in Secondary Schools

relationships of adults. The study of adolescent friendship may offer insights that could not be realized so readily at any other stage of development.

Another feature that makes adolescence ideal for analysis of friendship is the social setting in which adolescents spend much of their time. Until age 16—and much longer for many youths—young people's social interaction is structured by school. Practically, this means that the researcher has easy access to adolescents and their friends, and that most of the young person's social relationships will be formed and conducted in the school setting.

NEXT STEPS IN THEORY CONSTRUCTION

Our understanding of and theories about adolescence have developed to a point where it is both possible and promising to join developments in a number of disciplines for a richer, more densely textured theoretical formulation. In psychology, the contributions of Erikson (1950), Piaget (1932), and the social learning theorists have changed our perspective on the transitional period of adolescence and have sensitized us to content and process variables we must attend to if we want to understand friendships in young people's lives.

Erikson's critical-stage theory has focused attention on adolescence as a key stage for analysis of social interaction. The task of adolescence—identity development—and the central process by which it is accomplished—experimentation with various roles and ways of performing them (a period that Erikson calls the "psychosocial moratorium")—frame a set of questions about adolescence that place friendship high on the list of priorities for analysis and clarify the functions that friendship performs in development at this life stage.

Erikson as well as Piaget suggest that true interpersonal relations are unlikely to occur before adolescence. Because friendship involves the encounter between selves, the preadolescent chumship at the center of Sullivan's (1953) developmental theory does not qualify as truly interpersonal. The latency child has not consciously focused on self-development or identity issues. The outlines of a consistent and acceptable self-definition have not been drawn, nor is it the issue of central concern. The youngster does not distinguish self-as-subject from self-as-object and is not engaged, as the adolescent becomes, in distancing from the self, evaluating and critically judging the self, and taking steps to bring it into line with ego ideals and goals. The latency child is immersed in action but is not yet self-conscious.

Erikson's theory also leads to hypotheses about expected changes in friendship during the adolescent period. For example, friendship in early adolescence will focus on mutual self-exploration and issues of similarity and loyalty. Unsure of the lines of identity, the young partner uses friendship to discover and validate the self. The friend helps in this process by reflecting back similar tastes and characteristics. The process demands much similarity between partners, and, because it carries such critical self-involvement, the friendship must at all costs be secure.

Thus, loyalty becomes a key element of defining friendship and a key criterion used in judging and measuring it. In late adolescence, when identity is limned more clearly, the youngster can tolerate greater individuality in the friend (i.e., greater differences between the friend and the self) without feeling self-definition challenged or endangered by it. Loyalty is still an important part of the relationship, but it is now defined less rigidly, without so great an emphasis on similarity of tastes and attitudes. Variations can now be used to test and consolidate the sense of self; they do not automatically threaten the self-concept or lead to defensive rejection of the friend.

When we bring the issue of loyalty into our analytic frame—and adolescents themselves will force it on us—Piagetian theory becomes relevant to the discussion. Piaget's formulations about the cognitive capacities of various developmental stages direct us to adolescence for the analysis of friendship. Because such concepts as loyalty, similarity, mutuality, and variation are abstract, they require the achievement of abstract thought. And it is only at adolescence that the child fully achieves this capacity. The theory, then, urges a focus on the adolescent period, and Piaget's methods of investigation also offer models that can be applied to inquiry into friendship as well as thought about other aspects of social relationships. Kohlberg (1970), Gilligan (1980), and others have applied Piaget's methods and principles to the analysis of moral thought. Hoffman (1980) has extended the theory to the realms of empathy, altruism, and prosocial behavior—areas closely implicated in friendship.

Social learning theory can also contribute to analysis of adolescent social interaction. Friendship has not been a focus of concern to leading theorists of this school, but anthropologists and social psychologists who look at different styles of friendship imply social learning concepts in much of their theorizing. Thus, when J. C. Coleman (1974, 1980) and other investigators discuss differences between the adolescent friendships of males and females, they assume a social learning model that says that young men and women learn styles of interaction from adults who are similar to them—same-sex parent, teachers, and so forth. We assume that youngsters are socialized to adhere to sex-appropriate norms for behavior and also that a modeling process occurs in which same-sex adults are attended and imitated both consciously and unconsciously. Rewards are systematically attached to sex-linked and sex-appropriate behavior, and the young person learns to behave in the ways that yield reward.

When anthropologists, such as Graves and Eckert (see Graves, 1975), describe different cultural styles of friendship among adolescents—say, the inclusive style of Polynesian children contrasted with the exclusive style of New Zealand youngsters—they note the ways in which teachers act out and encourage the culturally preferred style, and the conscious and unconscious rewards that parents offer to reinforce the child's socialization to that style. Clearly, they implicitly use social learning theory as a central mechanism in the process.

On the side of structure, sociology, anthropology, and social history have all contributed insights and theory that can be useful in understanding adolescent friendship. Early theoretical work by Lewin (1935), Mannheim (1952), and K. Davis (1949) pointed to critical–structural aspects of the adolescent situation: the relation between generations, the marginal outsider status of the adolescent, the fact that the adolescent is neither child nor adult but some nether status between these two clearly stated normative positions.

Shellef (1981) extended and recast the view of generational exchange. The work of Eisenstadt (1964) in sociology and N. Davis (1971), Demos (1970), and other social historians has raised critical and pertinent questions concerning age grading and youth groups and their functions in social control and the social integration of youth to the larger social order. They have suggested the social conditions under which youth groups will assume significance as well as whom and how they will control.

Feminist critique of the family has exposed another insight about the situation of the adolescent: As she or he moves out of the family of origin (psychologically, if not physically) and has yet to establish a family of procreation, the adolescent or youth is, for the only time in the life cycle, outside the hierarchical–patriarchal authority system of the family. The adolescent's relevant social reference is horizontal rather than vertical. Authority rests in the peer group—the spread of horizontal relations—rather than vertically above in one's parents or exercised vertically downward to one's children.

This insight clarifies society's need for some form of social control over youths, the innovative quality of adolescent society, and the particular features of youth groups described by Eisenstadt and Davis. It also clarifies certain widely noted and empirically supported features of adolescent friendships: the improbable friendship choices of youngsters with dramatically different status and background characteristics, the touchiness of adolescents about parental criticism of their friends, their fierce generational loyalty, and Epstein's (Chapter 3) finding that social status is *not* a good predictor of either the choice of friends or the stability of friendship in adolescence. J. C. Coleman's (1974, 1980) finding that through early and middle adolescence youngsters overwhelmingly associate negative consequences and feelings with not being part of the group, and general observations about adolescent conformity fit the idea of authority invested in peers. We can speculate that this process of valorizing the peer group and peer norms would be even stronger and more long lasting in societies and settings that reinforce generational loyalty and responsibility, such as the Soviet classroom (Bronfenbrenner, 1970) and the Italian-American society (Gans, 1962). There is much to learn about the kinds of structural variables that will affect friendship formation during adolescence.

J. S. Coleman's (1961) early study of adolescent society provides a model for the investigation of the influence of peer norms. Although some of Coleman's conclusions and generalizations have been criticized, his approach to establishing the nature of norms and mapping the force of their influence (i.e., asking about the values of the leading crowd and using sociometric techniques) is extraordinarily imaginative and useful. J. C. Coleman and researchers in this volume have adapted these techniques effectively for use in large-scale studies. It is evident that peer values—the dominant value atmosphere of schools—have effects beyond those of close interpersonal interaction.

Although adolescence is a period during which friendship is critically important and is likely to be the focus of a high level of concern and action, it is nonetheless true that adolescents vary in their preoccupation with peer relationships. Girls are more absorbed in and more sophisticated about friendship than are boys of the same age. Commitment to friendship varies from early to late adolescence in a number of dimensions. The social status that a youngster holds in the larger high school social structure conditions the influence of various friendship patterns on behavior and adjustment.

There are other individual and extraschool factors that affect friendship that we will eventually want to enter into our analyses. It seems likely that youngsters will vary in their *need* of friendship and that this will be affected by, for example, the family situation. We might speculate that children in single-parent homes will have stronger motivation to establish stable, rewarding friendships as a substitute for family sociality. On the other hand, it may be that a disruption in family relationships will cause insecurity and defensiveness in the adolescent and that this insecurity will interfere with the ability to form and maintain friendships. R. S. Weiss (1975) notes that children of divorce "grow up a little sooner" and that this precocity may either help or hinder peer relationships. Youngsters from large reconstituted families may find enough opportunity for friendship among siblings, step-siblings, and half-siblings to satisfy their affiliative needs. They may, then, have less need to develop friendships outside the family.

H. Deutsch (1947) emphasizes gender as a determinant of the strength and importance of affiliative needs. She holds that special features of female development make the same-sex close friendship between girls a critical mechanism in the development of self. If the young woman makes a premature heterosexual commitment and misses or shortens the stage of exploration through intense friendship with other females, she may not achieve an articulated identity. Empirical findings from an early study support this suggestion: Early and middle adolescent girls who said they "went steady" (how dated that phrase sounds in these psychologically sophisticated times when even very young adolescents are more likely to say they have "a serious relationship" or a "committed relationship" with a boy) were undeveloped in their concepts and practice of friendship.

Thus, we have another hypothesis about a factor that affects friendship in adolescence: In females, the formation, stability, and quality of same-sex friendship will be influenced by the pace and nature of heterosexual interaction and in turn will influence identity formation. Some of the pseudobiological speculations of Tiger (1969) and their extensions in recent popular mythology about male bonding and the functions of team play among males would suggest that heterosexual events have less influence on male same-sex relationships.

On the side of structural variation, the chapters in this section by Karweit and Hansell and by Epstein, and chapters throughout the volume, make clear which variables have been examined and suggest others that should be examined. We know that the size and bureaucracy of schools will affect opportunities for friendship development. Barker and Gump's (1964) classic study compared large and small schools on formality of structure or bureaucratization as well as size. The large, formal school tends to restrict associations and to facilitate friendship choices on relatively restricting criteria. The small school shared many of the structural characteristics of the participatory or open schools studied by Epstein and her colleagues. Integrated and segregated classrooms or schools also obviously provide different opportunities for diverse and varied friendships.

To this point, we have looked at relatively few school structural variables and a narrow range of schools. For the most part, studies have looked at schools in middle- and working-class areas of cities and in middle-sized towns. Research in inner-city and rural public schools and in upper-class private schools is underrepresented in the literature of social science. Clearly these schools represent important variations on structural dimensions of interest in the study of friendship. To give just one example, McArthur (1955) suggests (and non-social science literature supports the suggestion) that upper-class private schools urge an impersonal, objective style of social interaction on their students. Cool, dispassionate, objective, and rational exchange is valued and modeled for youngsters by the teachers in such schools. We must ask how this style conditions friendship, and especially, what implications it has for development of loyalty, which is the essence of friendship and which is quintessentially nonobjective.

NEXT STEPS IN METHODS

We are at a stage in methodological development where we can handle complex sets of variables and interactions among them. In various chapters throughout this volume, we see examples of innovative and sophisticated methods used to analyze the effects on friendship of school structure variables (e.g., high- and low-participatory schools), individual variables (e.g., gender, age, intelligence), and the interactions among them. Multivariate techniques increase the possibility of extending and refining our understanding of the way in which friendship develops and functions for adolescents with varied individual and developmental characteristics in varied structures.

Longitudinal studies offer data with which we can analyze friendship stability and change over time. Developmental hypotheses can be logically and definitively tested only with longitudinal data, because analysis of age relationships in cross-sectional data can never disentangle the effects of age from cohort and historical effects. Epstein (Chapter 11) demonstrates specific instances in which conclusions drawn from cross-sectional data would be flawed and can be corrected only by means of data gathered over time.

Large-scale studies—and particularly large longitudinal studies—are expensive and complicated to do. They are most appropriately done when we have theories to test. But many of our ideas about friendship are not yet clearly formulated nor linked to other ideas in explicit theoretical frames. In the hypothesis-generating stage of theory development, the small ethnographic or participant observation study is still the approach of choice. How a friendship group responds to newcomers, how group norms are communicated and affect behavior, how conflict is resolved among friends, how specific situations test loyalty—all these are areas that lend themselves to the techniques of ethnography, observation, the use of informants, and intensive interviews. The sensitive ethnographic report can develop specific hypotheses and theoretical linkages that then can be subjected to analysis and testing in large-scale studies that control for extraneous variables and look at the full range of variation on focal variables. It is from a combination of the small, close-in, intensive study and the large, multiple-school study that we will gain the richest and most valid understanding of the nature of adolescent friendship.

CLASSROOM AND SCHOOL ORGANIZATION AND THE SELECTION PROCESS

JOYCE LEVY EPSTEIN

Selection of Friends in Differently Organized Schools and Classrooms

Parents worry about who their children's friends are. Most parents are concerned that their children's friends are "good kids" and good influences. When they select a neighborhood, families often consider the availability, characteristics, and potential influence of other children and of facilities and activities.

Proximity of families with children is one organizational feature in neighborhoods that affects children's selection of friends. If children live on the same block as other children about their age, chances are they will play together and some will become best friends. Young children who live many blocks or miles apart will probably not interact very often at home. *Size* of the available population is another organizational feature of neighborhoods that affects interaction and selection of friends. If only 2 children live near each other, chances are they will play together. If 22 are in the same vicinity, there will be different patterns of interaction and selection among pairs and groups.

The *facilities* available in neighborhoods organize potential friends around activities and projects. Neighborhood facilities may include a playground, ball field, skating area, bike path, swimming pool, pool hall, bowling alley, arcade, and organized or informal sports. These facilities define tasks, require decisions, and carry rewards that structure the way children interact.

Research on student peer groups has recognized that, like neighborhoods, schools and classrooms have organizational characteristics that affect the selection

73

FRIENDS IN SCHOOL
Patterns of Selection and Influence in Secondary Schools

of friends in school. Bidwell (1972), J. D. Campbell (1964), E. Campbell and Alexander (1965), Inkeles (1968), Picou and Carter (1976), and Woelfel and Haller (1971) provided early ideas about the importance of structural factors that alter the opportunities for student contact and define the pool of students from which friends in school are selected. K. L. Alexander, Cook, and McDill (1978), Rosenbaum (1976), and Sorensen (1978) discuss the effect of differentiation or tracking on friendship groups of secondary school students (also see Hansell and Karweit, Chapter 9, this volume). Hallinan and Tuma (1978) studied the consequences of grouping on friendship selection at the elementary school level. Tracking policies and other grouping practices affect the size and characteristics of the classroom population, the proximity of particular students in classrooms, and the facilities and activities that structure student interaction (Eder, 1981; Oakes, 1982).

In addition to broad structural conditions of schools, such as the tracking policy or size of the student population, the daily experiences of students in school and classroom settings may have important effects on friendship selection. This chapter examines the effects on selection of the authority structure in schools and classrooms. Specifically, we are interested in the degree to which teachers share decisions about academic activities with students—or the level of student participation in schools and classrooms. It is argued that variations in the organization of student participation in academic decisions affects the number and the purpose of the contacts students make in school and the friends whom they select.

Hallinan (1976a) shows in her study of friendship groups in open and traditional elementary school classrooms that the organization of open classrooms altered some of the patterns of friendship selection that had been documented in previous research conducted in traditional classrooms. This important research was limited, however, by its measure of "openness" and by its focus on the elementary grades. It did not examine the adolescent years, when strong peer group ties are made and when friends are assumed to be gaining in influence (Douvan & Adelson, 1966; Fine, 1980; Horrocks, 1976; Lipsitz, 1980; Sullivan, 1953). Also, because the selection processes were not analyzed by grade level, no information was provided about developmental patterns of peer group formation and friendship choices in contrasting school organizations. Finally, this research did not address how school and classroom organizations affect patterns of students' influence on their friends' behaviors. In general, if we are to understand the potential of the peer group as a socializing agent, we need research that not only examines the selection of friends and the formation of groups but also addresses directly the issue of *influence*. This requires longitudinal data on both the student and the students' friends on a variety of educational outcomes. In this chapter, we examine how patterns of friendship selection differ in high- and low-participatory school environments. Chapter 11 uses longitudinal data on these same students to examine patterns of influence.

DATA

Longitudinal data were collected from 4163 students surveyed in Grades 5, 6, 8, and 11 in 1973 and again in Grades 6, 7, 9, and 12 in 1974. The surveys collected information from each student on individual, family, and school characteristics, and on affective and academic outcome measures. School records supplied students' achievement test scores. Analyses of children's and teachers' reports show that there was significant variation between schools at every grade level in the formal organization of student participation in decisions about their academic activities (Epstein & McPartland, 1979; McPartland & Epstein, 1977). In high-participatory classes, students were given more frequent opportunities than in low-participatory classes to walk around the room in order to conduct and complete activities, talk to one another about their work, choose their own seats, choose their activities among many alternatives, work with each other in small groups, and monitor their progress.

The nonacademic and academic outcomes measured in the Time 1 and Time 2 surveys included self-reliance (an 18-item scale), satisfaction with school life (a short form of the Quality of School Life Scale, Epstein & McPartland, 1978), college plans (a dichotomized measure of definite versus no definite plan to attend college), report card grades in English and math, and standardized achievement test scores in English and math. In this chapter, we examine patterns of selection in the contrasting school environments in terms of friends' characteristics of sex, race, family SES, self-reliance, college plans, success in school, and achievement.

The friends' data from the two surveys were coded and merged with the individual's own longitudinal records to permit comparisons of respondents' and friends' characteristics and scores. We do not rely on the students' descriptions of their friends. Rather, the students' friends are included in the sample and report their own characteristics and behaviors.

Despite some unique coverage of the background and behaviors of students and their friends, there are important limitations in these data. First, only three spaces were allotted for the names of best friends in the students' school and grade level. Students may have more than three important friends.[1] Nevertheless, there is evidence that the three friends who were named were important to the students, usually in the order listed. In both years of the survey, the first friend a student named was more likely to be reciprocated than the second, who in turn was more likely to be reciprocated than the third. Similarly, the friends were listed in rank order of stability of friendship choices, with the first friend most

---

[1]Woelfel and Haller (1971) reported that students listed an average of 13 significant others for a single behavior (occupational aspiration). J. Cohen (1977) found an average of 5.2 friends under conditions of semi-fixed choice. Dunphy (1963) reported average clique size of 6.2 in an Australian sample. Verbrugge (1977) noted that adults' first-named friends are their best friends. Indeed, one could fruitfully use one best friend in research for many questions about the selection and influence processes (see Eder & Hallinan, 1978; Kandel, 1978).

likely to be the same friend chosen 1 year later. In addition, reciprocated friends were also more likely to be stable friends.[2]

Thus, although there may be other friends who are important to students, the friends named are likely to be especially significant choices for research on selection and influence of school friends. Of the 4163 students in the longitudinal sample, 3519 (85%) named at least one friend in school and 644 (15%) made no choice of a best friend in school. We use this information to study selection patterns and later (Chapter 11) to compare change over time in school-related outcomes of students who name *some* versus *no* friends in school.

Following Laumann (1973), the partial network that contains the individual student and up to three good friends is treated as the primary zone of the individual's total network. We are interested in how connected students are in terms of the reciprocity and stability of their friendships, and how students are connected in terms of the similarities and differences of their characteristics in the contrasting school environments.

PATTERNS OF SELECTION, RECIPROCITY, AND STABILITY

The means, standard deviations, and test statistics from the Time 2 survey on the number of friends selected, reciprocated, and stable are summarized for subgroups of students in Table 5.1. Females receive more choices ($F = 84.96$) and make more stable choices ($F = 21.81$) than do males, even after the total number of choices made is statistically taken into account. Younger students make and receive more choices ($F = 45.94$). The number of reciprocated and stable choices are not consistently associated with the grade level, although students in Grade 12 tend to make more stable choices. Students from high-SES families are selected significantly more often ($F = 31.17$), but patterns of reciprocated and stable choices are not significantly different for the SES subgroups. There are no significant differences in the numbers of black and white students who are selected as friends or as reciprocated friends ($F = 2.75$ and $F = 1.12$, respectively). However, white students have more stable friendships over the years ($F = 15.46$).

The patterns of sex differences noted in Table 5.1 were found in both years of the survey, but differences due to age (grade level) were more pronounced at Time 1, when the sample included a greater proportion of younger, elementary school

---

[2]Hallinan (1978/1979) reported that best friends and mutual choices are more stable. Stability of friendships over 1 year is upset by the natural upheavals and redistributions that occur when students enter new schools for middle and high school in Grades 6 and 9, and the natural attrition that occurs when families move from neighborhoods and children enter new schools. Stability of children's friendships is very much a function of the time span between measures (Busk, Ford, & Schulman, 1973). Hartup (1978) reported that about 50% of 11–15 year olds have stable choices for 2 weeks. Other fall-to-spring measures in year-long studies show a similar lack of stability over time of friends chosen as best friends. J. Cohen (1977), for example, found that 45% of the fall cliques disintegrated by spring.

TABLE 5.1
Mean Scores, Standard Deviations, and Test Statistics for Selection, Reciprocity, and Stability of Friends, by Sex, Race, SES, Grade Level, and Type of School Organization[a]

	Selection[b]			Reciprocity[c]			Stability[c]		
	Mean	SD	F	Mean	SD	F	Mean	SD	F
Sex									
Male	.431	(.499)		.360	(.362)		.131	(.249)	
Female	.546	(.531)	69.72	.467	(.360)	84.96	.169	(.267)	21.81
Race									
White	.513	(.530)		.428	(.380)		.160	(.263)	
Black	.474	(.499)	2.75	.450	(.364)	1.12	.109	(.242)	15.46
SES									
High	.537	(.534)		.430	(.364)		.145	(.257)	
Low	.454	(.517)	31.17	.414	(.368)	1.71	.158	(.263)	2.58
Grade									
6	.510	(.514)		.406	(.343)		.145	(.232)	
7	.570	(.561)		.426	(.366)		.146	(.296)	
9	.357	(.380)		.437	(.372)		.145	(.260)	
12	.493	(.600)	45.94	.395	(.394)	2.19	.180	(.330)	2.89

[a]From 1974 cross-sectional survey, based on 4163 students in secondary Grades 6–12.
[b]Standardized for number of choices made in school and grade.
[c]Standardized for number of selections made by student.

students. In the Time 1 survey, white students made and received more choices—a necessary precursor to the pattern reported of greater stability of friendships of white students at Time 2.

These patterns of selection confirm many of the findings in studies using data collected in traditionally organized schools (Asher, Oden and Gottman, 1977; Elder, 1968; Hartup, 1978; Schmuck, 1970; see Karweit & Hansel, Chapter 7, this volume). The basic patterns provide a background for the specific questions of differences in selection patterns of students in high- and low-participatory schools.

SELECTION IN HIGH- AND LOW-PARTICIPATORY SCHOOLS

In high-participatory schools, the physical setting and the instructional program are designed to permit and encourage frequent student interaction.[3] For

[3]Schools and classrooms attended by the students in this sample are categorized in terms of the extent of participation of students in classroom decisions. High-participatory schools are called "open" by some and were categorized that way by the school district in this study. High-participatory schools

example, *pods* (architecturally open spaces that are linked by a central meeting area) permit visual and/or direct contact among up to 150 students, sometimes from different grade levels. Learning centers, stations, or project areas are part of many participatory instructional programs, whether in architecturally open or regular buildings. These learning centers permit students to work in small, changing groups, to assist one another, and to move frequently to join new groups in different areas of the classroom. Groups of students with similar interests may work together on projects and form new groups for new projects. In empirical studies, open architecture and high-participatory instructional programs have been found to emphasize movement and fluid regrouping of students significantly more often than traditional instructional programs in elementary schools (Walberg & Thomas, 1972) and in secondary schools (Epstein & McPartland, 1975).

Participatory environments alter the students' role in classroom decisions. The nature and extent of peer interaction should measurably affect students' selections of friends and the structure of their friendship groups. In this chapter, we explore three assumptions about the selection and characteristics of friends.

First, there may be different distributions of accepted and isolated students in high- and low-participatory settings. Because of opportunities for wider social contacts in high-participatory instructional programs, students may become acquainted with greater numbers of students. This would enable more students to find at least one best friend, thereby producing fewer social isolates than in low-participatory school settings.

Second, there may be greater diversity in the characteristics of selected friends in high- than in low-participatory settings. Wider contacts among students on a greater variety of assignments and projects in high-participatory settings may lead to knowledge of and appreciation for the multiple talents or abilities of others. This better knowledge about others may make friendship choices more egalitarian, with students who are typically labeled disadvantaged included in friendship groups as they become better known for some skills that are useful to group efforts. Typical status characteristics, such as age, sex, race, and achievement, should be less the basis of selection in the more participatory organizations if more information about others is known and used in selecting friends.

Third, the determinants of status and selection may be based on the rewards issued for different behaviors in high- and low-participatory schools. For example, more students report rewards for self-reliant behavior and expressing opinions in high-participatory schools. If rewards create more self-reliant behaviors, then students' friendship groups will include more friends who are high in self-reliance. Self-reliance may be a pivotal variable for social status and selection.

---

were labeled "modern by Minuchin *et al.* (1969). The terms *open* and *modern* confound or confuse the architecture of the school with its educational program. More important, even when schools do not use the label "open" to characterize their instructional program, they may permit students to participate in academic decisions. Thus, high- to low-participatory schools is a useful theoretical and practical continuum.

RESULTS

Patterns of Selection

Table 5.2 presents means and standard deviations for the selection, reciprocity, and stability of students' friends across the grades in low- and high-participatory settings. The top panel of the table shows that, with selection standardized for numbers of of students chosen in each school and grade, there are, on the average, more students selected as friends in high-participatory settings. The middle panel indicates that, standardized for number of choices made by each student, there are, on the average, more reciprocated friendships in high-participatory settings. Grade 9 is the exception, with selections and reciprocations about equal in both settings.

The bottom panel shows no consistent significant difference in the average stability of friendship choices in high- and low-participatory settings, with scores standardized for the number of choices made by each student.

The rates of selection and reciprocity are consistently higher in high-participatory settings. This means that more students are selected and fewer are isolated or ignored in high-participatory settings and that the selections are more often mutual than in low-participatory settings. The results extend Hallinan's (1976a) re-

TABLE 5.2

Mean Scores and Standard Deviations for Selection, Reciprocity, and Stability of Friends in Low- and High-Participatory Schools, by Grade Level ($N = 4163$)[a]

| | \multicolumn{8}{c|}{Grade} | | | | | | | | | |
| | 6 | | 7 | | 9 | | 12 | | Total | |
	Mean	SD	Mean	SD	Mean	SD	Mean	SD	Mean	SD
Selection[b]										
Low-participatory	.430	(.481)	.546	(.556)	.343	(.385)	.452	(.543)	.447	(.499)
High-participatory	.566	(.528)	.607	(.566)	.355	(.370)	.771	(.839)	.545	(.544)
									$F = 48.66$	
Reciprocated choices[c]										
Low-participatory	.376	(.323)	.407	(.366)	.433	(.373)	.372	(.388)	.401	(.364)
High-participatory	.426	(.357)	.453	(.365)	.446	(.372)	.557	(.396)	.444	(.363)
									$F = 13.23$	
Stable choices[c]										
Low-participatory	.123	(.209)	.164	(.258)	.165	(.265)	.179	(.322)	.155	(.259)
High-participatory	.170	(.253)	.131	(.235)	.115	(.249)	.181	(.343)	.147	(.260)
									$F = 1.01$	

[a]The same patterns are noted when participatory organization of the school and grade is trichotomized for low, middle, and high participation.

[b]Standardized for number of choices made in each school and grade.

[c]Standardized for number of selections made by each student.

search conducted in the elementary grades that also showed patterns of fewer social isolates and fewer assymetric dyads in the more open settings. Patterns of results were less clear of mutual choices of elementary students in contrasting classrooms.

We look next at the differences in characteristics of selected friends *across* and *within* differently organized school environments. Chi-square statistics from tests of differences in the proportions of students selected as best friend in high- and low-participatory schools are reported in the top panel of Table 5.3. Males are more often selected as friends in high-participatory schools, but there is no significant difference in the proportion of females selected as friends in the high- versus low-participatory settings. In other analyses (not reported here), males were nominated by students for positive characteristics (e.g., popular, independent) more often in high-participatory schools, whereas no significant differences were found in the number of female nominations in the two settings. The top panel of Table 5.3 shows also that significantly higher proportions of students are selected in the more participatory settings at the middle school level, in Grades 6 and 7. At the high school level, the patterns differ in Grades 9 and 12. See Table 5.6 for effects of school organization on patterns of selection by grade level with student background characteristics and number of choices statistically controlled.

This information is supplemented in the bottom panel of Table 5.3 by the results of tests comparing selections *within* low- and high-participatory settings. In low-participatory schools, females are selected as friends significantly more often than males in three of four grade levels. In these schools, students high in self-reliance or achievement are more often selected, and students low in self-reliance or achievement are less often selected as friends. In high-participatory schools, across the grades, there is only one significant difference in selection based on students' sex or level of achievement. Males and females and students low and high in self-reliance or achievement are about equally selected as friends in high-participatory schools.

SES is not a consistently important variable for the selection or isolation of students, but high-SES students are selected significantly more often than low-SES students in Grades 6 and 7 in low-participatory schools.

These analyses suggest that more students are selected as friends in high- than in low-participatory schools. The rates are especially different for males and for younger students. Selections in high-participatory schools may be less dependent on typically recognized status characteristics (high SES, high achievement, high self-reliance). Boys, especially, may find it easier to accept and fit into the expected school behavior patterns in the more participatory settings, where the boundaries for acceptable behavior may be broader.

Students' reports of their own social status (how much "in the center of things" they felt in school) support these conclusions. Students in high-participatory schools with low and high scores on a measure of self-reliance are not significantly different in their self-reported social status ($\chi^2 = 1.94$). In low-participatory settings, however, students with high self-reliance report significantly higher social status than do low self-reliant students ($\chi^2 = 45.37$). Females and high-

TABLE 5.3
Summary of Chi-Square Statistics from Tests of Differences in Proportions of Students Selected as Best Friends

A. *Tests of differences in proportions of students selected as best friends* in *high- versus low-participatory settings, by sex and grade level*[a]

	Comparisons across settings χ^2 High- versus low-participatory
Males	34.08*
Females	2.25
Grade 6	14.97*
Grade 7	17.16*
Grade 9	−4.87*[b]
Grade 12	0.01

B. *Tests of differences in proportions of students selected as best friends* within *high- and low-participatory settings, by sex, SES, level of self-reliance, and achievement, by grade*[a]

	Comparisons within settings χ^2 Low-participatory	χ^2 High-participatory
Female versus male		
Grade 6	13.89*	7.27*
Grade 7	2.21	0.13
Grade 9	28.01*	0.58
Grade 12	29.77*	1.86
High versus low SES		
Grade 6	8.14*	3.20
Grade 7	11.93*	2.09
Grade 9	0.09	2.99
Grade 12	0.26	0.56
High versus low self-reliant students		
Grade 6	3.11	0.23
Grade 7	15.89*	2.12
Grade 9	5.88*	2.08
Grade 12	4.82*	0.95
High versus low achieving students[c]		
Grade 7	9.10*	2.45
Grade 9	5.04*	4.18*
Grade 12	10.86*	0.97

[a]Chi-square statistics of 3.84 are significant at .05 level; 6.64 at .01 level; 10.83 at .001 level. These are marked with an asterisk.

[b]A minus sign indicates that the proportions tested show the advantage in selection for students in low-participatory schools.

[c]Achievement tests were not administered to students in Grade 6.

SES students report they are more "in the center of things" in the less participatory settings. More specific research is needed to follow up these early suggestions that greater distinctions are made on observable status characteristics in low-participatory schools.

Patterns of Contact

Patterns of less isolation, greater selection, and greater reciprocation of friends in the more participatory settings may be the consequence of more opportunities for wider contact with greater numbers of students. Data were collected that identify whether students and their friends were in the same teachers' classrooms in English, math, social studies, and science. Students were assigned scores from 0 to 3 for each academic subject to indicate how many of their friends were assigned to the same teacher's class and from 0 to 12 for the number of friends who shared all four subject classes. Grade level, the number of different teachers for each subject in each school and grade, and the number of selections made were statistically controlled. Table 5.4 shows that students in high-participatory settings select fewer friends from their own teachers' classes; conversely, students in low-participatory settings select more of their friends from their own English, math, social studies, and science teachers' classrooms. The negative regression coefficients reporting effects of high-participatory environments on out-of-classroom choices are small but significant and consistent.

As would be expected, the fewer the number of teachers, the greater the number of friends selected from the same class ($t = -21.83$); when many friends are selected, a greater number of friends are in the students' own classes ($t =$

TABLE 5.4
Number of Best Friends from the Same Teachers' Classrooms Regressed on Level of Participation, with Controls on Grade Level, Number of Different Teachers' Classes in Each School and Grade, and Number of Friends Selected ($N = 2502$)[a]

Participatory level of subject	Effect on choices from same teachers' classrooms[b]	
	b	(t)
English	−.081	(−4.47)
Math	−.080	(−4.33)
Social studies	−.036	(−2.03)
Science	−.074	(−4.15)
All subjects	−.071	(−4.36)

[a]This table includes only students who selected at least one friend and who, with their friends, took all four academic subjects.

[b]b = standardized regression coefficient; (t) = associated test statistic.

TABLE 5.5
Average Number of Best Friends from Same
Teachers' Classrooms[a]

Grade	Low-participatory	High-participatory
6	4.90	3.96
7	5.58	4.05
9	2.99	2.97
12	2.49	2.06

[a]Standardized for number of choices made.

27.76). These demographic conditions mathematically define some obvious influences on selection. Beyond these, however, the selection of best friends in high-participatory environments is made from a wider set of contacts. Table 5.5 shows that at all grade levels, but especially in the middle school years, students in high-participatory schools more often select as friends students from outside the boundaries of their own teachers' classrooms, whereas students in low-participatory schools more often make restricted, within-classroom selections.

The patterns in Tables 5.4 and 5.5 suggest that when boundaries are fixed, as in track or group assignments, choices of friends will reflect the limits imposed by the organization. To some degree, schools determine patterns of selection in their decisions about curricular and class boundaries.

Effects of Organization on Selection

Table 5.6 summarizes regression analyses that impose strict statistical controls on the effects of participatory instructional programs on the selection, reciprocity, and stability of friendship choices, by sex and by grade level.

Clearly, high participation has a consistent, positive impact on the selection of students' friendship groups. In these regression analyses, grade level or sex of student (depending on the subgroup shown), SES, success in school, and total number of students selected as friends in each school and grade are statistically taken into account in order to identify the independent effect of participation on the selection of friends. There is a small but significant and consistent advantage for selection as friend for males and females in the more participatory educational settings and for students in three of the four secondary grades. Grade 9 is an exception to the pattern.

Additional analyses were conducted that also control for the size of the student population in each school and grade and for the number of students selected by each student. These additional statistical controls do not alter the results for males and females, but change the patterns of results for Grades 9 and 12, making the relationship less negative in Grade 9 and slightly less positive in Grade 12. School and grade size are potential influences on patterns of selection, but for the range of school sizes represented in this sample, size does not eliminate the

TABLE 5.6
Selection, Reciprocity, and Stability of Friendship Choices Regressed on the Formal Organization of Participation by Sex and by Grade Level[a]

| | Sex | | | | Grade | | | | | | | |
| | Female | | Male | | 6 | | 7 | | 9 | | 12 | |
	b	(t)	b	(t)	b	(t)	b	(t)	b	(t)	b	(t)
Selection[b]	.051	(2.50)	.063	(3.09)	.106	(4.31)	.099	(3.77)	-.039	(-1.39)	.176	(5.23)
Reciprocation[c]	.079	(3.98)	.075	(3.78)	.021	(0.74)	.076	(2.93)	.049	(1.87)	.179	(3.74)
Stability[c]	-.025	(-1.26)	-.028	(-1.43)	.033	(1.16)	-.091	(-3.58)	-.087	(-3.25)	.077	(1.59)
N	2822		2785		1688		1563		1437		919	

[a] b = standardized regression coefficient; (t) = associated test statistic.

[b] Grade (or sex), student SES, and success in school (report card grades) are controlled. The selection variable is standardized for number of choices made in each student's school and grade.

[c] Reciprocation and stability scores are standardized for the number of choices made by each student. Analyses take into account the number of students chosen in each student's school and grade.

positive effects of high-participatory programs on the patterns of selection of friends.

The independent effects of participation on reciprocation are presented next in Table 5.6, net of grade or sex, SES, success in school, and number of friends each student selected. High-participatory programs have significant positive effects on reciprocation of friendships for males and for females. This is true for three of the four grade levels, although these coefficients are not as strong as the effects of participation on selection.

Finally, Table 5.6 shows that the independent effects of participation on stability of friendship choices are inconsistent across the grades. There is an independent negative effect of participation on stability of friendships in Grades 7 and 9, a positive effect in Grade 12, and no effect in Grade 6. Stability of friendships is a problematic variable that should continue to challenge researchers in future studies. In this sample, for example, students at each grade level experienced significant physical change in school assignments over the year between the surveys that affected the potential for stability of friendships. Students in Grade 6, part of Grade 7, and Grade 9 entered new, larger schools for middle and high school. Grade 12 populations were the most stable within schools, but some students dropped out of school or graduated early. Thus, students' friends selected one year were not necessarily present in the same school the next year. We would guess that students make friends and reciprocate current friendship choices without considering whether the friendship will be stable.

Analyses were conducted also using a different measure of participation—the teachers' informal decision-making style (in contrast to the formal organization of academic decision making). This measure had no effect on patterns of peer association, whereas the formal organization of participation had clear and consistent effects. The informal teaching style has been shown to have strong direct effects on student development (Epstein, 1980, 1981, 1983; Epstein & McPartland, 1979) but may have nothing to do with peer interaction or patterns of selection or reciprocity. In contrast, the structural conditions that determine student placement, contact, movement, and purposes for interaction have significant effections on selection and reciprocity.

Correspondence of Teacher and Student Selections

Other features of low- and high-participatory school programs may affect the selection of friends. For example, different bases for status distribution can create more or fewer students considered "worthy" candidates for friendship. In many schools, high status is accorded by peers to students who meet the teachers' norms for behavior. This may be more true in schools where the teachers set the rules for classroom procedures and control all rewards for student progress. It may be less true in schools where students participate in defining acceptable classroom behavior and share responsibility with teachers for acknowledging and recording student progress. When children interact and identify each other's skills and talents, they may get to know each other better than in more restricted settings. We need to test empirically whether the teachers' choices of "stars" among students are the same as the student choices, whether discrepancies between teachers and students are greater in high- than in low-participatory environments, and whether any differences may be due to the fact that teachers classify students more broadly and identify more kinds of acceptable behavior or that students recognize a greater variety of acceptable, praiseworthy, attractive behaviors because of increased contact. The available data begin to address these difficult questions.

In low-participatory schools the characteristics of "stars" may be known to both students and teachers, and so the overlap in student and teacher positive nominations may be great (see Table 5.7). These tests may be interpreted to mean that more traditional, low-participatory schools have more restricted or well-defined groups of students who are singled out as "stars." In high-participatory schools, more, different students become known to teachers and students for their positive characteristics. We can guess about the reasons for these results, but the assumptions can be tested with more specific data in future studies. In low-participatory schools, the students who are favored by teachers for their ability to function independently in school may become known as "good" all-around students to their peers. In the more participatory schools, proportionately more students are highly independent in school and so the "good" or capable students are more numerous or less specifically identified by the teachers. Under these conditions, student choices of peers with positive characteristics will not necessarily match the choices of their teacher, and more (different) students may be nominated. Minuchin, Biber, Shapiro, and Zimiles (1969) reported more social independence and

TABLE 5.7
Chi-Square Statistics from Tests of Differences in Proportions of Student Teacher Nominations of "Stars" in Low- and High-participatory Schools

Students nominated by teachers as highly independent are more often selected as:	χ^2 Correspondence of teacher and student nominations	
	Low-participatory	High-participatory
Friends by students in traditional schools	10.39	NS[a]
Popular to a greater degree in traditional than in open schools	9.39	4.15
Independent by students in traditional schools	31.41	NS
Hard to fool by students in traditional schools	6.95	NS

[a]NS = nonsignificant.

flexibility of thought among students in more "modern" schools. Students had fewer stereotyped conceptions of their social roles. Similar characteristics may be guiding student nominations in high-participatory schools.

Diversity in Characteristics of Friends

Table 5.8 presents results of analyses of the effects of high- and low-participatory environments on the selection of friends with particular characteristics. First, the table shows that, on the average, with the students' own self-reliance statistically controlled, a student's friendship group is more likely to have highly self-reliant students in high-participatory settings. This is true for males and females and across the secondary grades.

There are greater numbers of more self-reliant individuals in high-participatory schools, so the school–grade pool provides more opportunities for selecting self-reliant friends. The larger pool may be due to the recruitment of initially self-reliant students to open schools, or it may reflect the educational practices in high-participatory schools that develop student self-reliance over time. By rewarding particular kinds of behavior, the school can affect the characteristics of the student body from which friends are selected. Students in high-participatory schools report significantly more rewards from teachers for original ideas and expression of opinions (Epstein & McPartland, 1979). Teacher rewards for independent thought and creative expression may contribute to the larger pool of self-reliant students in high-participatory schools.

The same pattern is shown in Table 5.8 for the average level of college plans and achievement of friends in differently structured schools. With statistical controls on the students' own aspirations or achievement, students in high-participatory schools are more likely than students in low-participatory schools to select friends who have definite plans to attend college or who are high achievers. This pattern is not evident for students' friends' report card grades—the effects vary for males and females and across grade levels.

Table 5.8 next presents results of analyses of the effect of attendance in high-participatory schools on the demographic characteristics of friendship groups. There are more frequent cross-sex selections in high- than in low-participatory schools; females (scored 0) select males (scored 1) more often and vice versa, as indicated by small but significant positive regression coefficients for females and negative coefficients for males. With students' grade and own race statistically controlled, males and females and students across the grades (except for Grade 12) in high-participatory schools select more black friends than students in low-participatory settings. Carter, DeTine, Spero, and Benson (1975) describe different rates of acceptance of black students in environments that are more or less integrated. It may be that black and white students in high-participatory settings have more positive interactions than do black and white students in low-participatory settings.

With students' own SES statistically controlled, males and females and stu-

TABLE 5.8

Average Friends' Characteristics Regressed on the Formal Organization of Participation, with Students' Initial Characteristics Controlled, by Sex and by Grade Level[a,b]

	Sex				Grade							
	Female		Male		6		7		9		12	
	b	(t)	b	(t)	b	(t)	b	(t)	b	(t)	b	(t)
Average friends' self-reliance	.134	(6.79)	.082	(3.64)	.114	(4.12)	.114	(4.02)	.225	(7.31)	.122	(2.84)
Average friends' aspirations	.161	(7.76)	.087	(3.65)	.154	(5.57)	.206	(7.35)	.102	(3.46)	.079	(2.02)
Average friends' report card grades	−.012	(−0.54)	.038	(1.52)	−.085	(−2.97)	−.032	(−1.04)	.037	(1.12)	.195	(8.50)
Average friends' achievement	.042	(2.10)	.059	(3.00)	NA[c]		.064	(3.15)	.057	(2.52)	−.002	(−0.07)
Average friends' sex	.070	(3.28)	−.056	(−2.36)	−.016	(−1.27)	.020	(1.79)	.018	(1.29)	.019	(0.59)
Average friends' race	−.037	(−2.92)	−.061	(−3.39)	−.069	(−3.74)	−.069	(−3.04)	−.043	(−2.36)	−.007	(−0.34)
Average friends' SES	.261	(13.31)	.267	(11.59)	.248	(9.37)	.249	(9.19)	.333	(11.73)	.198	(4.88)

[a] Sex subgroup analyses include statistical control for grade level. Grade level analyses include statistical control for sex of student.

[b] b = standardized regression coefficient; (t) = associated test statistic.

[c] Grade 6 was not administered standardized achievement tests.

dents at all grade levels in high-participatory schools select friends with higher SES than do students in low-participatory schools. The characteristics of race and SES (but not sex) are differently represented in the school–grade pool in high- and low-participatory settings—that is, more black students and more high-SES students attend the high-participatory schools.

Table 5.9 shows the scores of students' friends in the contrasting school settings. At each grade level, students low in self-reliance are more likely to have

TABLE 5.9
Average Friends' Self-reliance and College Plans for Students in Low-, Mid-, and High-Participatory Schools, by Students' Own Self-Reliance and College Plans and by Grade Level

	Low-participatory		Mid-level participatory		High-participatory	
	Mean	SD	Mean	SD	Mean	SD
Students' own self-reliance[a]						
Grade 6						
Low	9.54	(2.10)	9.16	(2.04)	10.49	(1.87)
High	9.70	(1.84)	9.85	(1.87)	10.90	(1.97)
Grade 7						
Low	9.49	(2.58)	10.14	(2.16)	10.91	(2.11)
High	10.91	(2.42)	10.60	(1.90)	10.90	(1.69)
Grade 9						
Low	10.15	(2.23)	10.88	(2.20)	11.29	(2.30)
High	11.12	(2.50)	11.70	(2.26)	12.17	(2.25)
Grade 12						
Low	12.36	(2.35)	11.62	(2.43)	12.46	(2.26)
High	13.07	(2.17)	12.52	(2.43)	14.12	(1.90)
Students' own college plans[b]						
Grade 6						
No	.40	(.35)	.45	(.34)	.65	(.35)
Yes	.58	(.35)	.58	(.35)	.66	(.28)
Grade 7						
No	.32	(.34)	.41	(.36)	.59	(.35)
Yes	.44	(.40)	.60	(.35)	.65	(.33)
Grade 9						
No	.24	(.32)	.39	(.37)	.40	(.35)
Yes	.66	(.32)	.62	(.36)	.70	(.36)
Grade 12						
No	.42	(.41)	.34	(.39)	.60	(.36)
Yes	.76	(.28)	.71	(.36)	.80	(.34)

[a] N's across rows in self-reliance are: Grade 6, Low 115/376/82, High 130/356/135; Grade 7, Low 145/351/97, High 101/367/94; Grade 9, Low 138/301/81, High 75/281/95; Grade 12, Low 76/15019, High 82/122/52.

[b] N's across rows in college plans are: Grade 6, No 128/345/91, Yes 124/401/127; Grade 7, No 159/344/67, Yes 93/383/123; Grade 9, No 141/314/77, Yes 76/273/105; Grade 12, No 66/124/20, Yes 97/154/53.

selected friends who are higher in self-reliance if they attend the more participatory schools. There are three exceptions, but the basic pattern is clear. Also, in high-participatory schools, students in Grades 6, 7, and 9 who are low in self-reliance have friends whose average self-reliance is as high as the friends of highly self-reliant students in the more traditional school settings. This selection pattern has implications for the influence of friends on students' self-reliance.

The bottom of Table 5.9 shows that, in the more participatory schools, students with or without college plans are in friendship groups with other students who have, on the average, higher aspirations for postsecondary education. The few exceptions to this pattern are in mid-level participatory high schools. In high-participatory settings, students in Grades 6 and 7 who *do not* plan to attend college have more friends *with* college plans than do students in low-participatory settings who do have college plans. These patterns of selection raise questions about influence on college plans that are addressed in Chapter 11.

Table 5.9 shows a steady decline in Grades 6, 7, and 9 in the average college plans of friends of students who do not plan to attend college. This suggests that non-college goers are increasingly picking friends more like themselves. In Grade 12, when whether or not to attend college becomes an imminent decision, the pattern changes. More non-college goers in low- and high-participatory schools have at least one friend with plans to attend college. Across the grades, students with college plans also increasingly pick friends more like themselves.

Tables 5.8 and 5.9 show that opportunities to select diverse or dissimilar friends differ in high- and low-participatory schools. This point is supported also in tests reported in Chapter 3 of differences in proportions of students who "pick up" (i.e., select as friends students higher than themselves on a particular characteristic). Students who are low in self-reliance, college plans, and SES more often select friends who are higher than themselves as best friends in high-participatory than in low-participatory schools. These patterns are important because earlier research assumed that status characteristics were important predictors of children's friendships, but did not consider environmental influences. Researchers who argue for similarity in friendship choices suggest that students from low-SES families or students who have no college plans will pick others like themselves. Those who argue for status-based selection suggest that low-scoring students will pick high-scoring friends. What our data suggest is that the organization of the school environment and the age/grade level of the student will influence how status criteria are reflected in students' friendship choices.

SUMMARY AND DISCUSSION

There are several differences in the patterns of selection of friends and the characteristics of selected friends in high- and low-participatory schools.

First, in high-participatory secondary schools, more students are selected and fewer are neglected as best friends. Hallinan (1976a) and Felmlee and Hallinan

(1979) report similar patterns for students in open elementary schools. Second, more students' friendships are reciprocated in high-participatory settings. Third, no consistent differences were found in the stability of friendships in contrasting settings over a 1-year period.

These patterns of selection and reciprocity of friends may be due to the increased opportunity in the more participatory settings to contact and work with more students, and to the official rewards for frequent and purposeful peer interaction. These conditions may help students know more students better, so that some choice of friends can be made and so that mutual regard can develop.

The results suggest that high-participatory schools have a less hierarchical structure with fewer students isolated. The specific patterns, however, are more interesting. For example, males and less advantaged students are more often isolated in low-participatory settings but more often selected as friends in high-participatory settings.

Fourth, there is evidence that friends in high-participatory settings are selected from a wider set of contacts. At all grade levels, students in high-participatory schools more often select friends from outside their own teachers' classrooms; students in low-participatory schools make more within-class selections.

Fifth, several developmental patterns are observed. As students get older, they select friends from a wider set of contacts and make more cross-sex choices. Their independence and dating behaviors influence their choice of best friends. High-participatory schools may create conditions for peer association and exchange that facilitate more diverse friendships, so students select friends from wider contacts and make more cross-sex choices earlier in their school careers.

In general, we find that the expected patterns of friendship choice based on similarities of social class, sex, and race, and selections reflecting similarity of achievement or of such personal attributes as self-reliance, are tempered by school organizations that create special conditions for peer interaction. Schools that arrange opportunities in academic classrooms (or in extracurricular activities, as suggested by Karweit in Chapter 8) for students to interact with many students on group assignments they choose and consider important, change the nature and extent of students' knowledge about other students. Students may learn about others' interests, goals, and values. The differences that are encountered in learning about others add to the "tension, zest, and enrichment" of social relations that Douvan and Adelson (1966) suggest are necessary to perpetuate friendships.

The wider contacts of older students and students in high-participatory environments suggest that there is a change in the meaning and importance of *proximity* for friendship choices. Pool and Kochen (1979) report that proximity is less important or differently defined for adults because the boundaries of their environments are limited only by the communications possible via letter, phone, or travel. Verbrugge's (1977) results also suggest that different occupational environments create different boundaries for selecting adult friends. For example, the choices of production workers are more homogeneous than those of sales persons because of the different ranges of contacts of the respective groups. We see in our data that the environmental conditions of schools change the proximity of certain students by organizational procedures that extend or limit the range of contacts.

Finally, students low and high in self-reliance have a greater number of self-reliant friends in high-participatory than in low-participatory schools. There is a higher proportion of self-reliant students in high-participatory schools because of self-selection, educational experiences, teacher rewards, or all these factors (Epstein & McPartland, 1979). Students who are themselves low in self-reliance select highly self-reliant friends more often in high-participatory than in low-participatory schools. More interesting is the fact that, although highly self-reliant students are selected as friends in all schools, students low in self-reliance are more often included as friends in high-participatory schools. Similarly, in high-participatory settings, the average of friends' college plans and friends' SES is higher for students who are low in their own aspirations or family status. These patterns may result from teacher rewards for inclusionary behavior or from group or team projects that require diverse students to work with each other.

Four environmental conditions may explain the different patterns of selection of friends in high- and low-participatory schools. These include:

1. The *physical* conditions of the architecture or room arrangements in high-participatory schools, which permit high visibility among students, greater space, and more places for purposeful interaction during class time.
2. The *instructional* conditions that require the grouping and regrouping of small groups of students to complete tasks and assignments for which students must rely on each other instead of on the teacher for directions and decisions.
3. The *psychological* conditions created by teachers or students that encourage and reward students for knowledge, tolerance, and acceptance of others.
4. The *demographic* conditions of the populations of students in a school, grade, or classroom.

These conditions are manipulable or alterable variables that can be controlled, designed, and directed by teachers and administrators. The natural variation that exists in this sample of secondary schools provides evidence that low- and high-participatory programs affect the ways students select friends and the friends they select.

ACKNOWLEDGMENTS

The author thanks William Spady, who, as discussant, offered helpful suggestions on an earlier draft of this chapter that was presented at an annual meeting of the American Educational Research Association. Many thanks, too, to James M. McPartland, with whom ideas and early drafts of this chapter were exchanged.

ROBERT E. SLAVIN
STEPHEN HANSELL

6

Cooperative Learning and Intergroup Relations: Contact Theory in the Classroom

In some cases, friendships are of such substantive importance that it is critical that we understand them as outcomes of individual and school characteristics, rather than as mediators between these characteristics and some other outcomes. Intergroup relations involving friendships between students of different ethnic or racial backgrounds are the best example of this. Although since the Coleman report (J. S. Coleman, Campbell, Hobson, McPartland, Mood, Weinfeld, & York, 1966) attention has focused on the effects of desegregation on achievement, the early social science argument for desegregation focused more on *relationships* between black and white students than on achievement. The Social Science Statement to *Brown* v. *Board of Education* (347 U.S. 483, 495, 1954) hardly mentions achievement, but dwells at great length on the intolerable social separation between the races. Although many researchers now feel that intergroup relations and minority achievement are intertwined (see Stephan, 1978), positive intergroup relations are still a primary goal of desegregation.

Despite the early and continuing emphasis on improving intergroup relations as a goal of desegregation, research has not tended to show any such effect (St. John, 1975; Stephan, 1978). If anything, race relations may deteriorate over time in schools in which nothing specific is done to improve them (Gerard & Miller, 1975). This disappointing result might have been predicted by the framers of the Social Science Statement, who wrote:

93

FRIENDS IN SCHOOL
Patterns of Selection and Influence in Secondary Schools

> Under certain circumstances desegregation not only proceeds without major difficulties, but has been observed to lead to the emergence of more favorable attitudes and friendlier relations between races. . . . Much depends, however, on the circumstances under which members of previously segregated groups first come in contact with others in unsegregated situations.

> Available evidence suggests . . . the importance of consistent and firm enforcement of the new policy by those in authority. It indicates also the importance of such factors as: the absence of competition for a limited number of facilities or benefits; the possibility of contacts which permit individuals to learn about one another as individuals; and the possibility of equivalence of positions and functions among all the participants within the unsegregated situation [*Minnesota Law Review*, 1953, pp. 437–438].

Gordon Allport, in *The Nature of Prejudice* (1954), made even more explicit the importance of the nature of interracial contact. He cited research indicating that superficial contact could damage race relations, as could competitive contact and contact between individuals of markedly different status. However, evidence also indicated that when individuals of different racial or ethnic groups worked to achieve common goals, when they had opportunities to get to know one another as individuals, and when they worked with one another as status equals, they often became friends and did not continue to hold prejudices against one another. Allport's contact theory of intergroup relations, based on these findings, has dominated social science inquiry in race relations for nearly three decades. He summarizes the essentials of contact theory:

> Prejudice . . . may be reduced by equal status contact between majority and minority groups in the pursuit of common goals. The effect is greatly enhanced if this contact is sanctioned by institutional supports . . . and if it is of a sort that leads to the perception of common interests and common humanity between members of the two groups [Allport, 1954, p. 281].

Traditional school organization hardly begins to fulfill the conditions outlined by Allport and by the Social Science Statement. Interaction between students of different ethnicities is typically competitive. Black, Anglo, Hispanic, and other groups compete for grades, teacher approval, and places on the student council or the cheerleading squad. Interaction between students of different ethnic groups is often superficial. In the classroom—the only setting in the school in which students of different races or ethnicities are likely to be sitting side by side—traditional instructional methods permit little contact between students that is not brief or teacher directed. Because black, Anglo, and Hispanic students usually ride different buses to different neighborhoods, participate in different kinds of activities, and go to different social functions, opportunities for positive intergroup interaction are structurally limited.

One major exception is sports; sports teams in integrated schools are almost always integrated. Sports teams create conditions of cooperation and interdependence among team members. Research by Slavin and Madden (1979) has shown that students who participated in sports in desegregated high schools were much more likely to have friends outside their own racial group and to have positive racial attitudes than were students who did not participate in integrated sports teams. Sports teams fulfill the requirements of Allport's contact theory of intergroup relations because interaction between teammates tends to be interdependent, cooperative, and of equal status. However, there are relatively few positions on sports teams; schools below the high school level may not have sports teams at all. A fundamental question is whether classroom organization can be changed to allow regular interdependent, cooperative contact to take place between students of different ethnicities.

This chapter describes the results of research designed to answer this question by systematically applying interventions based on Allport's contact theory to academic classrooms. The methods evaluated in this research are referred to collectively as "cooperative learning." The research on cooperative learning methods is reviewed, with an emphasis on understanding complex changes in classroom organization and in student friendship patterns caused by integrated cooperative learning groups in the desegregated classroom.

COOPERATIVE LEARNING

Cooperative learning methods explicitly use the presence of students of different races or ethnicities, which is the strength of the desegregated school, to enhance intergroup relations. Students work in groups of four to five students, with each group composed of students of different races, sexes, and levels of achievement, reflecting the composition of the class as a whole. Groups are evaluated in terms of how much they can increase the academic performance of each individual member and are rewarded or recognized on this basis. Cooperation between students is also emphasized by the teacher. These characteristics of cooperative learning contrast sharply with the interstudent competition for grades and teacher approval, characteristic of the traditional classroom.

Cooperative learning methods attempt to ensure that each student can make a substantial contribution to the group, so that members will be equal in the sense of role equality specified by Allport (1954). Cooperative learning methods are designed to make profound changes in classroom organization rather than temporary or cosmetic treatments. They provide daily opportunities for intense interpersonal contact between students of different races and ethnicities. When the teacher assigns students of different backgrounds to work together, unequivocal support for officially sanctioned interracial or interethnic interaction is communicated to students. Although race or ethnic relations may never be mentioned in the course of cooperative learning experiences, it is difficult for students to believe that their teachers endorse racial separation when they have helped set up multiethnic learning groups.

In theory, cooperative learning methods satisfy the conditions outlined in the Social Science Statement and by Allport (1954) for positive effects of desegregation: cooperation between races, equal-status roles of students of different races, interracial contact that permits students to learn about one another as individuals, and the communication of unequivocal teacher support for interracial cooperation.

The conditions of contact theory are not difficult to achieve in the social science laboratory. However, as Harrison (1976, p. 563) points out, "200 million Americans cannot be run through the laboratory one by one [to reduce prejudice]." A program designed to implement contact theory in classrooms must not only improve intergroup relations but also accomplish other educational goals. Cooperative learning methods would be of little use to schools if they did not also improve (or at least not hinder) student achievement or if they were too expensive, too difficult, too narrowly focused, or too disruptive to school routines to be practical as fundamental alternatives to traditional instruction. Thus, features of cooperative learning methods in addition to their effects on race relations are extremely important.

There are four major cooperative learning methods that embody the principles of contact theory, have been researched in desegregated schools, and have the practical characteristics outlined here: They are inexpensive and easy to implement in classrooms, widely applicable in terms of subject matter and grade levels, easily integrated into the existing school without additional resources, and have been shown to improve achievement more than traditional instruction does (see Slavin, 1980a). Two of these methods were developed and evaluated at the Center for Social Organization of Schools at the Johns Hopkins University. These are Teams-Games-Tournament, or TGT (DeVries & Edwards, 1973; DeVries & Slavin, 1978), and Student Teams–Achievement Divisions, or STAD (Slavin, 1978). These two methods have been extensively researched and are widely used in U.S. schools. A third technique, Jigsaw teaching (Aronson, 1978) has been evaluated in several desegregated schools and is widely used both in its original form and as modified by Slavin (1980b). Finally, methods developed and assessed at the University of Minnesota, referred to here as "Learning Together," (D. W. Johnson & R. T. Johnson, 1975) have been studied in desegregated schools. These techniques are described in the following sections.

Student Teams–Achievement Divisions (STAD)

STAD (Slavin, 1978) consists of five interlocking components: class presentations, cooperative groups or teams, quizzes, individual improvement scores, and team recognition. Academic material is initially presented in lectures by the teacher. Then students study worksheets in teams composed of four to five students representing all levels of academic achievement in the class, all racial or ethnic groups, and both sexes. The teams prepare their members to do well on individual quizzes that follow the team practice sessions. After approximately one class period of teacher presentation and one period of team practice, the students take individual quizzes on the material. The individual quiz scores are translated into team scores using a system that rewards students for improving on their own past performance, and the team scores are recognized in a class newsletter or on a bulletin board.

Teams-Games-Tournament (TGT)

TGT (DeVries & Edwards, 1973) is similar to STAD in basic rationale and methodology. Instead of the quizzes and improvement scores, however, it uses a system of academic game tournaments in which students from each team compete ′ with students from other teams of the same achievement levels to earn points for their teams. This competition with equals has the same rationale as the improvement score system of STAD; it gives every student an equal opportunity to contribute to the team score. The team assignments, lessons, team practice, and team recognition procedures are all the same for TGT and STAD.

Jigsaw and Jigsaw II

In the original Jigsaw method (Aronson, Blaney, Sikes, Stephan, & Snapp, 1975; Aronson, 1978), students are assigned to heterogeneous six-member teams, and each team member is given a unique set of information on a study unit. For example, for a unit on Spain, one student might be appointed as an expert on Spain's history, another on its culture, another on its economy, and so on. The students read their information and then discuss it in expert groups, which consist of students from different teams who have the same information. The experts then return to their home team to teach their information to their teammates. Finally, all students are quizzed, and students receive individual grades.

Learning Together

Methods developed by D. W. Johnson and R. T. Johnson (1975) are referred to in this chapter as "Learning Together." In these techniques, students work in small, heterogeneous groups. They complete a common worksheet and are praised and rewarded as a group.

MAIN EFFECTS ON INTERGROUP RELATIONS

Experimental evidence on cooperative learning has generally supported the conclusions of the Social Science Statement and of Allport (1954). With few exceptions, this research has demonstrated that, when the conditions outlined by Allport (1954) are met in the classroom, students are more likely to make friends outside of their own racial groups than they are in traditional classrooms, as measured by responses to such sociometric items as "Who are your best friends in this class?"

DeVries, Edwards, and Slavin (1978) summarized results from four studies of TGT in desegregated schools. In three of these, students in classes that used TGT gained significantly more in friendship choices outside of their own racial groups than did control students. In one study, no differences were found, although there were positive effects on the cross-racial helping reported by students (DeVries et al., 1978). The samples involved in the successful studies varied in grade levels (7–12) and in the percentage of minority students in the classroom (10–51%).

The evidence of gains in cross-racial friendships resulting from STAD is equally strong. In two studies, Slavin (1977a, 1979) found that students who had experienced STAD over periods of 10–12 weeks developed more cross-racial friendships than did control students. Slavin and Oickle (1981) found significant gains in white friendships toward blacks as a consequence of STAD, but no differences in black friendships toward whites.

One indication of the strength of the improvements in race relations over time caused by cooperative learning methods is provided by follow-up studies. Slavin (1979) assessed the effects of a 12-week STAD intervention 9 months after its completion. The follow-up study was conducted during the school year following the original study, so students were asked to name their friends from the entire school rather than from a single classroom. Because of the difficulty of locating students in an inner-city junior high school a year after the intervention, the follow-up concentrated on one experimental and one control class taught by the same teacher. However, despite this small sample, a statistically significant difference in cross-racial friendships favoring the experimental STAD class was found. Former STAD students named an average of 2.44 students of the other race, which was 37.9% of all of their friendship choices; former control students made only 0.80 cross-racial choices, 9.8% of their total choices.

Research on the effects of the original Jigsaw method has not directly investigated friendship choices between black and white students. Blaney, Stephan, Rosenfield, Aronson, and Sikes (1977) reported that students in desegregated classes using Jigsaw preferred fellow members of their cooperative groups over other classmates. However, because students' group members and other class mates had about the same racial and ethnic mix, it is impossible to assess the effects of Jigsaw on interracial or intergroup relations.

There have been two studies of the effects of a modified version of Jigsaw (Jigsaw II) on intergroup relations. In Jigsaw II (Slavin, 1980b), individual quiz scores are summed to form team scores, and winning teams are recognized in a class newsletter, similar to that used in STAD. Gonzales (1979) found that Anglo and Asian-American students had better attitudes toward Mexican-American classmates as a result of a Jigsaw II intervention, but no differences were found in attitudes toward Anglo or Asian-American students. Ziegler (1981) studied the effects of Jigsaw II on friendships in classes composed of recent European immigrants and Anglo-Canadians in Toronto. She found substantially more cross-ethnic friendships as a result of Jigsaw II both on an immediate posttest and on a

10-week follow-up. These follow-up effects were found both for "casual friend-ships" ("Who in this class would you call your friends?") and for "close friend-ships" ("Who in this class have you spent time with after school or on weekends in the last 2 weeks?").

The Learning Together method, in which students in small groups prepare a single report or worksheet and receive praise for working together, produced greater friendships across racial lines in a cooperative treatment than in an indi-vidualized method in which students were not allowed to interact (L. Cooper, Johnson, Johnson, & Wilderson, 1980). D. W. Johnson and R. T. Johnson (1981), using similar instructional methods, found more cross-racial interaction in cooperative than in individualized classes during free time. The Johnson and Johnson (1981) study is important because unlike most of the research on coopera-tive learning and intergroup relations, which depends entirely on self-reported sociometric data, they actually observed black and white interaction in school. Students were observed during a 10-minute free-time period immediately follow-ing either a cooperative intervention or an individualistic intervention (in which students were forbidden to interact). Black and white students in cooperative classes interacted far more frequently than students in the individualistic classes during their free-time activities. However, it is unclear whether these results have meaning outside the classroom setting, as students in the cooperative condi-tion may have simply stayed in their integrated groups during the observation sessions.

One of the largest and longest studies of cooperative learning was conducted by Weigel, Wiser, and Cook (1975) in tri-ethnic (Mexican-American, Anglo, black) classrooms. They reported that their cooperative methods had positive effects on white attitudes toward Mexican-Americans, but not on white–black, black–white, black–Hispanic, Hispanic–black, or Hispanic–white attitudes. They also found that cooperative learning reduced teachers' reports of interethnic conflict.

The effects of cooperative learning methods reviewed here are not entirely consistent, but each of the cooperative learning studies showed positive effects on some aspect of race relations. Eight of the nine TGT and STAD studies, for example, demonstrated that, when the conditions of contact theory are fulfilled, friendships between students of different ethnicities or races increase.

The pattern of findings in studies in which not all the hypothesized effects were found is an interesting one. In one case (DeVries et al., 1978), no intergroup relations effects were found. However, in three other studies (Gonzales, 1979; Slavin & Oickle, 1981; Weigel et al., 1975), positive effects of cooperative learning were found for attitudes toward minority students, but not for minority attitudes toward majority students. This may indicate that minority group members usually begin with better attitudes toward majority group individuals than the other way around (Slavin & Madden, 1979), but this trend needs to be explored in greater depth before firm conclusions can be drawn.

In most studies of cooperative learning in which achievement and intergroup relations were measured, achievement increased more in the cooperative groups than in the control groups. All four of the TGT studies (DeVries, Edwards, & Wells, 1974; K. J. Edwards & DeVries, 1972, 1974; K. J. Edwards *et al.*, 1972) found positive effects on achievement as well as on race relations, as did two of the three STAD studies (Slavin, 1977b; Slavin & Oickle, 1981). The Ziegler (1981) study of Jigsaw II also found positive achievement effects, as well as the previously noted effects on cross-ethnic friendships.

Thus, it is apparent that cooperative learning does stimulate positive relations between students of different races or ethnicities, while also increasing their achievement. In terms of implications for educational practice, these main effects are the most important findings of the research on cooperative learning. However, it may be possible to improve these techniques further and understand better how intergroup relations are formed in schools if we can discover how and why cooperative learning methods affect intergroup relations.

CONTACT THEORY IN THE CLASSROOM

In this section, we address the issue of how well the available evidence fits the predictions of the contact theory of intergroup relations. Our intent is to clarify what is and what is not known about how cooperative learning works and to explore some of the empirical and conceptual limits of these methods in actual classroom application.

All the cooperative learning methods described in the preceding pages use complex interventions but are based primarily on Allport's contact theory. Contact theory has been studied in the social-psychological laboratory for many years (see, for example, Cook, 1978). The field experimental research on cooperative learning methods in the classroom offers a new opportunity to explore many of the components and assumptions behind contact theory. Clearly, the evidence on cooperative learning confirms the expectation that a treatment based on contact theory would improve intergroup relations. We now consider how cooperative learning affects the conditions for contact, cooperation, equal status, normative climate in the classroom, and perceived similarity among students, which are major dimensions or derivitives of contact theory.

Contact

It is hardly surprising that friendships across racial or ethnic boundaries are rare, relative to friendships within these groups. Blacks, Hispanic, and Anglo students typically live in different neighborhoods, ride different buses, and prefer different activities. Secondary school students of different ethnicities often come from different elementary schools. Socioeconomic, sex, and achievement differences further separate students. These factors work against friendship formation even when race is not a factor (see Lott & Lott, 1965). Racial differences accentuate the tendencies for students to form homogeneous peer groups and sometimes result in overt prejudice and interracial hostility.

Given the many forces operating against the formation of cross-racial friendships, it would seem that, if cooperative learning influences these friendships, it would affect relatively weak relationships rather than strong relationships. Strong relationships take more time, involve more emotional intensity and intimacy, and are based on more reciprocal communications and exchanges of rewards than are weak relationships (Granovetter, 1973). Compared with competition, cooperation is known to increase strong, reciprocated friendships between individuals (M. Deutsch, 1949; Lott & Lott, 1965). However, it seems unlikely that a few weeks of cooperative learning would increase strong interracial relationships between students in the classroom at the possible expense of preexisting same-race relationships.

A study by Hansell and Slavin (1981) investigated this hypothesis. Their sample included seventh- and eighth-grade students in 12 inner-city language arts classrooms. The classes were randomly assigned to cooperative learning (STAD) or control treatments for a 10-week program. Students were asked on both pre- and posttests, "Who are your best friends in this class? Name as many as you wish," in a free-choice format. The study used two measures of the strength of student friendships, reciprocity and choice order. As suggested by Granovetter (1973), reciprocated choices tend to be strong, whereas unreciprocated choices tend to be weak. Hallinan (1979) has suggested that students typically name up to six best friends on sociometric questionnaires. Choices were defined as "close" if they were among the first six made by students and "distant" if they occurred seventh or later. Close choices tend to be more stable than distant choices (Hallinan, 1979; Moreno, 1934/1953; Epstein, Chapter 3, this volume) and are more likely to be strong friendship ties. The reciprocity and order of choices made and received were analyzed with multiple regressions, controlling for total pretest choices made or received, achievement, sex, race, and classroom racial composition. The results of these analyses are presented in Table 6.1.

TABLE 6.1
Cooperative Learning Effects on Strong and Weak Cross-Race Friendship Choices[a]

Reference	Total choices made	Total cross-race	Strong cross-race		Weak cross-race	
Hansell and Slavin (1981)	.09	.16*	.25*	.17[b]	.06	.11[c]
Hansell (1982)[d]	.17*	.12	−.04		.17*	

[a]Only the standardized regression coefficients are reported. Student sex, race, and achievement, and classroom racial composition and pretest choices were statistically controlled. The cooperative learning treatment was coded 1 and the control treatment was coded 0.

[b]Reciprocated and close choices on first six friends named, respectively.

[c]Unreciprocated and distant choices in seventh or later friends named, respectively.

[d]Based on three-point scale of how much they liked every student on the class roster. Strong choices were those liked "a lot" and weak choices were those liked "some."

*$p < .05$.

Positive effects of STAD on cross-racial choices were primarily due to increases in strong friendship choices. Reciprocated and close choices, both made and received, increased as a result of the treatment. In addition, there was a significant increase in distant choices received, but no significant changes in other types of weak friendship relations. Hansell and Slavin's study showed positive cooperative learning effects on strong friendship choices—the kind of friendship that should be most difficult to change.

A second study (Hansell, 1982) attempted to duplicate these results but, using an improved sociometric measure, found that cooperative learning increased weak rather than strong choices. The sample was 317 fifth- and sixth-grade children in 11 inner-city language arts classrooms. The overall procedure was very similar to that used by Hansell and Slavin (1981). Classes were randomly assigned to cooperative group learning (STAD) or control treatments for a 10-week program. Instead of the free-choice sociometric format used by Hansell and Slavin (1981) that asked students to name their best friends, Hansell (1982) gave students a complete roster of the classroom and asked them to indicate whether they liked each student a lot, some, or not much. Liking a lot was considered a strong relationship, whereas some liking was classified as a weak relationship.

The complete-list sociometric method yielded more total friendship choices, and, in particular, more weak interracial friendship choices, than the free-choice method. Hansell and Slavin (1981) reported that, on their pretest, students made an average of 10.51 total choices, 3.25 total cross-race choices, and 1.60 strong (reciprocated) cross-race choices. Hansell (1982) reported that, on the pretest, students made an average of 19.88 total choices, 9.68 total cross-race choices, 3.77 strong cross-race choices, and 5.80 weak cross-race choices.

Selected results from the Hansell (1982) study are also shown in Table 6.1. The cooperative learning treatment did not affect strong friendships (liking a lot). The treatment did increase weak friendships of all types—total weak friendships and weak same-race and cross-race friendships. In addition, cooperative learning increased weak cross-sex friendships. The differences in the findings of these studies could be due to the differences in sociometric definitions of strong and weak choices or to differences in the ages of the students. Further research is needed before we can reach a conclusion about the strength of new cross-race friendships caused by cooperative learning.

These studies concentrated on the strength of dyadic choices, but these structures are, of course, components of larger peer triads, peer groups, and friendship networks. An important topic for future research is whether cooperative learning affects larger peer structures, including relationships outside the classroom. Naturally occurring peer groups in schools tend to be relatively segregated and homogeneous. They consist of students of similar age, race, and sex (J. S. Coleman, 1961; Glidewell et al., 1966; Gronlund, 1959; Hansell, 1981; Schofield, 1978). Because there are relatively few contacts between naturally existing peer groups, the opportunities for intergroup communication and cooperation are structurally limited. An important issue is whether the beneficial effects of cooperative learning on dyadic peer friendships lead to extensive new interracial contacts across race lines outside of the context of the intervention.

The study by Hansell (1982) tested the hypothesis that cooperative learning would increase the social integration of peer groups within elementary classrooms. Network analysis was used to identify peer groups on the pretest and posttest, and the racial composition of each peer group was examined. A peer group was considered racially segregated if two-thirds or more of its members were of a single race. Peer groups with more even proportions of black and white members were classified as integrated. Using this criterion, the racial integration of peer groups in cooperative classrooms did not change, but the racial integration of peer groups in control classrooms decreased. Cooperative learning had similar effects on the sexual integration of peer friendships. Compared with students in control classrooms, those in cooperative classrooms made more choices as individuals of cross-sex friends, but the sexual composition of the identifiable peer groups did not change. Although this study did not include a longitudinal follow-up and we have no evidence about the permanence of these results, they suggest that cooperative learning stimulates new friendships between individual students of different races and sexes, but its effects on the racial and sexual composition of naturally existing peer groups may be somewhat limited. This is an issue for further research, with important implications for improving intergroup relations outside of the classroom.

Cooperation versus Competition

Allport's (1954) research documented many cases in which contact between races did not improve racial attitudes. School desegregation brings students of different backgrounds into regular interpersonal contact of some kind but does not lead by itself to improvements in intergroup relations (Gerard & Miller, 1975; St. John, 1975; Stephan, 1978). Thus, it can be stated confidently that not all interracial contact leads to favorable relations.

Allport (1954) emphasized that, if interracial contact is to improve race relations, the contact should be cooperative rather than competitive. Later research (e.g., D. W. Johnson & S. Johnson, 1972) showed that individuals working toward a cooperative goal begin to like each other in part because individuals like others who help them achieve important goals. In a cooperative group, each group member's efforts help the group to be rewarded, so the group members themselves are seen in a positive light by their groupmates.

However, it is difficult to separate the effects of cooperation from the effects of contact per se. When cooperative learning is introduced in a desegregated classroom, interracial interaction is drastically increased (D. W. Johnson & R. T. Johnson, 1981; Slavin & Wodarski, 1978). As students interact every day for many weeks, it is only logical to expect that many of them will become friends. But is it the interaction that produces the cross-racial friendships, or does the cooperative goal make an independent contribution to friendship formation?

There is some evidence that the critical variable is nonsuperficial contact, not cooperation. Cook (1978) found that, when mothers of disadvantaged nursery school students who previously had very few interracial contacts participated in weekly discussion groups of black and white mothers, cross-racial friendships tended to increase whether or not the groups were structured cooperatively. L. Cooper et al. (1980) compared a cooperative instructional intervention to competitive and individualistic methods. In the cooperative condition, students worked in heterogeneous groups, handed in a common assignment sheet, and received praise and rewards as a group. In the competitive condition, students were assigned to equal-ability clusters and received praise for being the best in their cluster. In the individualistic condition, students were forbidden to interact and received individual praise. Results showed that a much higher percentage of students in the cooperative and competitive conditions made friendship choices outside of their own racial groups than did students in the individualistic condition. However, there were no differences between the cooperative and competitive conditions; in fact, the proportion of students making cross-racial choices was somewhat higher in the competitive group than in the cooperative group.

This result supports a conclusion that assigning students to groups in which they may interact rather than providing them with cooperative goals affects intergroup relations. This result directly contradicts Allport's emphasis on cooperation (or at least noncompetition) as a criterion for positive outcomes of interracial contact. However, there are other issues involved. The cooperative groups in the Cooper et al. study were heterogeneous on academic ability, whereas the competitive clusters were homogeneous. Assuming that the clusters were racially mixed (this is not stated), this assignment might have created interaction between the black and white students most likely to become friends—those of similar academic achievement. The positive effects of this homogeneous cluster assignment on the chances of friendships forming across race lines may have offset the potentially negative effect of the competition. Also, competition in Allport's sense refers to a serious struggle for limited resources. Both the cooperation and the competition applied by L. Cooper et al. (1980) were mild and diffuse; if substantial rewards or grades had been attached to success in both conditions, the results might have been quite different. In fact, a series of laboratory studies by Cook (1978) and his associates suggested that, if success in a cooperative group was available to all groups, the use of substantial group rewards led to greater attraction among group members than did group cooperation without reward, which was the situation in the L. Cooper et al. study. From the students' point of view, the primary difference between the cooperative and competitive treatments might have been the homogeneous versus heterogeneous group assignment, not the difference in how rewards were assigned.

At present, the relative importance of contact per se versus cooperative contact for intergroup relations is unclear. On one hand, it seems likely that if regular, positive, equal-status interracial interaction can be created in a setting, relations between individuals of different races will be good. Holding that level of interaction constant, cooperative group goals may or may not add to the effect. However, cooperative goals increase the level and quality of interpersonal interaction (see D. W. Johnson & R. T. Johnson, 1974); in other words, if high-quality, nonsuperficial contact can be created by any means, race relations are likely to be improved, but setting cooperative tasks and goals may well be the most efficient way to bring about this level of positive interaction.

In the classroom, this last point may be particularly critical. It is difficult to imagine a classroom intervention that would be usable over the long term and would be likely to create frequent, positive interracial interaction that would not involve some form of cooperation. Further, there is evidence that well-structured cooperative tasks and clearly specified cooperative rewards are needed to create maximum peer interaction. Slavin (1980c) compared STAD to a condition in which students could study with anyone in the class but no rewards were given for doing well as a group. Despite the fact that the students in this condition were more likely to be with preexisting friends than were the students in the teacher-assigned heterogeneous STAD groups, peer interaction was substantially higher in the STAD condition. Thus, a laissez-faire classroom organization may not be enough to produce high levels of positive interpersonal interaction in the classroom. A structured group intervention with clear group goals and rewards may be the most practical way to create frequent, nonsuperficial interracial contact in the classroom. Despite the theoretical importance of contact per se versus cooperative tasks and goals, this distinction may have little meaning for practice.

Hansell, Tackaberry, and Slavin (in press) studied the effects of cooperative and competitive group learning on the structure of peer groups in a direct assessment of changes in intergroup relations. They based the research on Granovetter's (1973) conception of how the strength of dyadic relationships influences larger peer group structures. Granovetter reasoned that the strength of relationships among a set of people is associated with the overlap in their relationships. The set of people who all have strong relationships with any given individual will also tend to have strong relationships with each other. In contrast, the set of people with weak relationships with any given indiviudal will not generally have relationships with each other. Thus, relationships within peer groups tend to be reciprocated and strong, whereas bridging relationships between peer groups tend to be unreciprocated and weak.

Hansell et al. (in press) predicted that both cooperative and competitive group learning would increase total choice activity. Cooperative learning was expected to increase *strong* dyadic relationships and break down preexisting peer group structures, whereas competitive group learning was expected to increase *weak* dyadic relationships and enlarge preexisting peer groups. Results supported the hypotheses about the effects of competition on peer group structures, but cooperative group learning had no significant effects on either dyadic choices or peer group structures defined in terms of strong choices.

These results are consistent with the earlier Hansell and Slavin (1981) study. They found that cooperative learning increased strong *interracial* friendships, but they did not report an increase in *total* strong friendships, which was the focus of the later study. However, it may be easier to stimulate new weak cross-race relationships through realistic classroom interventions, as Hansell (1982) demonstrated. These studies suggest that cooperation and competition affect the structure of peer groups and may have important implications for intergroup relations. But the findings are complex, and research is needed before definite conclusions can be drawn.

One issue that has provoked a lively and continuing debate among cooperative learning researchers is the issue of intergroup competition versus pure cooperation. Slavin (1981), for example, defends the use of competition between learning groups as a practical means of motivating students to cooperate within learning groups. However, D. W. Johnson (1981b) criticizes such mixed strategies as unnecessary and potentially ineffective, and Weigel *et al.* (1975), who used group competition in their study, questioned whether group competition might inflame status-based rivalries (also see Miller, Chapter 12, for his contribution to this debate as it relates to the influence of friends in school).

The examples Allport (1954) cites to support his emphasis on cooperative contact as a precondition of positive race relations (e.g., sports teams, military platoons in battle) involve intergroup competition, not pure cooperation. In theory as well as in the actual research, however, it is clear that intergroup competition is not necessary; any superordinate goal should produce similar effects. In Sherif and Sherif's (1953) classic Robber's Cave experiment, intense intergroup rivalry was not broken down when the groups attended a party together, but it was dissipated when the groups were forced to cooperate on a task benefiting both groups. What is apparently critical in each case is not intergroup competition, but whether or not there is a salient, important mutual group goal with some kind of group reward (or an external threat). Cook's (1978) series of studies showed that cash payments to small groups for exceeding a preset standard significantly increased cross-racial acceptance in groups that succeeded. Cross-racial acceptance in groups that failed to earn the reward was lower, but not significantly different from acceptance levels in groups that did not have a chance to earn any money.

Success in intergroup competition is not likely to be as motivating as a monetary reward, but it is almost certainly more motivating than the informal group praise used in pure cooperative learning methods. Apparently, the greater the incentive for a group to succeed, the greater the positive affect within the group. Rabbie and Horwitz (1969) showed that losers as well as winners in intergroup competition liked their groupmates more than did students in similar groups not faced with a win–lose situation. In the cooperative learning methods that use intergroup competition, different teams can win each week, possibly producing the positive affect within teams seen in Cook's (1978) studies. If intergroup competition has a negative effect on intergroup relations, there must be some other compensating forces at work, because the most successful of the cooperative learning methods (e.g., TGT, STAD, Jigsaw II) use it.

One advantage of intergroup competition is simply a practical one. Educators generally object to giving students money or other tangible rewards for doing their schoolwork. Giving students grades based on their group performance would be unethical, as well as difficult for most teachers and parents to accept, because it would be possible for high-achieving, hard-working students on low-performing teams to receive low grades and lazy students on good teams to receive high grades; D. W. Johnson and R. T. Johnson (1975) and M. Deutsch (1979), however, do advocate some form of group grading. Barring tangible rewards and grades, public recognition for achievement is the reward of choice in schools. Recognition can be provided on the basis of a preset achievement standard, as employed by Madden and Slavin (1980), but this allows for fluctuations in individual rewards due to the varying difficulty of each week's tests and tends to be interpreted by students as group competition anyway. Clearly, research directly comparing intergroup competition to pure cooperation is needed to resolve the question of whether intergroup competition improves or impedes race relations relative to noncompetition.

Equal Status

One of Allport's (1954) theoretical criteria for contact to improve intergroup relations is that it occurs between individuals of equal status. Equal status has been emphasized by many as a critical aspect of contact theory as it relates to school desegregation (see, for example, Amir, 1969; E. G. Cohen, 1975). In Allport's use of the term, students in the same grade level have equal status, regardless of race, sex, or achievement levels. Allport was concerned more with occupational and socioeconomic status than with status associated with ascribed characteristics or innate abilities. The kind of equal status studied by Allport (1954) is referred to by Cook (1969) as "situational equal status."

However, E. G. Cohen's (1975) research introduces a new meaning to the term *equal status*. She is interested in the perceptions of competence that students of different ethnicities have about each other and whether students of different races and ethnicities have equal performance expectations for each other. In Cohen's sense, equal status may be impossible to achieve in an American school, because blacks are often seen as lower in competence by whites and low expectations for blacks generalize to situations in which there may actually be no achievement differences. Cohen (1975) states:

> The inference may be drawn that even though blacks and whites might be brought together in a desegregated school in an "equal status" manner, it is still quite possible for the racial difference to act as a strong status differential triggering expectations for whites to do better in a new situation and for blacks to do less well. If this occurs in the school situation, then the racial stereotypes which contribute to these expectations are only reinforced and confirmed by the interracial interaction in the desegregated school. It should be a matter of great concern if the process of desegregation actually does result in reinforcing such stereotypes of racial incompetence [p. 294].

Cohen's argument implies that equal-status interaction between black and white students is very unlikely, particularly when actual black–white differences in reading and mathematics performance confirm racial stereotypes. She has often stated that placing students in small work groups would make racial differences in achievement even more salient, thereby eliminating any chance that black and white students might treat one another as equals. She evaluated an alternative approach to the desegregated classroom in which blacks were given unique and important skills that they could then teach to their white classmates. This treatment produced equal-status interaction on an experimental task, although a cooperative group condition also had this effect (E. G. Cohen, Lockheed, & Lohman, 1976). It should be noted, however, that Cohen's cooperative intervention was implemented during the summer; her small groups were not academic groups and did not require reading or mathematics skills, If, as Cohen suggests, cooperation on academic tasks in small groups leaves preexisting perceptions of unequal status intact, or makes them even more salient, then equal status in Cohen's sense may not be critical for intergroup relations. Of course, it is possible that reducing differential perceptions of ability could further enhance the effects of cooperative learning on intergroup relations.

Most of the cooperative learning methods reviewed in this chapter contain mechanisms to diminish the salience or effects of ability differences within cooperative activities. In STAD (Slavin, 1978), the scores students contribute to their teams are based on individual improvement, which is equally available to all students. In TGT (DeVries & Edwards, 1973; DeVries & Slavin, 1978; DeVries, Slavin, Fennessey, Edwards, & Lombardo, 1980; K. J. Edwards *et al.*, 1973), students compete against classmates who are equal in past performance to add points to their team scores. This gives all students an equal chance to contribute to their team scores, regardless of performance level. Jigsaw (Aronson, 1978) and Jigsaw II (Slavin, 1980b) give each student a unique piece of information, making all students of value to the group.

These elements of the major cooperative learning methods may reduce or soften the impact of any racial differences in achievement. However, it should also be recognized that such differences may not exist or may not be very large in many classes, both because of tracking and because lower-class minority students are often integrated with lower-class whites. Even when black–white performance differences exist on the average within a group, there are almost always blacks among the highest performing students and whites among the lowest performing students, making a racial generalization difficult for students to make.

Finally, there is some evidence that cooperative learning methods reduce the achievement gap between black and white students, which may act to reduce differential performance expectations. In two STAD studies, initially significant differences between blacks and whites in academic performance disappeared on the posttest in the experimental groups, while remaining or increasing in the control groups (Slavin, 1977b; Slavin & Oickle, 1981). Similar reductions in black–white achievement differences were found for Jigsaw (Lucker, Rosenfield, Sikes, & Aronson, 1976) and for the improvement score system used in STAD (Beady & Slavin, 1981). These reductions in actual black–white achievement differences may cause (or be caused by) changes in intergroup perceptions brought about by the cooperative intervention and the improvement score system.

At present, the evidence about the role of equal status in cooperative learning interventions is inconclusive. Unfortunately, cooperative learning researchers have not measured status perceptions directly, and Cohen and her colleagues have not measured student relations directly. It seems unlikely that positive race relations absolutely require equal performance status (as opposed to situational status) between blacks and whites, but future research could establish this link.

Institutional Norms

Allport (1954) hypothesized that cross-racial contact would be more likely to improve race relations if the institutions in which the contact took place clearly supported racial interaction and racial equality. Allport felt that most whites had conflicting feelings about desegregation. On one hand, they may be uncomfortable about interacting with blacks or others different from themselves, but on the other hand, they may feel shame about this discomfort, because most Americans believe in fair play and equality. Allport therefore reasoned that whites would most strongly accept desegregation when they themselves did not have to initiate interracial contact and when such contact was externally mandated by institutional norms and policies.

In schools, one might assume that institutional support for interracial contact would always be present. Certainly, few school officials openly advocate segregation. However, teachers and administrators are often quite uncomfortable about the issue of race, being unsure whether race should simply be ignored ("We're all the same here") or whether the issue of race relations should be openly discussed and confronted. Students in such schools may get the idea that, while racial conflicts are not permitted in school, positive cross-racial contacts are not really encouraged either.

One simple change that cooperative learning methods may make in the desegregated classroom is to clearly legitimize positive interracial contact. Students of different races may hold few overt prejudices but still be reluctant to take the first step toward making friends of another race. Such students might welcome the teacher's establishing a normative climate that supports and encourages interracial interaction and labels it as normal and desirable. This climate may be created without a word about race being spoken; the fact that the teacher assigns students to racially mixed learning groups clearly indicates teacher approval of interracial interaction. Should the teacher allow students to choose their own teams (which would often result in racially and sexually homogeneous teams), the opposite implicit message might be communicated.

Perceived Similarity

In the absence of research directly investigating the contribution of cooperative learning methods to classroom norms supporting interracial contact, we speculate that such norms may be a function of student perceptions of similarity. One of the strongest determinants of friendship in general (after contact) is the perception by two individuals that they share important characteristics, world views, favorite activities, and so on (see Lott & Lott, 1965). A persistent problem is that students of different races or ethnicities are likely to be dissimilar on many important attributes, such as sociometric status, values, and preferred activities. Even if students could be made color-blind, these other differences would perpetuate the tendency for students to make friends primarily within their own racial groups. Allport (1954) referred to perceived similarity as a criterion for improved race relations that "leads to a perception of common interests and common humanity [p. 281]." However, few of the basic racial dissimilarities likely to exist in desegregated classrooms can be easily overcome.

In one sense, cooperative learning methods create a new basis of perceived similarity among relatively dissimilar students. The fact of being assigned to cooperative groups automatically gives students a common identity. Social-psychological laboratory research has shown that simply announcing group assignments can induce individuals to evaluate groupmates more positively than nongroupmates, even before they interact (Gerard & Hoyt, 1974). Students entering adolescence associate with peer groups for a sense of identity and worth. In some cases, prior cross-racial friendships that existed in elementary school are broken in junior high, as students identify more with their own ethnic group. Cooperative learning provides each student with a peer group that is not based on racial or sexual identity, but on shared goals. The mere announcement of group assignments may begin to break down racial barriers to friendship as students perceive their shared identity as cooperative group members. The direct contribution of shared perceptions of group identity to improved race relations may be difficult to separate from the effects of contact. However, this may be an important, largely unanticipated result of cooperative learning methods that deserves careful study.

A MODEL OF EFFECTS OF COOPERATIVE LEARNING ON INTERGROUP RELATIONS

The preceding section discussed the components of contact theory and of cooperative learning methods in terms of their impact on intergroup relations. Research exploring the mechanisms that cause the effects of cooperative learning on intergroup relations is sketchy. However, enough is known at this time to present a causal model that links the elements of cooperative learning to intergroup relations. Such a model is presented in Figure 6.1.

In this model, cooperative learning is represented by primary components that

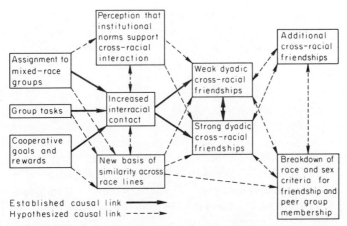

FIGURE 6.1. Contact theory model of effects of cooperative learning on intergroup relations.

usually operate together in practice but are distinct in theory. These are the assignment to mixed-race groups, the provision of group tasks, and the setting of cooperative goals and rewards. As discussed earlier, the simple assignment of students to mixed-race teams, even without contact, is likely to give them a new basis of status similarity across race lines and to communicate an unmistakable institutional norm that interracial interaction is normal and desirable, both of which may increase cross-racial friendships independently of contact per se.

The provision of a group task (which could be made without group assignments or cooperative goals) is hypothesized to operate primarily through interracial interaction (contact), although working on a group task may provide students of different races with similar status as well. However, the true effects of group tasks may depend on their particular characteristics. For example, if students are allowed to choose partners for a task, they may choose students within their own race groups, potentially reducing interracial interaction. If the task encourages interaction among students, and students of different races are likely to interact, the effect of the group task (through the increased contact) may be positive even without group assignment or cooperative goals.

Cooperative goals and rewards are hypothesized to affect intergroup relations in part by increasing interracial interaction, in part by giving students a new basis of status similarity, but also in part directly by creating a common, cooperative goal that is likely to increase mutual positive feelings among those who share the goal (see D. W. Johnson & S. Johnson, 1972).

We emphasize the centrality of interracial contact in the model depicted in Figure 6.1. In schools, where situational status differences are unlikely to exist between students in the same grade, meaningful interracial contact is probably the critical mediating variable linking cooperative learning to improved intergroup relations. If cooperative learning did not create conditions of frequent positive and close interaction between students of different races, the effects produced by assignment to groups or provision of cooperative goals and rewards might be weak and temporary. The various elements of cooperative learning probably affect inter-racial relations primarily through the mediating variable of close interracial contact.

One limitation of existing research on cooperative learning, and on contact theory in general, is the exclusive focus on dyadic relationships involving students of different races or ethnicities. However, the impact of cooperative learning almost certainly involves networks of friendships rather than simple dyadic friend-ships. New preliminary analyses of the data from the Slavin (1979) STAD study have revealed that many of the new cross-racial friendships made over the course of the STAD intervention were formed between students who had not been in the same cooperative group. A moment's reflection would support the inevitability of this result. In a four-member team that has two blacks and two whites, each student could only make two new friends of a different race if he or she made new friends only within the team. At least one of those teammates of a different race is also likely to be of a different sex, but cross-sex friendships are even less frequent than are cross-race friendships (L. Cooper et al., 1980; DeVries & Edwards, 1974). It is also possible that two or more teammates of different races were already friends, further restricting the possible number of new cross-racial choices within teams, and any deviation in team composition from an even racial split reduces the possibilities still further.

Apparently, cross-racial friendships formed outside of cooperative groups ac-count for some of the effects of cooperative learning on dyadic interracial friend-ships. In theory, this should not happen; after all, the teams are usually in competition with each other. However, there are at least two ways this could happen. First, a cooperative learning experience often exposes students to their first (or best) cross-racial friendships. Racial groups in classrooms are charac-terized by many friendship ties within each racial group but few across groups. However, once a cross-racial friendship is formed, the new friend's friends of his or her race become likely candidates as friends as well. In other words, if a white student makes friends with one black student, this relationship bridges formerly isolated black and white peer groups and opens up an entirely new pool of potential friends, possibly reaching beyond the confines of a particular classroom. Also, even a small number of cross-racial friendships may make peer group boundaries, formerly based on race and sex, less well defined, allowing for new, smaller cliques to form based more on mutual liking than on race and sex. These patterns were found in the analysis of sociometric data conducted by Hansell et al. (in press); clique sizes tended to diminish as a result of a cooperative intervention similar to STAD.

This interpretation assumes that secondary effects of cooperative learning on interracial friendship outside of the cooperative group depend on the development of strong friendships within the group. However, this is not necessarily the only route by which new interracial friendships might be formed as a result of cooperative learning. Granovetter (1973) pointed out that friendships between individuals of different cliques tend to be weak, but they are critical in bridging the cliques and eventually allowing for more cross-clique relationships, which are, at first, also weak. Naturally occurring, racially homogeneous peer groups in schools are characterized by many strong friendships within the groups and few friendships of any kind across racial boundaries. Under these circumstances, large numbers of weak cross-race friendships might be just as important as strong ones in breaking down cross-racial barriers to friendship by providing numerous bridges between the race groups. Hansell and Slavin (1981) found that the effects of STAD were stronger on close, reciprocated interracial friendships than on distant or unreciprocated choices. However, even if these relatively strong relationships weakened over time, or were limited to the classroom settings in which cooperative learning is applied, they could still have important outcomes on intergroup relations in general. In fact, it is interesting to speculate whether or not an intervention designed to foster large numbers of weak cross-racial friendships might have more positive or more lasting effects on intergroup relations than cooperative learning, which is primarily directed at producing relatively small numbers of strong interracial friendships (but see Hansell, 1982, for evidence that cooperative learning increases weak cross-race friendships).

NEW DIRECTIONS

We would like to emphasize that, although the effects of cooperative learning methods on intergroup relations are positive and reliable, the theoretical model underlying and explaining these effects is preliminary. Research is needed that tests and extends this model and that evaluates the usefulness of cooperative learning. Research on ethnic groups other than blacks and whites, research at the elementary and high school levels, and observational research is needed to extend recent work. The most critical task now is further research, in actual classroom application, on why cooperative learning works and in what forms it works best. We list some of the important questions in need of exploration.

—What is the impact of the size and type of group reward on the effects of cooperative learning on intergroup relations outcomes? Does intergroup competition increase or decrease the effect? Would tangible rewards or grades dependent on group success increase or decrease the effect?

—Does cooperative learning increase or decrease perceived performance status differences between black and white students? What is the effect of initial performance expectations between students of different races on subsequent friendships between them?

—What is the effect of cooperative learning on general prejudice? What is the effect of initial prejudice on initial and subsequent cross-racial friendship choices in cooperative learning?

—How are new cross-racial friendships outside of students' teams formed? Are such friendships as strong and reciprocated as within-team friendships? Are some preexisting cross-racial friendships broken by cooperative learning, particularly when intergroup competition is used? What is the effect of cooperative learning on social networks beyond the mixed-race dyad? Do race and sex diminish as criteria for friendship? Does cooperative learning make student friendship choices less hierarchical, more reciprocal, and more widely distributed?

—What is the impact of teacher prejudice, attitudes, and expectations on the effects of cooperative learning on intergroup relations? What is the effect of cooperative learning on these prejudices, attitudes, and expectations?

—Can effects on intergroup relations similar to those of cooperative learning be produced using methods that do not include teams, scores, cooperative goals, etc.? Can contact be directly manipulated to achieve these outcomes?

—What are the roles of perceived institutional support and perceived similarity across race lines in the effects of cooperative learning on intergroup relations?

Understanding and extending the effects of cooperative learning on intergroup relations will be a long and difficult process. Some of these questions might be addressed in laboratory studies, although in such a socially complex area as intergroup relations it is doubtful that generalizable results can be produced from brief encounters among strangers in an artificial environment. On the other hand, continued theory-based research of the kinds of extended field experiments emphasized in this chapter allows social scientists a unique opportunity to study change in interpersonal relations in school settings. A desegregated classroom undergoing a cooperative learning intervention is a real-world laboratory in which social forces are being manipulated to bring about social change; understanding how that change occurs is an exciting and important undertaking.

This chapter has described a series of cooperative instructional methods based on Allport's contact theory, summarized their effects on intergroup relations, discussed components of contact theory in the light of this research, and presented a model of the effects of cooperative learning on intergroup relations. Much more remains to be done, but the research on cooperative learning is important both for exploring practical ways to improve intergroup relations in desegregated schools and for developing theories of interracial contact and friendship formation.

NANCY KARWEIT
STEPHEN HANSELL

7

Sex Differences in Adolescent Relationships: Friendship and Status

The topic of sex differences in forming and maintaining friendships has not often been addressed directly. Most discussions of sex differences in friendships have evolved as a minor part of studies that focus primarily on child or adolescent development or on student peer relationships. Sex differences tend to be noted in passing, with little exploration of their bases or consequences. It is difficult to judge the generalizability of specific findings, because comparable studies are rarely conducted across ages or grade levels. If, for example, a sex difference in the average size of the friendship group were detected in a study of sixth-grade students, it is unlikely that there would be a comparable study of the average size of friendship groups of tenth- or twelfth-grade students.

Also, most discussions of sex differences are guided by either a developmental orientation or an environmental orientation, and these perspectives are rarely combined in the same work. Researchers interested in developmental aspects of friendships have not usually considered the significance of the settings in which they occur. Researchers interested in the effects of social contexts or school organization have usually not been sensitive to developmental differences and have treated friendships among children, adolescents, and adults in an undifferentiated manner.

This chapter has two objectives. First, we review relevant literature on sex differences in adolescent friendships, focusing on four major areas in which sex differences have been reported—sex segregation, size of group, reciprocity of choice, and bases of friendship selection. This review identifies differences associ-

115

FRIENDS IN SCHOOL
Patterns of Selection and Influence in Secondary Schools

ated with developmental processes and environmental conditions. Second, we illustrate the usefulness of attending simultaneously to environmental and developmental points of view in an examination of how sex differences and school organization interact on student adjustment to the transition from elementary to junior high school.

STUDIES OF SEX DIFFERENCES IN FRIENDSHIP PATTERNS

Previous research has identified four major sex differences in the nature of friendship ties. First, friendships tend to be segregated within same-sex groupings. Second, males typically have larger friendship groups than do females. Third, females have more cohesive friendship groups than do males, based primarily on reciprocated choices. Fourth, female friendships are oriented toward issues of loyalty, intimacy, and commitment, whereas male friendships are geared toward achievement, leadership, and status acquisition. These four topics are reviewed with specific emphasis on the consistency of the findings across developmental (age) levels and environmental conditions.

Same-Sex Friendships

Many studies document that a preference for same-sex friends persists from nursery school through adulthood. Serbin, Tonick, and Sternglanz (1977) note that same-sex play groups have been found so consistently in all cultures that this tendency may be a universal characteristic of human social behavior. However, they suggest that it is possible to change the extent of cross-sex play in a nursery school setting. Same-sex friendship preferences are found in the elementary years (J. D. Campbell, 1964; Eder & Hallinan, 1978; Gronlund, 1959; Parsons, 1966). Eder and Hallinan (1978), for example, find that about 75% of the friendship choices in a fifth-grade class were within the same sex, and Foot, Chapman, and Smith (1980) note preferences for same-sex friendships in the range of 62–81%.

Dweck (1981) speculates about the causes for segregation by sex and the subsequent emergence of different social interaction patterns. She notes that in the preschool years, girls become "interested in prosocial behavior—in complying with and propagating social regulations [p. 326]." Boys, not interested in this behavior, tend not to comply with rules and are soundly rejected by girls' friendship groups. Gunnarsson (1978) reports that girls in day-care centers were encouraged to have more one-to-one contacts with adults than were boys. Boys spent more time in peer-oriented activities and tended to interact individually with an adult mainly when they caused trouble. These studies suggest that different sexual cultures begin to evolve at an early age, and as sex segregation persists, the interests and activities of boys and girls diverge further. Thus, tendencies that were small and tractable at first become translated into larger, relatively stable differences.

Do the daily experiences in elementary school classrooms contribute to this divergence into separate sexual cultures, and if so, how? If, as the studies cited suggest, young girls are more interested than young boys in complying with and propagating social regulations, then classrooms provide an ideally suited environment for the practice of these skills. Females are praised and positively rewarded more often than boys in the early elementary grades for obeying the rules and being good citizens in the classroom. This behavioral pattern frequently causes young girls to be cast in the role of tattlers and enforcers (Grant, 1982) and to conduct their interactions with boys in the classroom in specific sex-stereotyped patterns. Thus, some classroom environments facilitate and strengthen the development of different sexual cultures. Particular classroom instructional techniques, such as whole-group, teacher-directed instruction, make girls' compliance behaviors and boys' noncompliance behaviors more visible, and reinforce and validate emerging sex differences. This type of traditional classroom not only may reinforce existing patterns but may further encourage sex segregation by limiting opportunities for cross-sex interactions. As peer groups become more sexually homogeneous, this pattern is accentuated and becomes, in turn, an important criterion for membership in the peer groups.

Segregation of students into same-sex friendship groups is not entirely a consequence of individual student preferences but also an outgrowth of classroom structure. Classroom organizations that foster cross-sex interactions, such as high-participatory classes, contribute to a higher incidence of cross-sex friendships than is found in traditional classrooms (Eder & Hallinan, 1978; Epstein, Chapter 5, this volume).

In a direct manipulation of classroom organization, Hansell (1982) assigned students in elementary classrooms to sexually mixed groups and instructed them to work together on cooperative learning tasks for a 10-week period. Four-member groups had two students of each sex, and five-member groups had three students of one sex and two of the other. Results indicated that students in the cooperative groups increased their cross-sex friendship choices compared to students in control classrooms. However, an analysis of peer clique structures showed that student cliques did not become more sexually integrated as a result of this experience. Although the persistence of these effects over a long period of time has not been established, these results suggest that some of the usual segregation of male and female friendships can be decreased under alternative modes of classroom organization.

The preference for same-sex friends is perhaps even more pronounced in early adolescence (Hartup, 1970). Martin (1971) comments that "twelve-year-olds hang around in groups by sex. It is a rare exception when a member of one sex risks associating with members of the opposite sex. The students make the issue an important one, for example, when they work in groups and strongly prefer one-sex grouping [p. 1099]." Schofield (1981), in her study of a middle school, confirms the overwhelming segregation of peer groups by sex. Norms against informal association by peers of opposite sex are well entrenched. She notes, for example, the strong tendency for same-sex seating patterns in the cafeteria, commenting that "during any particular lunch period, there were about 200 students in the cafeteria and fewer than ten cross-race adjacencies occurred and significantly fewer cross-sex adjacencies [p. 62]." Thus, sex is a powerful grouping factor in early adolescence.

Given the strong preference for same-sex friends at this age, the finding of positive effects of cooperative learning teams on cross-sex interaction (DeVries & Edwards, 1974) is particularly important. Using a sample of 115 seventh-graders in a large urban junior high school, DeVries and Edwards assigned males and females to work together in small groups on classroom learning tasks and rewarded them for cooperative group performance. Pre- and posttests comparisons with control classrooms showed that students in cooperative groups named significantly more cross-sex friendships. This study also suggests that classroom organization can reinforce or alter sex groupings, but, like the Hansell (1982) study, it provides no evidence about the duration of such effects or the difficulties of implementing such interventions over a longer period of time.

Some researchers report that during middle and late adolescence, same-sex groupings give way to more heterosexual peer groups based on dating couples (Dunphy, 1963). The transition to mixed-sex groupings is argued to be prevalent by age 16 (Savin-Williams, 1980, citing Hollingshead). However, the frequency, extent, and duration of mixed-sex groups is not clear, and many studies indicate that same-sex friendship patterns extend through high school and college. Specific findings depend partly on different data collection techniques. In sociometric studies, Kandel (1978) finds that 91% of the friendship choices in her sample of high school students were of the same sex, and Hansell (1978) reports that 81% of friendships in his high school sample were sexually homogeneous. Montemayor and Van Komen (1982), in an observational study of adolescent peer interaction, indicate that most of the friendships are confined to members of the same sex. Wheeler and Nezlek (1977) also report interactions among college freshmen to be mainly within the same sex. In a study combining observational and sociometric techniques, Gordon (1957) documents that most cliques within the high school were of the same sex. Other major studies of adolescent peer groups (J. S. Coleman, 1961; McDill & Rigsby, 1973) do not shed light on this issue because they restricted choices to same-sex school friends. Epstein, Chapter 3, this volume, shows that there is an increase in cross-sex friendship choices over the middle to high school years, but the majority of best friends remain of the same sex.

Taken together, the results of these studies indicate strong sex segregation in peer friendships from nursery school through early adolescence, but the findings for adolescents are more complicated. Adolescents clearly engage in heterosexual behavior and interact in mixed-sex groups at times, but they also participate in sexually homogeneous groups at other times. Most of the studies cited have used crude measures of peer relations and have not charted the duration, frequency, and size of mixed- versus same-sex groupings in detail.

Sex segregation probably depends heavily on the nature of activities and settings available to adolescents, which none of these studies attempted to measure. Student norms concerning peer relationships probably specify which school settings are appropriate for mixed-sex groups and which confine interaction to same-sex groups. It is likely that current conflicting evidence on this topic results from the general failure to consider the organizational and normative context in which peer relationships occur.

Size of Group

Although the conventional view is that boys have larger friendship groups than do girls, the research indicates that this may be only partially true. Foot *et al.* (1980) reviewed sex differences in the size of friendship groups and found that, until age 7, boys are actually situated in smaller groups than are girls. Other evidence, cited by Montemayor and Van Komen (1982), indicates that the size of groups prior to elementary school is comparable.

The pattern of small friendship groups for girls and larger ones for boys emerges consistently, though, in studies of elementary school students. Tuma and Hallinan (1979) find that fifth-grade boys name more friends than do the females in their classes. Douvan and Adelson (1966), in an influential statement about sex differences in friendship patterns, similarly observe that boys have larger friendship groups. Summarizing the existing work on friendship groups, Maccoby and Jacklin (1974) suggest that boys in elementary school years are likely to have larger friendship groups than girls.

Lever (1976) relates sex differences in games children play to the emergence of different sized groups. She finds that among fifth-graders, boys more often play outdoors and in larger groups than do girls. The nature of boys' games require a larger group to play than do girls' games. Baseball, for example, involves more people than hopscotch or jump rope. Also, Dweck (1981) observes that girls, through the elementary school years, engage in small-group games in small spaces, in "games that allow them to practice and refine social rules and roles directly [p. 326]." For boys, play is concentrated in competitive games with extensive and externally determined rules. Because of the differences in the games played, girls learn social behaviors that are functional for small groups and for intimate personal relationships, whereas boys learn social skills appropriate for achievement in larger groups functioning to meet externally mediated goals.

These sex differences in activity structures, with attendant emphases on different skills, promote sex differences in the content of friendships. Females are concerned with developing interpersonal skills and find these skills best practiced in dyadic relationships. Males, however, are more concerned with developing autonomy and independence, best worked out in a larger group context (Savin-Williams, 1980; Waldrop & Halverson, 1975).

However, it is not clear that these differences in average size of peer groups persist into adolescence. If the nature of the activity, in this case the structure of play, affects the size of friendship groups, then once these activities become less prevalent, so too may the sex differences in the size of group. Hansell (1981) reported no significant difference in the average size of male and female friendship cliques in a high school sample. Montemayor and Van Komen (1982), in an observational study of adolescent friendship groups, found no sex difference in the size of groups, and they suggest that both male and female adolescents are concerned with such leisure time pursuits as talking and socializing, which are more easily pursued in small than in large groups. They suggest that "the presence of sex differences in group sizes occurs when males and females engage in activities which require different numbers of participants and does not appear to be the result of a difference in a general orientation toward others [p. 13]."

Both J. S. Coleman's (1961) study and McDill and Rigsby's (1973) study of 20 high schools document that females name *more* friends than do males. Both studies collected sociometric data on survey questionnaires in which a fixed number of lines were supplied for naming the "boys(girls) you go around with most." The possibility that the differences in the number of friendship choices was simply evidence of greater response rates for females was explored in the McDill and Rigsby data (Karweit, 1976), but it was not found to be a likely explanation. Another possibility is that the restriction of friendship choices to friends within school may have affected cross-sex choices because males made more out-of-school friends than did females (Karweit, 1981). Although these data have limitations, they suggest that, by adolescence, sex differences in friendship group size are minimal.

The size of adult male and female peer groups also tends to be similar. Booth (1972) examined the number of choices made by men and women and found no significant difference between the averages, with men naming an average of 3.0 friends and women naming an average of 3.5.

Some of these studies suggest how the settings in which the friendships take place affect the size of the friendship groups that emerge. For example, Eder and Hallinan (1978) point out that in open-space elementary classrooms the total number of choices made increases for both sexes and the sex difference in the size of peer groups decreases. Karweit (1981), using McDill and Rigsby's (1973) data for 20 high schools, documents that the number of friends named within school is negatively related to school size but that there are no sex differences in this pattern. School size was negatively related to the proportion of total friends located within the school to a much greater extent for males than for females ($r = -.85$ for males; $r = -.12$ for females).

Other school settings, such as college curricular tracks, also affect the size of the friendship groups by constraining friendship choices to subgroups of students. Hansell and Karweit (Chapter 9, this volume) report that students of both sexes who are in college curricular tracks have more extensive networks than do students in noncollege tracks, although this difference was slightly more pronounced for males than for females.

Collectively, the evidence of previous studies does not indicate a clear or consistent sex difference in the size of friendship groups. Males tend to associate in larger groups than do females during the elementary school years, but this is probably a function of sex differences in games and activities that vary in the number of people required. The research on this topic generally suffers from not considering in detail environmental constraints on group size, although we noted several studies that did include environmental measures. Socialization differences may orient girls toward small groups and boys toward large groups, as some of the earlier work suggests, but the personnel requirements of high school activities may override these preferences and result in comparable group sizes for adolescent males and females.

Reciprocity of Friendship Choices

Several authors suggest that the focus, interests, and social skills of members of sex-segregated peer groups tend to diverge. Compared with male peer groups, female groups tend to become more concerned with loyalty, commitment, and intimacy. Major concerns of females during adolescence are security in interpersonal relationships and peer acceptance, which are clearly reflected in the values that emerge in peer groups. Booth's (1972) analysis of sex differences in adult friendships also finds sex differences in intimacy and disclosure—females are more likely to confide in their friends than are males.

The different functions of friendships for adolescent males and females suggest that the internal structure of their peer groups will differ along predictable lines. Intimacy, loyalty, commitment, and strong interpersonal ties are best practiced and realized in dyadic relationships. Achievement, leadership, and competitive advantages are best explored in loosely coupled groups. These differences in the structure of adolescent peer groups were recognized by J. S. Coleman (1961), who stated

> Perhaps the most striking difference is the difference between boys and girls in each school. Anyone familiar with teenagers knows the extreme importance of friends, cliques, groups and crowds for girls. Nevertheless, the complexity of the clique structures among girls in these schools, compared to the relative simplicity of the boys' associations, is startling. The networks of girls . . . are extraordinarily elaborated compared to those of boys [p. 185].

Coleman points out that several peer groups in which all members were connected by mutual choices were found for girls, but none were found for boys. These results are consistent with Hansell and Karweit's finding (Chapter 9, this volume) that the social networks of adolescent girls exhibit higher reachability than do boys' networks.

J. Cohen's (1977) detailed analysis of the clique structure of one of J. S. Coleman's (1961) high schools confirms that there are different peer group structures for males and females. Defining a clique as a group of four or more persons in which at least two are involved in a mutual choice relationship, Cohen finds

that girls had more cliques than did boys (38 versus 11). Karweit (1976), comparing the extent of density within friendship groups, documents that females have
higher rates of density than do males (.583 versus .457).[1] Density was negatively
related to school size, and substantially more so for females than for males ($r =$
$-.49$ versus $-.16$). Hansell (1981) and Epstein (Chapter 5, this volume) also
report that adolescent females have more reciprocated friendships than do boys.

These studies indicate that the internal structure of friendship groups, specifically the extent of reciprocity, differs for adolescent males and females. Moreover,
the internal structure appears to be affected by the larger school setting in which
the friendships take place. Several studies (Karweit, 1981; Lindsay, 1982; Simmons, Blyth, Van Cleave, & Bush, 1979) suggest that adolescent females are
affected more by traditional school organization than are males. Simmons *et al.*
(1979) introduced the concept of the "stress of multiple role transitions" to explain the negative effects on self-esteem for their young adolescent (seventh-
grade) sample. The high school samples used by Lindsay (1982) and Karweit
(1981), however, were not undergoing multiple transitions and therefore suggest
the generally greater susceptibility of females to such organizational conditions as
school size and curricular tracking. Epstein (Chapter 5, this volume) suggests that
participatory school organization may have positive effects on patterns of selection
of male students as friends. It is not yet clear, however, how deleterious effects of
size or effects of school organizations are differentially transmitted to males and
females.

Bases of Friendship Selection

Research on the importance of individual characteristics for friendship formation concentrates on the similarity of attributes in friendship dyads. The attributes investigated in different studies vary widely because there has been no
systematic attempt to discover which attributes are the most important for friendship formation. Also, there is little evidence about potential sex differences in the
importance of attributes.

Many studies document that similarity of attitudes, values, and behaviors is an
important element guiding friendship selection (Byrne, 1969; J. Cohen, 1977;
Hansell, 1981; Kandel, 1978; Newcomb, 1961). Cohen (1977) stresses that
friendships tend to be formed among those who are similar on a broad range of
characteristics, primarily because of the interdependence of these characteristics.
Examining the extent of similarity of clique members, he found that, on all 20
items considered, the members of boys' cliques were more similar to each other
than to the rest of the school and that members of girls' groups exhibited greater

---

[1]*Density* was defined as the ratio of the number of actual ties to the number of possibilities within
each student's personal network. Thus, if a student named four friends, and they all named each other
as friends, density would be 1.0. If none of the students' friends named each other, density would be
0.0. High density among one's friends, defined in this way, depended highly on the reciprocation of
choices among one's friends.

similarity on 19 of these same 20 measures than did other students. He suggests that students can be classified into distinct high school social types corresponding to "fun," "academic," and "delinquent" subcultures and that students select friends from within their social type, thus assuring homophily on a broad range of attributes.

It seems likely that student choices of specific social types can be made only after sufficient information about attributes is obtained. Until then, choice patterns probably depend on more easily recognizable attributes of the individual, such as grade in school, age, sex, and race. Studies of adolescent friendship pairs (J. Cohen, 1977; Hansell, 1981; Kandel, 1978; Karweit, 1976; Epstein, Chapter 5, this volume) indicate that similarity on demographic characteristics of sex, race, and age is highest of all traits considered. Kandel finds correlations of .85 (girls) and .81 (boys) between grade levels of students and first-named friends, and correlations of .68 (girls) and .60 (boys) between race of students and first-named friends. Karweit (1976) and Hansell (1981) report similar homophily for grade level.

This probably results from the fact that most activities in schools are organized by grade level. Students in the same grade take classes together, eat lunch together, perform in sports together, and get into trouble together. In the few studies in which comparisons can be made, girls' friendships appear to be more similar on these attributes than are boys' friendships. The higher similarity within female dyads may reflect the fact that reciprocated choosers tend to be more similar than nonreciprocated choosers, and girls have more reciprocated choices than do boys.

In examining the effect of similarity as a basis of friendship selection, existing research has not been guided by a specific theoretical orientation. Instead, studies take a host of attributes, determine the similarity of pairs of friends on these attributes, and conclude that certain traits are important for friendship selection. Post hoc theoretical explanations of the importance of behaviors (Kandel) or the importance of student social types (J. Cohen) are then introduced to explain the patterns. These empirically derived models are bound by the context and measures of particular studies and probably have limited generalizability, although they have substantial heuristic value. Because these models have not been deduced from any general theory of adolescent friendship selection, they use a variety of different variables and constructs, which makes comparisons of results across studies difficult.

STATUS AND FRIENDSHIP

The criteria for relationship choice can be usefully organized in terms of the dimensions of affiliation (friendship) and status. These basic dimensions of human social relationships have been of long-standing theoretical interest in sociology (e.g., Bales, 1970; Homans, 1974) and have been the focus of studies of adult relationships (e.g., Laumann, 1966). Perhaps because of its atheoretical orientation, most research on children and adolescent relationships has focused exclusively on friendship and has neglected other content dimensions of social relationships that shape social structure.

This section considers how friendship and status interact in adolescent relationships. One goal is to show how research in this area can benefit from sociological theory on relationships. Another aim is to show how the status dimension of relationships, in particular, requires a consideration of the organizational and normative context in which these relationships occur. Affiliation is most conveniently studied at the dyadic level of analysis, and this approach has been used by almost all studies in this area. However, the essence of status is the linkage between an individual and larger social and organizational entities. Thus, status provides a conceptual wedge for understanding the development of relationships within the constraints of larger social and environmental settings.

A recurring, implicit theme in many studies of sex differences in adolescent development is that females, in their quest for establishing their own identity, are concerned with issues of love, personal and social intimacy, and commitment. Males are often depicted as primarily concerned with issues of status, power, leadership, and autonomy. Simply stated, the female adolescent prefers to orient her relationships around issues of *affiliation*, whereas the male adolescent is most concerned with *status*. Deaux (1977) suggests that males attempt to assert status in social interaction, whereas females prefer more egalitarian relationships based on mutuality and intimacy. McClelland (1975) argues that powerful males learn to assert themselves with other people and their environment, whereas "the female high in power focuses on building up the self which may be the object of that (male) assertiveness [p. 51]." If females are more concerned about affiliation and males are more concerned about status in their relationships, sex differences in patterns of selection should be consistent with these orientations.

The ranked-cluster model of J. Davis and Leinhardt (1972) is a general model of social relationships that incorporates both affiliation and status and is based on the interpersonal theories of Homans (1974). The model states that:

> a) groups tend to form levels (like floors in a building) and within levels all relationships are mutual positive or mutual non-positive, b) within levels, clusters or cliques occur (like rooms on a particular floor of a building) such that all pairs are mutual positive, and between clusters all pairs are mutual non-positive, c) asymmetric relations all flow between levels, running in the same direction and creating a hierarchy of choice [Davis & Leinhardt, 1972, p. 844].

The Davis and Leinhardt model postulates a series of ordered levels in which mutual relations connect people on the same status level and asymmetric relations connect people on different status levels. The recipient of an asymmetric relationship is always at a higher status level. Thus, mutual relations form clusters within

status levels. Clusters are interconnected by unreciprocated choices from mem-
. bers of lower status clusters to members of higher status clusters. A diagram of the
ranked-cluster model, illustrating the relationship between friendship and status
relations, is shown in Figure 7.1.

Based on the Davis and Leinhardt model we would expect:

1. For both sexes, reciprocity of friendship choices occurs more frequently
   among individuals with similar traits.
2. For both sexes, unreciprocated friendship choices occur more frequently
   from lower to higher status individuals than from higher to lower status
   individuals.

We now use the Davis and Leinhardt model and our review to derive an additional
hypothesis about sex differences in adolescent relationships. If status is more
salient to the formation of male relationships than female relationships, we would
expect that status differences would organize male friendship clusters more clearly than female friendship clusters. Our hypothesis is that the Davis and Leinhardt
model describes the structure of male relationships more accurately than the
structure of female relationships. Specifically, we expect that:

3. Males will exceed females in the number of unreciprocated choices made
   from lower to higher status peers.

Some evidence supports this hypothesis. Hansell (1978) charted the friendships
of males and females in one high school. First, male dyads exhibited homophily in
the status characteristics of SES and academic achievement, whereas female
dyads did not. In contrast to males, members of female dyads were highly similar
in the personality characteristic of ego development. Second, males made more
unreciprocated friendship choices to higher status peers and fewer unreciprocated

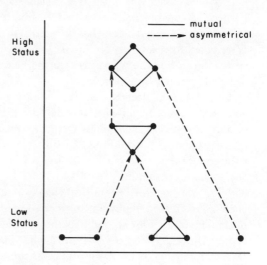

FIGURE 7.1. Ranked-cluster model
of status and friendship.

choices to lower status peers than did females. These results suggest that status characteristics are more important bases for male friendship selection than for female friendship selection and that the ranked-cluster model depicts male relationships more accurately than female relationships.

We used the McDill and Rigsby (1973) sociometric data from 20 high schools to test these hypotheses. These schools are not a random sample but were purposely selected to maximize variation on educational and social status variables. Questionnaires administered to 20,345 students, 1029 teachers, and 20 principals yielded extensive information about social climate and student activities. Further details about the sampling design and the questionnaires are available in McDill and Rigsby (1973).

The sociometric data can be linked to the rich information about individual student status. Boys were asked, "Of the boys here in this school, who do you go around with most?" Girls were asked the same question with the appropriate shift in gender. Four lines were provided for students to name their friends, but no limit was put on the number of friends to be named. Cross-sex choices were not allowed.

In our analyses, we determined the similarity of the respondent and his or her first-named friend for those attributes that could unambiguously be considered status criteria, such as college plans, curricular track, father's education, father's occupation, and a school status index. The school status index consisted of 16 items that gauged the student's position in the informal social system of the school. The items included nominations from other students as leading crowd member, other popularity measures, and self-report measures of leading crowd membership. To determine the similarity of peers, each variable was treated as a dichotomy. Curricular track was coded as noncollege or college preparatory program. For college plans, the categories were no college plans or college plans. Father's education was coded as some college attendance or no college attendance. Father's occupation was classified as blue or white collar. The school status measure was treated somewhat differently. An average student status value was determined for each school. Then students were classified low in status if they scored lower than the school average and high in status if they scored greater than or equal to the school average.

Percentages of friends who were similar and nonsimilar on each of these variables and rates of reciprocity were determined. Table 7.1 presents the proportions of mutual choices among similar students (Column 1) and among dissimilar students (Column 2). According to our first hypothesis, we would expect Column 1 to be greater than Column 2. This hypothesis is strongly supported for each of the five attributes examined.

Next, we examined friendship choices that are not reciprocated. As Column 3 shows, the greatest number of unreciprocated choices are still emitted to persons of similar status. Our second hypothesis states that there should be a greater rate of unreciprocated choices made to higher status individuals. If this were true, then Column 4 of Table 7.1 would be greater than Column 5. We do find that the

TABLE 7.1
Similarity of Friendship Pairs on Selected Status Characteristics, by Sex and Reciprocity of Choice

	Reciprocated		Not reciprocated		
Attribute/sex	Similar status	Not similar status	Similar status	Choices to higher status	Choices to lower status
College plans[a]					
Females	.428	.143	.309	.065	.055
Males	.343	.100	.414	.083	.060
Curriculum[b]					
Females	.408	.161	.296	.067	.067
Males	.303	.141	.377	.092	.087
Father's education[c]					
Females	.375	.198	.282	.075	.069
Males	.268	.175	.323	.120	.114
Father's occupation[d]					
Females	.393	.181	.293	.072	.061
Males	.343	.100	.414	.083	.060
School status[e]					
Females	.564	.221	.147	.059	.016
Males	.412	.207	.227	.118	.036

[a]College plans: high status = yes, definite college plans; low status = no definite college plans.
[b]Curriculum: high status = college preparatory; low status = not college preparatory.
[c]Father's education: high status = no college; low status = at least some college.
[d]Father's occupation: high status = white collar; low status = blue collar.
[e]School status: high status = above the school mean; low status = below the school mean.

choices made to higher status students exceed or equal those made to lower status students in every case, although the magnitude of these differences is not very large. Nonetheless, the evidence for the hypothesis is consistent in all cases, suggesting that unreciprocated choices are modestly related to status differences.

Finally, our third hypothesis predicts that males will make more unreciprocated choices than will females, in which case the value of Column 4 for males should exceed that of Column 4 for females. This expectation is supported consistently and confirms that status is indeed a more important dimension of friendship selection for males than for females.

These results support our hypothesis of a fundamental sex difference in the organization of informal friendship networks. Students of both sexes usually associate with status-equivalent peers. If association with similar students were the only factor present, however, the school would be subdivided into mutually isolated cliques. The preference for choosing higher status students prevents· this complete segregation from occurring, and this is where a sex difference is evident. We find that males more frequently choose up the status hierarchy than do females. Thus, female networks are likely to be composed of tightly knit groupings of equal-status peers, whereas male networks will more closely resemble a clustering of cliques tied together in a loose, but discernible, status hierarchy.

The tendency of males to select higher status students is initial evidence of the differential importance of status for each sex. Males may use friendships for status acquisition and maintenance more than do females. This idea has often been suggested in the literature on adolescent sex differences, but the present study offers one of the first empirical demonstrations of this pattern of selection.

The results suggest that the ranked-cluster model of Davis and Leinhardt (1972) applies better to male friendships than to female friendships. In particular, unreciprocated choices may function differently in the integration of male and female cliques. Consistent with the model, male cliques in our sample were connected into a vertical status hierarchy by unreciprocated choices. However, females' unreciprocated choices connected cliques primarily at the same status level and contributed to the horizontal, or affiliative, integration of female cliques. A reasonable speculation is that male networks are generally more elaborated in the vertical status dimension, whereas female networks are more completely developed in the horizontal, affiliative dimension. More research is needed to clarify adolescent sex differences in the relationship between friendship and status.

INTERACTION OF STUDENT DEVELOPMENT AND SCHOOL ORGANIZATION

The developmental literature suggests the general importance of friendship associations for adolescent development and the particular importance of strong, dyadic friendship ties for the development of adolescent females (Douvan & Adelson, 1966; Hansell, 1981). Some authors suggest that females who go through adolescence without close friendship ties are at a particular disadvantage, whereas males do not need these strong friendship ties and do not suffer as much stress if such ties are lacking. Thus, the developmental perspective points to sex differences in the function of and need for friendships in early adolescence and suggests differences in the consequences of failing to acquire such friendships.

What has frequently been omitted from this discussion is how the organization of the environments in which relationships occur influences these friendships. Because many adolescent friendships exist within the school context, the organization of the school during early adolescence is of special interest, and it is important to examine how school organization interacts with developmental processes and needs for friendship at this age. This joining of developmental and organizational perspectives is particularly useful for understanding the nature and function of friendship in early adolescence, because this is a period when the need for friendship ties appears to be strong, when rapid pubertal and developmental changes are occurring, and, finally, when marked environmental changes occur as students transfer from elementary to junior high school.

In a study of the effects of these multiple transitions on adolescent self-esteem,

Simmons *et al.* (1979) found that young females are particularly vulnerable to the stresses induced by developmental and environmental shifts. Young female students who went from elementary to junior high schools, who had recently experienced puberty, and who had begun to date had lower self-esteem than females who were not experiencing multiple role transitions. Simmons *et al.* argue that these decrements in self-esteem derive from the multiple life changes that occur. These changes focus the attention of the young girl on her popularity with peers, her physical attractiveness, and her appearance—in short, on external standards of her definition of herself.

Although this argument is highly plausible, we suggest that an additional source of stress resulting in the lowering of female self-esteem is the disruption of strong friendship ties by the transition to a new school that is organized in a different way. Elementary classrooms make possible the reciprocated dyadic friendships preferred by many young females by establishing a stable set of peers all day long. Females in elementary classrooms have ample time to establish individual relationships with the single teacher, who is also often a female. Males of this age are already heavily engaged in peer group activities located primarily outside of the classroom, and the friendships formed in these activities do not involve much classroom activity or teacher involvement.

In the shift to junior high school, with six different classes and teachers per day, the social world of the female may be dramatically reversed. The new schedule interferes with the formation and maintenance of reciprocated, classroom-based, dyadic friendships with peers, and there is much less opportunity to establish intimate friendships with teachers. Females must learn different ways of relating to friends than they used successfully in elementary school. The transition to junior high school is probably less stressful for males, who can continue activity-based patterns of relationships that they learned in elementary school, often in the same team-oriented activities outside of classroom settings.

Thus, specific elements in the junior high school organization, such as larger size and scheduling practices, may contribute to the dissolution or instability of friendships at this age, especially for females. Also, specific organizational factors, most notably size, may affect the nature of the friendships that emerge. For example, the reciprocity of friendship choices, argued to be important for female development at this age, has been found to be affected by the size of the school (Karweit, 1981). The transition to junior high school may be particularly difficult for young females precisely because of the interruption in strong interpersonal ties at which they are adept. To address this issue in greater detail, longitudinal data on friendships in elementary and junior high schools need to be collected, as well as information about activities and friendships inside and outside of classrooms. (See Epstein, Chapter 3 in this volume for an analysis of data on this issue.)`

Many developmental processes will not interact with school organization as clearly as the ones discussed in this chapter. In some instances, developmental processes will overshadow the constraints of the school environment. In others, the effects of school organization will predominate and may obscure or alter the effects of individual development. We would like to emphasize, however, the need to examine developmental processes within the context of school organization in order more fully to understand both areas and to be more fully aware of the limitations of each orientation when both kinds of influences are operating.

SUMMARY AND DISCUSSION

This chapter reviews the major ways in which adolescent friendships differ for males and females. Four dimensions along which sex differences have been reported are: the extent of same-sex friendships, the size of the friendship groupings, the extent of reciprocity of friendships, and the bases of friendship selection. We discuss conditions of age and school environments under which the expected sex differences are and are not observed, and suggest the benefits for research of joining developmental and organizational perspectives for the study of friendships in schools. Two examples are offered to illustrate the benefits of such an approach. First, sex differences are reported in the importance of status for friendship selection. Measures of status specifically linked to school tracking practices and school status measures were included in our analysis; they suggest that patterns of friendship selection are the result of both school organizational and developmental influences.

In a second example, friendship ties are considered to be an important, but neglected, mediating variable in explaining the changes in self-esteem noted by Simmons *et al.* (1979). We suggest that a major, unanticipated influence of school organization may be the disruption of strong dyadic interpersonal ties at a time when such relationships are most needed, especially by females.

Our review of sex differences in patterns of friendship selection indicates the need to consider environmental and developmental effects jointly. Size of group, extent of same-sex groupings, and reciprocity of choice were all influenced by properties of the school environment in which students were situated. What is less clear is how schools could be structured either to inhibit or accentuate sex differences. This decision is less a matter of discovering the impact of specific environments than it is a matter of deciding what types of friendships should be fostered by school environments. Although such value questions are not easily addressed, they require the kind of basic knowledge about sex differences in relationships reviewed in this chapter.

NANCY KARWEIT

Extracurricular Activities and Friendship Selection

Extracurricular activities within the school provide settings in which adolescents can meet one another, participate in activities of common interest, and learn and practice skills other than strictly academic ones. Although these activities, like curricular ones, are formally controlled and sanctioned by the school, they differ in important ways from curricular settings for student interaction.

First, participation in extracurricular activities, in contrast to curricular ones, is voluntary. Students select activities that suit their purposes; these may be activities that interest them, that have high student status, or that provide numerous social opportunities. Because participation is voluntary and because the existence of the activity depends on participation, members are likely to be committed to the activity initially and to continue their involvement in order to keep the activity alive. Thus, voluntarism affects student commitment through self-selection of interested students and through the continued involvement that is necessary to sustain the activity.

Second, extracurricular activities make a wider range of student aptitudes, skills, and interests visible than is possible or desirable in academic classrooms. Classroom instruction is typically carried out in groups of 20–40 students. For group instruction to succeed, the teacher has to maintain a precarious balance between attending to individual student's needs and attending to the needs of the entire group. In this context, the display of a particular individual's talents, skills, or aptitudes may be dysfunctional for the instructional goals of the teacher. Thus,

131

FRIENDS IN SCHOOL
Patterns of Selection and Influence in Secondary Schools

classrooms tend to allow students to display only a narrow set of attributes. Extracurricular activities, on the other hand, permit students to demonstrate a range of skills, such as musical or theatrical talents, or the ability to work well with a group of people. Acquisition of interpersonal and behavioral skills is an important part of adolescent socialization that is aided by participation in extra-curricular activities.

Finally, because extracurricular activities may be more closely aligned with the interests of adolescents than are the strictly academic pursuits of classrooms, the recognition and visibility gained in these activities are important for social stand-ing among adolescents (Spady, 1970a). Membership in clubs and activities may increase student status and lessen such typical status distinctions as those associ-ated with family background or curricular track. Extracurricular participation, then, is an important avenue for the social integration of the school.

Participation in extracurricular activities may influence friendship selection in two ways. First, extracurricular activities provide additional information about the interests, skills, and personalities of the participants, which may guide the choice of friends. Given that friendships are formed in part among individuals with similar characteristics, sharing extracurricular activities may reveal addi-tional information and salient attributes around which friendships may be formed. Second, participation in these activities increases student status. Because friend-ship choices are more likely to be made to higher status than to lower status students and because participation in extracurricular activities alters student status, participation may affect friendship selection patterns.

PARTICIPATION EFFECTS ON SELECTION: SIMILARITY

Mutual interests, shared values, and common activities are important ingre-dients in the making of friendships. Students spend most of their schoolday in classroom activities that display a limited range of each student's interests and capabilities. A broader range of student interests is made visible by participation in school activities. Because these activities are voluntary, student operated, and more closely aligned to student interests than are classroom activities, the traits made visible by these activities are also probably highly salient to students. Thus, extracurricular activities provide significant settings for friendship selection.

Are friends likely to be members of the same school clubs and activities? To address this question, we use the data from McDill's survey of 20 high schools, which includes both sociometric and extracurricular activity data. Complete de-tails of the sample and variables are found in McDill and Rigsby (1973). The 20 public, coeducational high schools were purposely selected to maximize variation on certain educational and social variables.

Questionnaire data were obtained from 20,345 students, 1029 teachers, and the 20 principals of these schools. The student data included information on background, attitudinal, and achievement variables. Sociometric information on friendship choices was obtained from responses to the question "Of the boys (girls) here in this school, who do you go around with most?" Four lines were left for answers, but no specific request to name four friends was made. Cross-sex choices were not allowed. Additionally, sociometric nominations were made of the student one would most like to be like, the student one would most like to date, the student named as best athlete, and the student named as member of the leading crowd.

These data were used to determine the extent to which friends were found in the same extracurricular activity. The number of friendship pairs that share an activity were compared with the number expected by chance. This exercise indicates that friends are more likely than random pairs of schoolmates to be in the same activity. For example, 4.7% of all male students participated in newspaper and journalism activities. Of the friendship choices, 1.9% of all friends participated jointly in newspaper and journalism activities. If friends were selected at random, then the number of pairs in the activity should mirror the chance occurrence of finding two individuals in the same activity given the distribution in the population, or 0.2% in this case. Table 8.1 provides the number of friendship pairs in particular activities and the number expected by chance. Across all activities, the proportion of friendship pairs who share an activity exceeds the proportion expected by chance. These comparisons suggest at least two interpretations. Students who are friends may join the same activity, and thus participation may have little to do with the selection of friends. Or it may be that students who are not friends join an activity and through the sharing of the activity come to be friends. Because the McDill data pertain to only one point in time, it is not possible to tell whether friends joined an activity together or became friends as a result of the activity. The data indicate only that friends are likely to belong to the same extracurricular activity.

TABLE 8.1
Percentages of Friendship Pairs in the Same Activity and Percentages Expected by Chance

	Males		Females	
Activity	Observed pair percentage	Expected pair percentage	Observed pair percentage	Expected pair percentage
Newspaper and journalism	1.9	.2	5.9	.8
Student government	8.6	1.7	18.1	5.2
Hobby clubs	4.0	1.4	3.2	.5
Sports	19.4	6.4	—	—
Service clubs	8.6	1.5	24.1	7.8
Social clubs	2.5	.1	11.9	2.7

PARTICIPATION EFFECTS ON SELECTION: STATUS

We speculate that membership in extracurricular activities affects student status and consequently patterns of friendship selection. Participation in these activities is seen here as a mediating device, tempering the opportunities for interaction imposed by curricular tracking and diluting the impact of track placement or family background on peer student status. The model discussed in Chapter 2 is the framework for the present investigation. Here, we are concerned with the effect of curricular track placement on friendship selection, student status, and extracurricular participation and the mediating effect of extracurricular participation on friendship selection.

Curricular track placement segregates students for the majority of the schoolday. Not surprisingly, most friendships are formed among students in the same curricular track. For example, in the McDill data set, about three-quarters of the friendship choices are among students in the same curricular track. Proximity is one reason for the preference of same-curricular classmates as friends, but the difference in status accorded students by curricula is no doubt another factor that influences this pattern. Curricular track differentiates students and also helps define the status of students within the school. On items that measure peer popularity, peer esteem, and leading crowd choices, college preparatory students receive, on average, more choices than non-college preparatory students, as shown in Table 8.2. Thus, placement in the college preparatory track is clearly related to peer status within the school.

Track placement is also related to rates of participation, with students in non-college preparatory tracks participating less often than college preparatory students (Schaefer & Olexa, 1971). These participation differences are interpreted as the consequence of track placement and not just as selection differences. If

TABLE 8.2
Average Number of Peer Status Choices Received, by Sex and Curricular Track

	Males		Females	
Nominations as:	Not college preparatory	College preparatory	Not college preparatory	College preparatory
Friendship choice	2.8	3.1	3.0	3.4
Member of leading crowd	1.4	2.4	1.6	3.4
Person most like to be like	.5	.8	.5	.9
Best athlete	.5	.8	.5	1.0
Best student	.2	1.0	.2	1.3
Like to be friend's with	.4	.6	.4	.8
Like to dance	.5	.7	.5	.8

tracking does affect participation in this manner, differences in participation should increase with the length of time in the track.

To examine whether track placement accentuates participation differences, we conducted several analyses with the data from a High School and Beyond study (1980). This data set is a national longitudinal sample of the high school senior and sophomore clases in 1980. Questionnaires were administered to sampled students, their teachers, and principals. Details of the sample design and content of the questionnaire are available elsewhere (High School and Beyond, 1980). The questionnaire items on student activities were summed for the total number of activities in which each student participated. The school size was obtained from the principal's questionnaire.

Analyses using the High School and Beyond data indicate that college preparatory students participate in more activities than do non-college-going students (for seniors, 2.63 activities versus 1.85; for sophomores, 1.89 activities versus 1.59). Because the differences in participation between college goers and non-college goers are larger for seniors than for sophomores, it may be argued that tracking itself appears to influence participation.

Track placement is related to participation and to popularity and esteem with one's peers, but the question remains whether participation in activities per se is related to popularity and student esteem. In particular, we need to understand better the relationships among curricular track placement, participation, and student status. Table 8.3 presents the peer status choices received by sex, by level of participation, and by curricular track for the various nominations. The results in the table suggest that both participation and curricular track placement contribute to peer popularity and esteem nominations. It is noteworthy that the nominations received by the non-college preparatory students with high participation are very similar to the nominations received by college-bound students with limited participation. This finding suggests that the distinctions made by curricular track can be ameliorated by participation in the extracurricular arena.

A more systematic examination of the relationship between student status, curricular track, and school activities was conducted in other analyses (not presented here) in which nominations received were regressed on track placement and number of activities. For all nominations, the amount of variance explained by these factors was small, around 5%. Of the two independent variables, the number of extracurricular activities was consistently more important than was track placement in explaining the number of nominations received. These regressions suggest that extracurricular participation is important for student status and may significantly counteract the status distinctions associated with track placement.

Is participation in particular activities or participation in a number of activities more important for enhancing student status? To examine this issue, we regressed the number of status choices received on participation in activities that have been considered prestigious—athletics for males and service clubs for females. Comparing the regression weights for select activities versus total activities indicated that total activities were more influential in explaining peer popularity and esteem

TABLE 8.3

Average Number of Peer Status Choices Received, by Sex, Curricular Track, and Number of Activities

	Males								Females							
	Not college preparatory				College preparatory				Not college preparatory				College preparatory			
Nominations as:	0	1	2	3+	0	1	2	3+	0	1	2	3+	0	1	2	3+
Friendship choice	2.7	2.8	3.2	3.2	2.7	3.1	3.4	3.5	2.6	3.0	3.4	3.7	2.6	3.1	3.4	3.8
Member of leading crowd	.8	1.6	3.9	2.8	1.0	2.0	3.2	4.6	.6	1.1	2.4	4.7	.7	1.4	2.8	4.5
Person most like to be like	.4	.6	1.2	.8	.4	.7	1.0	1.6	.3	.4	.6	1.3	.3	.5	.7	1.2
Best athlete	.2	.8	1.7	.5	.3	1.0	1.2	1.3	.3	.5	.8	1.2	.4	.7	.9	1.2
Best student	.1	.2	.3	1.0	.3	.7	1.3	2.2	.2	.1	.2	.7	.3	.6	1.0	1.5
Like to be friends with	.3	.4	.7	.4	.3	.5	.8	.9	.3	.3	.6	1.0	.3	.5	.7	1.0
Like to date	.4	.5	1.0	.6	.4	.6	.9	1.1	.3	.4	.7	1.1	.4	.6	.8	.9

Number of activities

than participation in select activities alone. These findings suggest that it is the number of activities in which the students participate, rather than participation in any one particular activity, that is responsible for the positive association between extracurricular participation and student status.

There are clear relationships among peer popularity, extracurricular activities, and track placement. A related question is how the status or visibility gained via participation in extracurricular activities alters the choice of friends, in particular, the tendency for friends to be chosen from within the same curricular track. Track placement often limits the opportunities for contact to students in the same track and, by conferring different status according to track placement, may also curtail contact even when there are opportunities for cross-track interaction. One major function of extracurricular activities may be to reduce these boundaries between the tracks by permitting students to meet in nonacademic situations. If extracurricular activities serve such a function, then participation should encourage tolerance of students in differing social positions. We argue that the number of cross-curricular choices should increase as a function of involvement in extra-curricular activities.

To test this, the choice patterns for students participating in none, one, two, and three or more activities are examined. Table 8.4 shows that the extent of cross-curricular choosing increases uniformly with increasing participation. The pattern holds for both males and females and for cross-curricular choices in both directions. Thus, membership in activities appears to be a significant way in which cross-curricular friendships may be initiated and maintained.

The results in Table 8.4, combined with the examination of the effect of participation on student status, suggest that the major status benefit from extracurricular activities comes about from participation in multiple activities and not just from participation in high-status ones. Athletics is an interesting example of this. Because participation in athletic teams requires a lot of time, student athletes may have to limit their participation in other activities. We note that 51% of

TABLE 8.4
Proportion of Students Naming Other-Curricula Students as Friends, by Participation in Extra Curricular Activities[a]

Number of extracurricular activities	Males		Females	
	Not college prep picking college prep	College prep picking not college prep	Not college prep picking college prep	College prep picking not college prep
0	.139 (2007)	.272 (1695)	.073 (1639)	.368 (692)
1	.175 (1343)	.461 (1014)	.089 (1564)	.383 (1313)
2	.194 (309)	.537 (1101)	.124 (764)	.492 (1319)
3+	.327 (107)	.648 (518)	.175 (503)	.545 (1036)

[a]Figures in parentheses indicate N's.

students in athletics engaged only in this extracurricular activity. The rate of participation in only one activity for other activities were: newspaper, 24%; subject matter club, 29%; hobby club, 42%; drama club, 22%; service club, 26%; and social club, 29%. Thus, athletes are more likely than other students to participate in only one activity. If participation in multiple activities is important for status in the school, then athletes may not obtain the same status benefits for the same amount of time involved as do students who participate in less demanding, but more, activities.

SCHOOL SIZE EFFECTS ON PARTICIPATION

Several studies document that school size negatively affects participation in extracurricular activities (Barker & Gump, 1964; Lindsay, 1982; Morgan & Alwin, 1980). Because participation affects friendship selection, school size may be an important school organization variable that affects friendships.

The concept of "manning" is typically used to explain the finding that students in smaller schools participate more often in the activities of the school than do students in larger schools. According to this view, smaller schools have the same types of activities as larger schools but relatively fewer students to operate the activities, resulting in an "undermanned" situation. Because the activities are important to the students, this undermanning creates greater pressure for participation in smaller than in larger schools. That is, students in smaller schools participate more often because their effort is felt to be important and needed for the existence of the activity.

In analyses using the McDill data, we find the expected negative relationship between school size and the extent of extracurricular participation. The correlation between school size and number of activities was −.29 for males and −.35 for females. In large schools, we also find a greater tendency for students not to participate in any activities at all. The correlations between school size and percentage of the students not participating at all was −.37 for females and −.45 for males.

Because school size affects participation, we expect that patterns of friendship selection may differ in large and small schools. In particular, students in larger schools may have fewer friendships within the school than do students in smaller schools. To examine this hypothesis, we determined the correlation between school size and the number of friendship choices made to students within the school. The correlation between number of friends named and school size was −.23 for males and −.30 for females. Although these correlations suggest that school size affects friendship selection patterns, many conditions associated with school size, such as urbanity of location, may be responsible for the observed results.

Studies by Schaefer and Olexa (1971) and Wicker (1971) indicate that the negative effects of size on student participation are particularly felt by "marginal" students. To test this, we designated the non-college preparatory students in the

High School and Beyond survey as marginal. We then determined the average number of activities by curricular track within schools. Across 741 schools, the average number of activities was 1.95 for college preparatory students and 1.60 for non-college preparatory students. As predicted, size is negatively related to these participation rates, the correlation being $-.35$ for college preparatory students and $-.47$ for non-college preparatory students. The difference between these correlations was statistically significant ($z = 2.68$; $p < .05$). These results are important because they indicate that school size has an additional depressing effect on participation for the non-college preparatory students.

SUMMARY

Extracurricular activities are important locations for the selection of friends within the school. These activities allow the display of a greater range of student talents and interests than is possible in curricular settings and thus expand the base upon which friendships may be formed. Because these activities are voluntary and often student operated, they assume special significance to students. For this reason, participation in clubs is particularly important in defining student status. Several analyses reported here suggest that membership in extracurricular activities is important for student status. Further, the analyses indicate that extracurricular activities lessen other status distinctions and permit the initiation of friendships among students who differ in academic status. Major evidence of this effect was the finding that participation alters cross-curricular choosing patterns. This indicates that extracurricular activities can serve the important function of socially integrating the school. Whether this effect was due to status enhancement, increased visibility, or sharing of activities of mutual interest could not be determined from the available data. The visibility gained by involvement in a number of activities was one likely means through which cross-curricular friendships arose.

Differences in participation and, by implication, differences in both the number and the type of friends made do not depend solely on individual preferences, idiosyncracies, and tastes. Schools provide different opportunities for interaction among students that can greatly affect what friendships will emerge. School size influences student participation in extracurricular activities by creating a climate in which different pressures to participate and belong are perceived. Track placement is also an important determinant of participation. And the effect of tracking on participation seems to depend on the size of the school as well. These findings suggest that differences in organizational environments create different internal conditions that influence the selection of friends within the school.

STEPHEN HANSELL
NANCY KARWEIT

9

Curricular Placement, Friendship Networks, and Status Attainment

Curricular placement is a feature of school organization that has a long history of research for several reasons. First, curricular placement is a ubiquitous characteristic of American secondary education. Nearly all public high schools separate college-oriented youths from general education students and provide them with different programs varying in academic difficulty. Second, curricular placement is a dimension of school organization that, in principle, can be changed. Criteria for student placement can be adjusted, study materials of different types can be selected, and the schedules of students and teachers can be manipulated.

Finally, curricular tracking has important implications for social mobility and status attainment. Students in college preparatory tracks aspire to and achieve higher educational and occupational levels than do students in other curricular tracks, controlling for background characteristics (K. L. Alexander, Cook, & McDill, 1978). Although researchers disagree about whether this reflects only a selection process or represents a true socialization process (e.g., K. L. Alexander et al., 1978; Bowles & Gintis, 1976; Kerckhoff, 1976; Rehberg & Rosenthal, 1978), there is no doubt that curricular track placement is associated with adult status attainment.

Despite this widespread interest in curricular tracking, we have limited knowledge about how it affects learning or status attainment. In part, this is because researchers have conceptualized curricular placement as an individual attribute rather than as an organizational characteristic. This psychological bias in the conceptualization of curricular tracking means we know little about how tracks

141

FRIENDS IN SCHOOL
Patterns of Selection and Influence in Secondary Schools

function as organizational environments to provide different educational experiences for specific groups of students. Few studies have examined the social structural constraints on status attainment imposed by curricular tracking or other features of school organization. It is likely that curricular tracking affects status attainment not only through psychological effects on individuals but also through structural constraints on the social and academic opportunities available in different tracks.

The fact that most research on curricular tracking has focused exclusively on achievement outcomes (E. Morgan, 1977; Rosenbaum, 1980) represents a second gap in our understanding of tracking effects. Students not only master academic skills in school but also have a range of social experiences with peers and adults that prepare them for future work roles. These experiences provide a context for the development of interpersonal relationships that may be as important as academic achievement for later success (Jencks, Acland, Bane, Cohen, Gintis, Heyns, Michaelson, & Smith, 1972; Lavin, 1965). It is highly likely that college and noncollege curricular tracks expose students to different social as well as academic environments, which results in systematic differences in the development of peer relationships.

This chapter investigates the structural constraints of curricular tracks on student social relations in high school and how this may affect future status attainment. We develop a rationale for predicting curricular tracking effects on personal friendship networks and status attainment in several steps. We review prior research on the effects of curricular tracking on student relationships. Then, we begin to develop a conceptual linkage between socialization experiences in adolescent networks and future status attainment by considering the association between the structure of adults' personal networks and their attained status. Next, we identify two causal mechanisms underlying this linkage. First, experience in complex network structures may stimulate the development of individual cognitive and interpersonal skills that are advantageous in higher status occupations. Second, specific friendship structures facilitate the process of finding a good job and thus contribute directly to higher status attainment. Both processes contribute to status attainment for adults.

Finally, we consider analogous relationships between student network structures and curricular placement in high school. Specific hypotheses suggest how curricular placement encourages the formation of personal friendship networks that are most appropriate for eventual occupational placement:

1. Students in college preparatory tracks, who will work in white-collar and professional occupations in the future, will have friendship networks similar to those reported for adults in these roles.
2. Students in noncollege tracks will have friendship networks similar to those reported for adults in blue-collar occupations.

These hypotheses are tested with a secondary analysis of a large set of data on high school students (McDill & Rigsby, 1973).

Thus, this chapter examines how the social organization of school affects patterns of social relationships that are associated with adult status attainment. Although family influences undoubtedly affect the acquisition of varying styles of relating to others, the onset of curricular tracking coincides with a critical developmental period in which adolescents need peer group membership to strengthen and develop their identities (Douvan & Adelson, 1966; Douvan, Chapter 4, this volume). During this developmental period, the structure of friendship networks is especially likely to reflect or influence individual personality development (Hansell, 1981). Constraints on or opportunities for social relationships during adolescence, such as those provided by curricular tracking, may have especially powerful effects on the structure of social interaction—effects that may persist into adulthood. Curricular tracking may thus have especially strong although now unrecognized influences on adult status attainment.

Changes in friendships across grade levels are also explored in order to examine the socialization versus selection issue. If tracking reflects selection factors only, we would expect no differences across grade levels in social relationships. If time spent in curricular tracks represents a true socialization experience, then we would expect curricular tracking differences to increase during the high school years. The chapter concludes with some observations about the intended and unintended long-term consequences of curricular placement.

EXISTING RESEARCH ON CURRICULAR TRACKING AND NONACADEMIC OUTCOMES

Recent interest in nonacademic outcomes of curricular tracking has been stimulated by arguments that schools are organized not to maximize student effort and achievement but rather to maintain the prevailing economic and social order. In this view, often called revisionist theory, students are separated into curricular tracks primarily by their SES and are then exposed to learning experiences that prepare them with the knowledge, values, attitudes, and behaviors necessary to fill roles at appropriate, predetermined levels of the socioeconomic hierarchy. Bowles and Gintis (1976), for example, argue that schools foster "legitimate inequality" by ostensibly rewarding students for achievement and effort, while in fact allocating them to positions in the occupational hierarchy on the basis of ascriptive rather than achieved criteria.

Despite the strident ideological and political overtones of revisionist theories, their unique contribution is to focus our attention on social as well as academic outcomes of schooling. In fact, Bowles and Gintis (1976) viewed social relations as the driving mechanism of cultural reproduction. Schools do not consciously subvert merit and maintain inequities. Rather, the educational system has these effects "through a close correspondence between the social relationships which govern personal interaction in the workplace and the social relationships of the educational system [p. 12]." This key idea differentiates this line of work from earlier status attainment perspectives by highlighting a very important issue—the effects of curricular placement on student social relationships.

Bowles and Gintis (1976) analyzed the social worlds of work and school in terms of power and authority relations. For them, the most important dimensions of social structure were relationships of dominance and subordination. They drew analogies between the hierarchical structure of business organizations and the hierarchical organization of students in college versus noncollege curricular tracks. Compared to blue-collar jobs, white-collar jobs are characterized by more self-direction, greater freedom from immediate supervision, higher degrees of initiative and individual judgment, and more complex and varied job tasks. They made the corresponding argument that, in schools, the college curricular track emphasizes internalization of norms, more student participation and freedom, less direct supervision, and more student electives, whereas vocational and general curricular tracks emphasize rule following, close supervision, the use of coercive power, and immediate rewards and punishments.

The hypothesis that similar attitudinal and behavioral differences exist between white- and blue-collar workers and between students in college and noncollege curricula is provocative and suggests possible causal relationships. However, the revisionists are vague when trying to specify how curricular tracks channel individuals into occupational roles. Bowles and Gintis (1976) invented the mediating psychological mechanism of "consciousness," and argued that "it is the overall structure of social relations of the educational encounter which reproduces consciousness [p. 139]." Consciousness includes modes of self-presentation, self-images, aspirations, and class identifications. At some point, consciousness becomes a self-fulfilling prophesy, and people "tend to adjust their aspirations and self-concepts accordingly, while acquiring manners of speech and demeanor more or less socially acceptable and appropriate to their level [p. 141]." This includes seeking particular occupations. Consciousness is thus defined as an abstract and complex combination of the personality traits, attitudes, and values held by an individual.

For McDonald (1977), consciousness, or "cultural capital," includes forms of language, styles of good taste, and certain kinds of knowledge and abilities that are unequally distributed in society and largely determined by SES. Although there is some intriguing evidence that such personality traits as cognitive complexity are associated with the complexity of the jobs people have (Kohn & Schooler, 1978), personality characteristics are notoriously poor predictors of specific occupational choice, especially once the confounding effects of SES have been controlled. From our viewpoint, the revisionists present an overly psychological and incomplete explanation of how economic advantage is transmitted through curricular tracking.

Bowles and Gintis (1976) focused on similarities between power structures in work and school. Other researchers have investigated the internal conditions of schools in more detail, particularly the qualitative differences between learning environments in different curricular tracks. Morgan (1977) assessed how successfully curricular environments taught the democratic norm of social interdependence, which includes positive feelings of affiliation, tolerance for others' views, the ability to compromise, a willingness to form coalitions to pursue one's goals, and a willingness to cooperate.

Morgan (1977) developed a persuasive argument that students in noncollege curricular tracks are systematically excluded from participating in many school activities and are constrained from interacting with a broad range of fellow students. These constraints inhibit their intellectual and social development. As a result, they tend to become alienated and bored and refuse to commit themselves to any academic purpose. In contrast, the participation of college track students in school life is encouraged and rewarded by adults in the school. As a result, these students show more involvement both in class and in student activities, which are run primarily by their college-oriented peers. These students have more opportunities to learn interpersonal, organizational, and political skills that may help them in future white-collar jobs and have more contacts with guidance counselors (Heyns, 1974) and other adult sources of job information. In Morgan's (1977) view, curricular tracking largely eliminates these opportunities for students in noncollege tracks.

In addition to constraining participation in school activities for noncollege youths, curricular tracking segregates groups of students for most of the schoolday. For example, Karweit (Chapter 8, this volume) shows that students choose about 75% of their friends from their own curricular track. Of the choices made across tracks, there is a slightly greater tendency for students in noncollege tracks to choose higher status college track friends than for college track youths to name noncollege peers as friends. However, most peer friendships occur within curricular boundaries. Rosenbaum (1980) has pointed out that tracking helps structure the use of time differentially. College-bound students are assigned more homework than are non-college-bound students, therefore the time available to them to associate with non-college-bound students outside of school is limited. Curricular tracking thus erects academic, extracurricular, and time barriers to student interaction between curricular tracks.

Several authors have suggested that there are qualitative differences in the classroom environments of different curricular tracks. Rosenbaum (1980) documented that classrooms in noncollege tracks are most likely to be tightly controlled and highly regimented, with the teacher the single authority figure, imposing a single task and reward structure. Active participation in classroom activities tends to be low, and feelings of alienation and boredom run high. Thus, both the setting for instruction and student responses to the setting are quite different in college and noncollege track classrooms. Rosenbaum's work also points to possible socialization differences across tracks. Rosenbaum characterized college tracks as presenting complex environments requiring student self-direction, whereas noncollege tracks present simpler, homogenizing environments in which student conformity is encouraged. These differences parallel those found in comparisons of the work environments of white- and blue-collar workers. Thus, tracking is a differentiated socialization experience that prepares students for later allocation to a differentiated labor market.

Metz (1978) reported similar qualitative differences in learning environments in an ethnographic study of two junior high schools. Teachers in different curricular tracks varied markedly in their expectations about the future success of their students and exhibited different styles of interaction with students. Noncollege track classrooms had relatively more highly structured individual seatwork and less class discussion. Teachers mainly supervised routine student work. In contrast, teachers in college track classrooms tried to motivate students to stretch their cognitive perspectives in active class discussions. Teachers were also more likely to question, probe, and interpret text materials in class. Freiberg (1971) also studied student–teacher interactions across curricular tracks. Students in college tracks received more empathy, praise, and recognition from teachers than did students in noncollege tracks. Teachers were also less likely to criticize or direct college track students than students in noncollege classrooms.

Oakes (1982) examined differences in classroom climate across curricular tracks and measured student perceptions of their relationships with peers on questionnaire scales. In a series of discriminant analyses, friendliness and non-exclusiveness consistently characterized high-achievement tracks compared to low-achievement tracks, although cliquishness did not discriminate between curricular tracks. These results are difficult to interpret because they are based on self-reports aggregated at the classroom level, but they do suggest some differences in the quality of peer relationships across curricular tracks.

The cited studies suggest that curricular tracking affects interpersonal skills and personal relationships as well as achievement in school. Although these studies differed in methodology and conceptual approach, a common theme emerged—curricular tracking constrains the kinds of educational experiences and social relationships available to students. In particular, tracking limits opportunities to form friendships to specific pools of relatively homogeneous students, and it limits the opportunities of non-college-bound students to become involved in curricular and extracurricular activities that can provide a focus for the formation of peer relationships. It is therefore highly likely that tracking also affects the structure of personal friendship networks in school.

A major challenge in this area of research is to link these outcomes of curricular tracking to future occupational attainment and occupational roles. To demonstrate that the social constraints of curricular tracking affect future occupational choice, it is necessary to develop an explicit causal hypothesis about how such social structural effects can occur in terms of clearly measurable and quantifiable constructs. In the following sections, we develop such a rationale from a detailed analysis of social structures in adolescence and adulthood. The first step is to consider the association between the structure of adult social networks and status attainment.

PERSONAL NETWORKS AND ADULT STATUS ATTAINMENT

The nature of everyday adult social relationships is a rapidly growing field of study because of its implications for such important sociological concerns as status attainment. Pool and Kochen (1979), for example, discussed how such basic dimensions of relationships as the simple number of acquaintances shapes a person's status, power, opinions, and politics. Although "there is a very finite number of persons with whom any one psyche can have much cathexis [p. 7]," the content and structure of those relationships can vary dramatically and influence the outcomes of interpersonal interactions.

Social structure limits opportunities for contact to people who share common social settings. As a consequence, people tend to form relationships with others who have similar status measured in terms of a wide variety of characteristics (Verbrugge, 1977). Gurevich (1961) asked blue-collar workers, white-collar workers, and professionals to keep detailed diaries of all their interpersonal contacts for 100 days. Each group tended to interact with people of the same social class. The total contacts made by each group were about the same, but there were large differences in their structure. Blue-collar workers had many repeated contacts with the same, relatively small set of people. Professionals tended to have fewer repeated contacts, but with a larger set of people. Professionals were also somewhat more likely to meet people in other social classes than were blue-collar or white-collar workers, although most of their contacts were with professionals like themselves. These results suggest that SES is associated with the structure of personal social networks—blue-collar workers live in a relatively restricted social world, whereas professionals have contacts with a wider range of people.

Other studies have reported similar results. Fischer, Jackson, Stueve, Gerson, Jones, and Baldassare (1977) used two large surveys to study the decline in the sense of community purportedly occurring in American society. They hypothesized that communal social relations—defined as involving intimacy, emotional depth, moral commitment, and continuity in time—would be enhanced when there were social or spatial constraints on the range and number of social relationships available to individuals. People who had limited opportunities to enter new relationships would compensate by investing more time and energy into relationships with a few people, often kin or close neighbors.

Fischer et al. found complex interdependencies among the intimacy, duration, and frequency of relationships. However, for our purpose, the most interesting finding was a negative association between SES and constraints on personal friendship networks. People with higher SES had friends from more diverse sources, and they named fewer kin and neighbors as friends than did individuals lower in SES. Their higher status provided these people with more opportunities for and fewer constraints on forming the kinds of friendships they preferred. By participating more in organizations, high-status persons generated more contacts and were able to find friends similar to themselves. With their greater financial and social resources and geographic mobility, people with high SES tended to live relatively far from their most intimate friends, while maintaining cordial but relatively casual friendships with their immediate neighbors.

Blue-collar workers' opportunities for establishing new associates were more restricted to family or the neighborhood, therefore decreasing their chances of finding friends with similar interests and preferences. Their friendships were based more on convenience than commitment, tended to be relatively dense, and were physically concentrated in the neighborhood. Of course, there were also variations within the structure of each individual's personal friendship network. Relationships that formed in more constrained contexts, such as the family or at work, resulted in relationships of high density and low social similarity, whereas less constrained contexts, such as voluntary clubs, produced relationships of low density and high similarity.

Allan (1979) compared the friendship structures of middle- and working-class individuals. His in-depth interviews with families revealed that working-class friendships were generally restricted to family, neighbors, and a few colleagues at work. Middle-class respondents had friends from a wider variety of contexts who tended not to be members of the family or neighborhood. The friendships of middle-class people were not as constrained by specific social contexts as were working-class friendships. Middle-class people developed relationships that emphasized the individuality of their friends rather than the context in which they met, whereas working-class people tended to have friends linked to specific interactional settings. The social life of middle-class individuals was often planned in advance, because it frequently required traveling. Interestingly, middle-class individuals discontinued relationships as easily as they formed them. In contrast to the high stability of working-class friendships, middle-class people expected to change their friends as a result of a job move or promotion. The loss of old friends was counterbalanced by the continual addition of new friends.

Allan (1979) observed that middle-class husbands and wives often formed joint friendships with other couples, whereas there was less overlap among the friends of working-class spouses. These results parallel Bott's (1971) findings about conjugal roles and family networks. Bott reported that working-class families had the most close-knit networks of kin and neighbors and also tended to have high conjugal role separation. Husbands and wives spent their leisure time with same-sex friends from the neighborhood, secure in the knowledge that their spouses were in good company. Middle-class husbands and wives tended to share more leisure time activities and chores at home and to have a joint set of loose-knit friendships from a wider variety of social settings.

Taken together, these studies portray a coherent image of social class differences in the structure of personal friendship networks. People with lower SES tend to have fairly close, intimate friendships with a small, stable set of people often concentrated within the immediate neighborhood. Their relationships are constrained by limited opportunities to participate in wider social contexts and to meet new people. Their friends also tend to be friends with each other. In contrast, middle-class and professional people have more extensive, but looser, personal networks. Their participation in a broader range of work and voluntary associations, often involving substantial geographic and social mobility, brings them into contact with more new people with whom they may form friendships. Their networks are characterized by lower density, but higher reachability. They enjoy relationships with friends in different social circles who do not know each other.

PSYCHOLOGICAL AND ORGANIZATIONAL EXPLANATIONS OF STATUS ATTAINMENT

Differences in personal friendship networks probably affect status attainment indirectly, by shaping psychological values and attitudes suitable for work in either simple or complex organizational environments, and directly, by influencing the status of the job actually attained through social structural constraints. The first process assumes that experience in different social environments has psychological effects on the individual. Long-term experience in different network structures probably shapes individual intellectual self-direction and flexibility in ways that mediate the kind of job they seek.

Coser (1975) presents detailed hypotheses about how the complexity of the social roles in which a person functions contributes to the development of individual autonomy, the ability to take the role of the other, and the ability to participate in multiple settings. Coser suggests the intriguing notion that a coherent, stable self-image results from experience in shifting, complex, ambiguous roles. Specifically, "the fact that an individual can live up to expectations of several others in different places and at different times makes it possible to preserve an inner core, to withhold inner attitudes while conforming to various expectations [p. 241]." In contrast, individuals who have lived primarily in simple social milieus may never develop the cognitive ability to evaluate their environments with any degree of objectivity. These individuals may be unaware of external influences on their relatively small social worlds and have difficulty imagining different styles of life.

Coser argues that the social life of lower-class people involves relatively simple cognitive skills. Because everyone knows everyone else and how they will behave in a cohesive neighborhood, little effort must be expended to maintain smooth social discourse. In contrast, middle-class and professional people involved in wider social networks and meeting new people cannot take so much for granted. They must present a fuller explanation of their intentions and behavior to prospective friends and be prepared to take the role of others who are quite different from themselves. Coser (1975) concludes that long-term experience in complex social structures facilitates the development of intellectual flexibility and self-direction for middle-class individuals, whereas lower-class individuals, whose social experience is constrained to simple, cohesive networks, do not develop these traits.

Hansell (1981) showed that psychological development is positively associated with involvement in more extensive and complex network structures in a sample of high school students. Individuals at middle levels of ego development had the greatest number of reciprocated choice dyads. The progression to higher levels of ego development was associated with the development of liaison roles between peer cliques, which required balancing multiple, sometimes competing, social roles. Although this study was cross-sectional, and selection factors cannot be ruled out, the results were consistent with the socialization process suggested by Coser (1975).

Thus, blue-collar and white-collar social networks may provide qualitatively different socialization experiences that help match individual psychological development to the interpersonal requirements of various occupational settings. However, there is a second reason that personal social networks are important for status acquisition and maintenance. The structure of a person's social contacts directly influences the kind of job he or she is able to get. In a series of papers, Granovetter (1973, 1974, in press) formulated the theoretical implications of strong and weak relationships between individuals for the structure of larger networks and demonstrated that weak contacts, in particular, help people find better jobs. In this view, social structure directly affects status attainment.

According to Granovetter (1973), strong relationships take more time and energy and involve more intimacy and reciprocal rewards than do weak relationships. For example, most reciprocated friendships are strong relationships, whereas most unreciprocated friendships are weak relationships. Relationships within friendship groups tend to be strong, whereas contacts between groups, called "bridges," are necessarily weak. Granovetter (1973) further hypothesized that the existence of bridges facilitates communication between friendship groups or social circles, and pointed out that cohesion within and between groups tends to be inversely related. Groups whose members all have strong interrelations lack bridging relationships to other groups, and such groups tend to be isolated from one another. In contrast, groups whose members have bridging relationships to other groups can communicate and cooperate with these groups.

This theory has many interesting implications, but most important for our present purpose is Granovetter's (1974) demonstration that individuals with high-status professional, managerial, and technical jobs were more likely to hear about new jobs through weak contacts than through strong friendship ties. Because 80% of all jobs are found through personal contacts, individuals with more contacts are likely to have access to more information about potential job openings. Weak contacts with persons outside one's usual friendship group, such as professional or business acquaintances, are probably most useful, because they tend to provide new information. In contrast, close friends and other strong contacts tend to provide the same information that one already has.

Although Granovetter's (1974) sample was limited to professional, technical, and managerial workers, the implication for lower-class individuals is clear. Any constraint on the reachability of personal networks imposed by individual preferences, social structural boundaries, or economic conditions will interfere with the transmission of job information and diminish occupational mobility. Individuals with many weak contacts will be better able to transcend these constraints. People who cannot develop and use weak ties to reach beyond their close friends and relatives will have a substantial disadvantage in the acquisition of job status and rewards.

These studies suggest that middle-class and professional people are better able to use weak contacts to find jobs than are lower-class people because they already have more weak contacts and because they have cognitive and interpersonal abilities that enable them to form new weak contacts. Granovetter (in press) has reviewed some evidence supporting this hypothesis. Langlois (1977) found that 43% of his sample of Canadians obtained their jobs through personal contacts and that the strength of these contacts varied by occupational level. Administrative and managerial employees used weak contacts more than strong ones. These were exactly the people most likely to form weak ties by dealing with business acquaintances in organizations or departments other than their own. Professionals and office workers used weak ties to get jobs, but they also frequently used strong contacts. Blue-collar workers rarely used weak ties.

Ericksen and Yancey (cited in Granovetter, in press) found that, in their probability sample of Philadelphia, individuals with less education tended to use strong contacts (relatives and friends) to find jobs, whereas the tendency to use weak contacts (acquaintances) was greatest among college graduates. The interaction effects of education and the use of weak ties on income were interesting. There was a negative effect on income of the use of weak ties for those with the least education, a slight positive effect for high school graduates, and a strong positive effect for college graduates, who were also most likely to use weak contacts to find their jobs. Thus, better educated persons benefited more from the use of weak ties than did people with less education.

Lin, Ensel, and Vaughn (1981) studied a representative sample of adult men in upstate New York and reported that weak ties had indirect effects on the status of the job attained. Weak ties were instrumental in getting better jobs if they connected the job seeker to a person with high occupational status. The direct effect of weak ties was less than the indirect effect, indicating that, although most weak contacts were made to higher status individuals, job seekers also established some weak contacts with low-status persons.

The results of these studies are substantially more complicated than can be reported here, and Granovetter (in press) raised many issues for further clarification and research. For example, although weak ties are clearly important for accessing job information because they may provide bridges to new social circles, many people get jobs through strong contacts. We need to understand better what characterizes effective contacts of both strong and weak types. However, Granovetter (in press) concluded that the available evidence indicates a positive association between the use of weak contacts and higher occupational attainment.

CURRICULAR PLACEMENT AND PERSONAL FRIENDSHIP NETWORKS

Social structures in different curricular tracks resemble those found in white-collar and blue-collar jobs. However, existing research has not described this correspondence in any detail and has not specified the social processes that cause it. We suggested that the causal linkage between curricular tracking and status attainment involves psychological predispositions working within social structural constraints. Recent research has suggested that individuals with more extensive networks, who can reach more people through strong and, especially, weak contacts, tend to get higher status, better paying jobs. These are the people who find positions in white-collar or professional occupations. However, there have been no studies of these kinds of differences in personal network structures across curricular tracks in high school.

On the basis of above discussion, we predict that the personal friendship networks of college track students will be more extensive than those of students in noncollege tracks. College track students will reach more students than will students in noncollege tracks. The remainder of this chapter presents some preliminary evidence on this hypothesis and the structure of personal networks in high school.

Data

The McDill and Rigsby (1973) sociometric data from 20 high schools were used for secondary analysis. These schools were not a random sample but were purposely selected to maximize variation on educational and social status variables. Questionnaires administered to 20,345 students and 1029 teachers yielded extensive information about social climate and student activities. This sociometric data base is one of the largest in existence with which curricular track comparisons can be made. Further details about the sample and questionnaire are available in McDill and Rigsby (1973).

Boys were asked, "Of the boys here in this school, who do you go around with most?" Girls were asked the same question with the appropriate shift in gender. Four lines were provided for students to name their friends, and cross-sex choices were not allowed. Because of the limited choice format of the sociometric questionnaire, we cannot use the data to examine friendship density or the relative frequency of strong versus weak choices—many friendships, particularly weak friendships, obviously were not reported.

Analyses

Four indices of reachability were calculated for each student. First, the number of students reachable through direct choices, or one-choice paths, were counted. Second, the number of friends of friends, or new students uniquely reachable in two-choice paths, were counted. Third, the number of friends' friends of friends, or new students uniquely reachable in three-choice paths, were counted. Finally, we added together the total number of students reachable in one-, two-, or three-choice paths. The fixed-choice format undoubtedly yielded low estimates of actual reachability, but it is reasonable to assume that these estimates were directly proportional to actual reachability.

The means and standard deviations of reachability are shown in Table 9.1 for each sex, grade level, and curriculum. Almost every comparison of means is statistically significant. Instead of reporting many specific comparisons, we will discuss only the major trends.

The hypothesis that students in college tracks reach more students than those in noncollege tracks was supported for both sexes and across grade levels. With one exception, every index of reachability in Table 9.1 is higher for college track students than for students in noncollege curricula. The weighted mean of students reachable in one-choice paths, pooled across sexes, was 2.93 for students in noncollege curricula and 3.18 for college track students. The weighted mean of students reachable in two-choice paths was 5.36 for students in noncollege curricula and 5.88 for college track students. Noncollege track students reached a weighted mean of 9.88 new students in three-choice paths, whereas college track students reached a weighted mean of 10.55 new students. Finally, when students uniquely reachable in one-, two-, or three-choice paths were added together, noncollege track students reached a weighted mean of 18.17, whereas college track students reached a weighted mean of 19.60.

There were sex differences in all four indices of reachability. With two exceptions, every index of reachability in Table 9.1 is higher for females than for males. The weighted mean reachability in one-choice paths, pooled across curricular tracks, was 2.94 for males and 3.20 for females. The weighted mean number of students reachable in two-choice paths was 5.40 for males and 5.91 for females. The weighted mean reachability in three-choice paths was 9.50 for males and 11.00 for females. Finally, when students uniquely reachable in one-, two-, or three-choice paths were added together, males reached a weighted mean of 17.84 and girls reached a weighted mean of 20.11.

The effects of grade levels on reachability were curvilinear. The weighted mean number of students reachable in one-choice paths was 3.10 for freshmen, 3.12 for sophomores, 3.08 for juniors, and 3.01 for seniors. In two-choice paths, freshmen reached a weighted mean of 5.64, sophomores reached 5.99, juniors reached 5.65, and seniors reached 5.29. In three-choice paths, freshmen reached a weighted mean of 9.86, sophomores reached 11.07, juniors reached 10.33, and seniors reached 9.36. Finally, when the numbers of students uniquely reachable at one-, two-, or three-choice paths were added together, freshmen reached a

TABLE 9.1
Mean Reachability by Curriculum, Grade, and Sex[a]

	Reachable at 1		Reachable at 3	
	Males	Females	Males	Females
Non-college prep	2.71 (1.29)	3.08 (1.07)	8.63 (6.76)	10.74 (8.05)
Grade 9	2.57 (1.32)	3.08 (1.05)	8.41 (6.42)	9.99 (5.82)
Grade 10	2.73 (1.30)	3.16 (1.05)	9.16 (6.96)	11.70 (8.40)
Grade 11	2.78 (1.26)	3.04 (1.09)	8.94 (6.76)	10.49 (7.98)
Grade 12	2.64 (1.31)	2.99 (1.08)	7.79 (6.56)	9.96 (8.21)
College prep	3.06 (1.16)	3.31 (.96)	9.96 (6.92)	11.22 (8.07)
Grade 9	3.14 (1.04)	3.42 (.82)	10.48 (5.94)	9.92 (6.23)
Grade 10	3.04 (1.17)	3.38 (.93)	10.42 (7.13)	12.20 (8.23)
Grade 11	3.08 (1.16)	3.29 (.97)	10.02 (6.98)	11.45 (8.42)
Grade 12	3.05 (1.19)	3.19 (1.00)	9.17 (6.78)	10.09 (7.70)

	Reachable at 2				Total reachability		
	Males		Females		Males		Females
Non-college prep	4.89	(3.39)	5.68	(3.31)	Non-college prep	16.23	(3.81)	19.50	(4.14)
Grade 9	4.82	(3.33)	5.44	(2.99)	Grade 9	15.80	(4.79)	18.51	(3.29)
Grade 10	5.06	(3.42)	6.11	(3.39)	Grade 10	16.95	(3.89)	20.97	(4.28)
Grade 11	5.04	(3.39)	5.56	(3.29)	Grade 11	16.76	(3.84)	19.09	(4.12)
Grade 12	4.57	(3.37)	5.31	(3.26)	Grade 12	15.00	(3.75)	18.26	(4.18)
College prep	5.67	(3.38)	6.12	(3.29)	College prep	18.69	(3.82)	20.65	(4.11)
Grade 9	5.98	(3.09)	6.00	(3.02)	Grade 9	19.60	(3.36)	19.34	(3.36)
Grade 10	5.85	(3.45)	6.54	(3.28)	Grade 10	19.31	(3.92)	22.12	(4.15)
Grade 11	5.64	(3.36)	6.14	(3.35)	Grade 11	18.74	(3.83)	20.88	(4.25)
Grade 12	5.40	(3.37)	5.60	(3.23)	Grade 12	15.23	(3.78)	18.88	(3.98)

[a]Students reachable in one-choice paths are direct choices. Students reachable in two-choice paths are indirect choices through one intermediary. Students reachable in three-choice paths are indirect choices through two intermediaries. Total reachability is the total number of students reachable in one-, two-, or three-choice paths. Cell frequencies are: Non-college prep Grade 9 girls 433, boys 257; Grade 10 girls 1639, boys 946; Grade 11 girls 1476, boys 1089; Grade 12 girls 1121, boys 911; college prep Grade 9 girls 392, boys 472; Grade 10 girls 1793, boys 1968; Grade 11 girls 1690, boys 2069; Grade 12 girls 1455, boys 1603. Standard deviations are in parentheses.

weighted mean of 18.60, sophomores reached 20.18, juniors reached 19.05, and seniors reached 16.90. Thus, mean reachability increased from Grade 9 to Grade 10 and remained relatively high in Grade 11. Mean reachability decreased considerably for seniors, who reached substantially fewer students than members of any other grade level, including freshmen.

The association between curricular tracking and reachability could be due to student SES or ability, because curricular tracking is positively correlated with these factors (e.g., K. L. Alexander *et al.*, 1978). Therefore, the association between curricular tracking and reachability was tested in regressions that controlled for father's education, abstract reasoning ability, grade levels (coded as three dummy variables), and extracurricular participation. Separate regressions were run for males and females.

The means, standard deviations, and intercorrelations of variables are shown in Table 9.2 for each sex. Curricular tracking was positively correlated with father's education, extracurricular participation, and reasoning ability for both sexes. The four indices of reachability were positively correlated with curricular tracking for both sexes, although slightly more strongly for males than for females. For males, reachability had positive correlations of about equal magnitude with curricular tracking and extracurricular activities. For females, reachability was more highly correlated with extracurricular activities than with any other factor.

Regression analyses of reachability on student characteristics for males and females are summarized in Table 9.3. The regressions were run both with and without the independent variable of extracurricular activities to determine whether the effects of curricular tracking on reachability were mediated by extracurricular participation. First, the regressions without extracurricular activities taken into account show that curricular track has weak positive effects on reachability for both sexes, although they are slightly stronger for males than for females. Curricular track placement effects are significant for all four indices of reachability for males and for three of the four for females. However, the absolute sizes of these effects are small.

Second, the regressions that take extracurricular activities into account show that there are differences in the effects of curricular tracking for males and females. When the number of extracurricular activities was added to the equation for females, two of the three coefficients linking curricular track to friendship reachability became nonsignificant, but this did not occur for males. Thus, extracurricular participation mediates the effects of curricular tracking on reachability for females. This finding is consistent with the effects of extracurricular participation on friendship selection documented by Karweit (Chapter 8, this volume).

Extracurricular activities had a strong positive association with reachability for both sexes. Students who participated in more extracurricular activities reached more students as friends in one-, two-, or three-choice paths and had higher total reachability.

The curvilinear association between grade levels and reachability was weakened by the statistical controls on other variables in these regressions, but the curvilinear pattern was still evident. Controlling for all variables, including extra-

TABLE 9.2
Means, Standard Deviations, and Intercorrelations of Variables for Analyses of Reachability, by Sex[a]

Variable	CT	EA	FE	RA	G10	G11	G12	R1	R2	R3	TR
					Males						
Curricular track (CT)											
Extracurricular activities (EA)	.26										
Father's education (FE)	.18	.14									
Reasoning ability (RA)	.27	.19	.13								
Grade 10 (G10)	.03	−.10	.04	−.10							
Grade 11 (G11)	.00	−.01	.00	.06	−.48						
Grade 12 (G12)	−.03	.13	−.02	.10	.41	−.43					
Reach 1 (R1)	.13	.15	.01	.10	.00	.01					
Reach 2 (R2)	.10	.14	.02	.08	.04	.00	.01	.63			
Reach 3 (R3)	.09	.10	.02	.07	.05	.01	−.04	.51	.83		
Total reach (TR)	.10	.12	.02	.08	.05	.01	−.06	.65	.93	.97	
Mean	.66	1.02	4.56	10.20	.33	.36	.26	2.93	5.44	9.59	17.99
SD	.47	1.10	1.62	2.59	.46	.48	.44	1.22	3.39	6.88	10.62
					Females						
Curricular track (CT)											
Extracurricular activities (EA)	.35										
Father's education (FE)	.24	.14									
Reasoning ability (RA)	.32	.25	.15								
Grade 10 (G10)	−.02	−.10	.03	−.07							
Grade 11 (G11)	.00	.01	−.02	.05	−.49						
Grade 12 (G12)	.04	.18	.00	.09	−.42	−.40					
Reach 1 (R1)	.11	.20	.03	.08	.08	−.01	−.07				
Reach 2 (R2)	.06	.12	.02	.05	.06	−.02	−.05	.53			
Reach 3 (R3)	.03	.06	−.01	.05	.10	−.01	−.08	.37	.81		
Total reach (TR)	.05	.09	.00	.06	.10	−.01	−.07	.50	.91	.97	
Mean	.55	1.64	4.65	9.76	.34	.34	.25	3.20	5.97	10.95	20.12
SD	.50	1.45	1.78	2.77	.47	.47	.43	1.03	3.38	8.01	11.41

[a]Noncollege curricular track was coded 0; college track 1; dummy variables for grade levels were coded 1 for each grade, 0 otherwise, with Grade 9 as the reference category; R1, R2, R3, and TR are reachability in 1, 2, or 3 paths and total reachability, respectively. Listwise deletion of cases was used. N for girls = 9308; N for boys = 8744.

curricular activities, male seniors had significantly lower reachability than freshman in terms of all four indices. For females, juniors and seniors had lower reachability than freshmen in one-choice paths. The curvilinear pattern was most evident for reachability in two- and three-choice paths, and in total reachability. Female sophomores had significantly higher reachability than freshmen, whereas seniors had significantly lower reachability.

Stephen Hansell and Nancy Karweit

TABLE 9.3
Regression of Reachability on Student Characteristics, with and without Extracurricular Activities, by Sex[a]

Variable	Reachability at 1		Reachability at 2		Reachability at 3		Total reachability	
			Males					
Curricular track	.12*	.09*	.08*	.06*	.07*	.05*	.08*	.0(
Extracurricular activities	—	.13*	—	.13*	—	.09*	—	.1(
Father's education	−.02	−.03*	−.01	−.02	.00	−.01	.00	−.0(
Reasoning ability	.07*	.06*	.06*	.05*	.06*	.05*	.07*	.0(
Grade 10	−.01	−.01	.00	.00	−.02	−.02	.01	.0(
Grade 11	−.01	−.02	−.03	−.04	−.02	−.02	−.02	−.0(
Grade 12	−.03	−.05*	−.07*	−.09*	−.07*	−.09*	−.07*	−.0(
R^2	.02	.04	.02	.03	.01	.02	.02	.0(
			Females					
Curricular track	.09*	.03*	.05*	.01	.02	.00	.04*	.0(
Extracurricular activities	—	.21*	—	.13*	—	.07*	—	.1(
Father's education	.00	−.01	.00	−.01	.02*	−.03*	−.02*	−.0(
Reasoning ability	.06*	.04*	.05*	.03*	.05*	.04*	.06*	.0(
Grade 10	.01	−.02	.09*	.08*	.12*	.11*	.11*	.1(
Grade 11	−.05	−.09*	.01	−.01	.05*	.04	.03	.0(
Grade 12	−.08*	−.13*	−.04*	−.08*	−.00	−.02	−.02	−.0(
R^2	.02	.06	.02	.03	.01	.02	.02	.0(

[a]N for females = 9308; for males = 8744. Standardized betas are shown.
*$p < .05$.

The background characteristics of father's education was weakly associated with one index of reachability for males and with two indices for females. Contrary to our expectations, students with lower SES tended to have slightly higher reachability than their higher status peers. Individual reasoning ability was weakly but consistently associated with reachability for both sexes. Students with greater ability exhibited higher reachability when other variables were controlled.

Although these regressions yielded significant effects, the proportions of variance in reachability accounted for by our independent variables was relatively low (less than 10%), and caution must be used in interpreting these results. Clearly, variables not included in our model may be more important influences on reachability and must be included in future research to improve the explanatory power of the model.

Discussion

These results provide limited support for the hypothesis that students in college curricular tracks have more extensive personal networks than those in non-college tracks. Mean reachability was higher for college track students of both sexes, but when student SES, reasoning ability, and extracurricular activities were controlled, the effects of track on reachability remained significant primarily for males.

The heterogeneity and large size of the McDill and Rigsby (1973) sample substantially increase our confidence in these preliminary results. The wide range of student backgrounds represented in the sample reduced the likelihood that these results are limited to a single social class. The fact that 20 schools were sampled means that the results do not depend on the curricular tracking system in any one school.

These data also had some limitations. They were collected in the mid-1960s and are now somewhat dated. It is possible that the structure of typical student networks has changed since then, but we are not aware of any systematic evidence showing this. The fact that the McDill and Rigsby (1973) data set is still one of the most recent, large-scale sources of information about peer friendships in school demonstrates how sorely we need further research in this area. These data are excellent, however, in providing multiple indicators of student status characteristics and attitudes, and they contain much information that has not yet been analyzed.

A more serious problem is the fixed-choice format of the sociometric questionnaire. As noted, this format limits the number of friends named, and we did not attempt to analyze friendship density or the relative frequency of strong versus weak choices because of possibly serious measurement errors in these indices. The fixed-choice format almost certainly yielded lower estimates of reachability than actually existed, and it probably also reduced the variance in these estimates. However, we made the reasonable assumptions that these estimates of reachability were directly proportional to actual reachability and that these estimates were not differentially biased across curricular tracks.

The major limitation in our analysis is that we counted the number of students reachable up to a maximum of three-choice paths. Even in small high schools, choice paths as great as 17 have been observed (Hansell, 1981), and the greatest differences between curricular tracks may involve relatively long choice paths. The fact that the hypothesis was supported over relatively short choice paths may mean that curricular tracking has stronger effects on personal friendship networks than those reported here. Clearly, further research using better sociometric instruments is needed before definite conclusions can be drawn. However, the present results suggest the potential usefulness of a new theoretical linkage between curricular tracking in school and adult status attainment.

The results revealed an unanticipated sex difference in the extent of personal networks that is not consistent with sexual stereotypes about networking ability. Males are often assumed to be better team players and to have more extensive personal networks than females (e.g., see Karweit and Hansell, Chapter 7, this volume). However, these stereotypes typically contrast adult men who work in business organizations with adult women who are housewives and have fewer opportunities to form extensive relationships. Our results suggest that, in settings in which the opportunities to participate in activities and form relationships are roughly equal for each sex, such as in high school, females have relatively more extensive personal networks than do males.

One possible explanation of this result is the mediating effects of extracurricular participation. Females participated in more extracurricular activities than did males, and this participation mediated the effects of curricular tracking on reachability. Thus, females in college tracks were involved in more activities than those in noncollege tracks, which gave them more opportunities to form relationships with a wider set of peers. Females in noncollege tracks were constrained from participating in many activities and thus had fewer opportunities to meet new friends.

The curvilinear distribution of reachability across grade levels did not suggest a simple interpretation of tracking as a socialization or selection process. There was no evidence that socialization experience in different curricular tracks caused increasing differences in reachability from Grade 9 to Grade 12. However, we cannot rule out socialization effects that may have occurred prior to the freshmen year or socialization effects that might be detectable in a true longitudinal study. The results were consistent with the interpretation that curricular tracking effects are caused by selection, but without longitudinal data collected before and after the selection process, alternative explanations cannot be ruled out. Clearly, we need longitudinal studies of the development of peer relationships within the context of the opportunities and constraints of school organization.

The curvilinear association between grade level and reachability may reflect floor and ceiling effects. Freshmen and seniors have a limited range of age-mates from which to choose friends, whereas sophomores and juniors can form relationships with students both younger and older than themselves. Even a small number of direct choices across grade levels could markedly increase students' reachability. Interestingly, freshmen had higher reachability than seniors, suggesting a prestige bias in choosing activity. If seniors were the least likely to name friends in a different, necessarily lower, grade level, they would have the lowest reachability. Ironically, seniors may be constrained against achieving high reachability by their relatively high status in the high school. Of course, we measured reachability in choices *made*. If reachability had been measured in choices *received*, seniors may have scored higher than students in other grades.

An important issue is why curricular tracking was more strongly associated with reachability than with SES (measured as father's education). In the world of the adolescent, curricular track may be a more proximal and possibly more potent status characteristic than family background, except perhaps in schools with unusually heterogeneous student populations. Family background may influence student reachability indirectly through the mediating influence of curricular tracking, but longitudinal data are needed to address this issue. Longitudinal data would also reveal directly the impact of curricular tracking and personal friendship networks on the status of the first job after high school or college.

CONCLUSION

This chapter suggests a new theoretical linkage between school organization and adult status attainment. Most previous research on status attainment has treated curricular tracking as an individual status characteristic. Although this approach has provided much valuable empirical information, it has not provided a detailed explanation of how school organization affects the transmission of status. Recent research by the revisionists has focused attention on social outcomes of education, and particularly on the correspondence between social structures in school and work. However, most of these theories also use psychological explanations of how students learn social skills that prepare them to assume white- or blue-collar work roles in the future. Although this research is provocative, it fails to specify how economic advantage is transmitted through social structure.

These perspectives are plausible but incomplete. Their strength is their focus on how individual motivation is generated. However, they do not consider in detail how the opportunities and constraints provided by social structure affect the motivation of individuals. This chapter developed a perspective that explicitly considers how school organization may affect later status attainment, and tested this perspective on a large-scale data set. The results indicated that students in college tracks have more extensive personal networks than students in noncollege tracks, and we suggested that this may give college preparatory students a substantial advantage in future status attainment.

Limitations in these data suggest caution in the interpretation of the results, and many important questions remain to be addressed. However, if future longitudinal research replicates the present results, then school organization will assume a much more important role in theories of status attainment than is now the case. Also, such research may alert educators to the unintended consequences of scheduling and grouping practices that may have important effects on the future status attainment of students. In particular, students in noncollege curricular tracks who are constrained from participating in school activities with a wide variety of peers may lack practice in forming extensive personal networks that would help them achieve higher occupational success. It may be possible to reorganize schools at relatively small expense to provide all students with opportunities to enlarge their social worlds.

JERE COHEN

10

Commentary:
The Relationship between Friendship
Selection and Peer Influence

The study of interpersonal selection and sociometric choice, although a topic of sociological interest for years, takes on new significance through the research in this volume. These studies make it clear that selection is no isolated event but rather has lasting consequences for the social relationships it spawns. Perhaps most importantly, subsequent interpersonal influence depends on the circumstances of interpersonal choice. Hence, a felicitous by-product of the investigation of the selection process is a greater understanding of social influence.

Toward this end, the studies in this volume rightly emphasize the relationship between interpersonal selection and influence and contribute to the specification of this relationship. This commentary builds on the other chapters to move toward a more detailed and systematic enumeration of the ways in which influence depends on selection. Evidence and examples are drawn primarily from research on high school and college friendships.

INFLUENCE OF SELECTED AND NONSELECTED PEERS

Before concluding that peer influence depends on selection, it must first be shown that *selected friends* have more influence on an individual than *nonselected acquaintances*. The relatively impersonal influence of nonselected others has been conceptualized in a number of ways—for example, as the impact of (a) an inter-

163

FRIENDS IN SCHOOL
Patterns of Selection and Influence in Secondary Schools

personal environment, (b) an elite, (c) a school or peer context, and (d) a value climate. Evidence is mixed on the effectiveness of these types of peer influence.

Wallace (1966) studied the impact of a college's interpersonal environment on students. A student's interpersonal environment consisted not of selected friends but of everyone registered at the college whose name the student recognized. Wallace showed that freshmen's attitudes toward grades were influenced over time by their interpersonal environment and that their closest friends had no more influence than did acquaintances they spent little time with. At the same college, however, graduate school aspirations were primarily influenced by intimate friends; so, at least on this aspiration item, ultimate influence depended on choice of close friend. A replication of Wallace's study in a high school (J. Cohen, 1971) found little peer influence, but whatever there was came from respondents' best-liked friends and not from the interpersonal environment as a whole.

The second type of nonselected peers who are believed by some to have influence are school elites. Newcomb (1943), who showed that students at Bennington College grew more politically liberal during their college years, believed that they were most influenced by the emulation of campus leaders, not by relationships with personal friends. Attempting to become leaders themselves, Bennington students conformed to liberal campus norms in hopes that conformity would be rewarded with leadership. Those who most desired leadership (i.e., those most influenced by campus leaders) changed most readily to Bennington values. J. S. Coleman (1961) developed a similar hypothesis at the high school level: Students desiring membership in the leading crowd wanted most to change. However, a secondary analysis of Coleman's panel data (see J. Cohen, 1976) found no tendency at all of students to emulate the leading crowd. Furthermore, unpublished panel data from the Coleman study show that, despite high school students' desires to emulate leading students and athletes, they become in fact no more academic nor athletic. What all these studies indicate is that peer emulation that involves no actual friendship selection results in little peer influence. This supports the conclusion that most influence stems from those who have been selected as close friends.

A third type of influence that short-circuits the friendship selection process is the influence of peer contexts. Contextual effects, like interpersonal environments, have been said to affect students by establishing a certain ambience. A high school's social class context was once believed to significantly affect its students' achievements and aspirations. More recent research, however, attributes little influence to the broader student context and more to selected close friends.

The belief that social class context affected school achievement stemmed from the work of J. S. Coleman (Coleman, 1961; Coleman, Campbell, Hobson, McPartland, Mood, Weinfeld, & York, 1966; Wilson, 1967). However, Jencks (1972) and M. Smith (1972) pointed out defects in the Coleman et al. (1966) design, and M. Smith's (1972) reanalysis found that Coleman et al. had substantially overestimated student body effects on achievement. Moreover, other studies (e.g., Hauser, 1969; McDill, Meyers, & Rigsby, 1967) found no student body effects on achievement.

The effects of social class climate on college plans have been shown to be quite small. Initial findings that such effects existed (Boyle, 1966a, 1966b; Krauss, 1964; Michael, 1961; Rogoff, 1962; Turner, 1964; Wilson, 1959) were challenged when McDill et al. (1967) and Sewell and Armer (1966a) found little or no effect; debates revolving around the proper interpretation of Sewell and Armer's (1966a) data (see Boyle, 1966a; Hauser, Sewell, & Alwin, 1976; Michael, 1966; Sewell & Armer, 1966b; R. Smith, 1972; Spady, 1970b; Turner, 1966) have brought no agreement. More conclusively, Meyer (1970), Nelson (1972), Jencks & Brown (1975), and K. L. Alexander and Eckland (1975) have each shown that the positive effects of peer context on college aspirations are cancelled by contradictory negative effects; and Hauser (1971), Duncan, Featherman, and Duncan (1972), Jencks and Brown (1975), and Alwin and Otto (1977) have shown that between-school variability (and thus the peer context effect) on the college aspiration variable is small.

E. Campbell and Alexander (1965) found that the socioeconomic composition of the student body did not affect college plans directly, but it did affect them indirectly, by providing greater or fewer opportunities to associate with friends with high status or high educational aspirations. Close friends were found to influence a student's college plans by Herriott (1963), C. N. Alexander and Campbell (1964), Duncan, Haller, and Portes (1968), Kandel and Lesser (1969), Hauser (1972), Picou and Carter (1976), Kahl (1953), and Simpson (1962). Similarly, friends' influences on occupational aspirations have been found by Haller and Butterworth (1960), Hauser (1972), and Duncan et al. (1968). These studies show that the influence of selected close friends is strong and actually accounts for the influence that was previously attributed to the broader peer context.

This dominance of selected friends over nonselected peers in the influence process has been disputed by McDill and Rigsby (1973), who preferred the concept of school value climates over the concept of school context. They found that when they used "academic emulation," a scale derived through factor analysis, as a measure of normative value climate, the direct effect of the normative value climate remained statistically significant even when influence of close friends was controlled. They concluded, therefore, that Campbell and Alexander had overstated the case in arguing that *no* important structural effect exists independently of interpersonal influence, and they inferred that there was something more to schools' intellectual climates and their influence than simply student interpersonal processes. However, the "something more" that McDill and Rigsby had identified was not clearly peer influence but included the influence of teachers as well. Thus, McDill and Rigsby did not so much contradict Campbell and Alexander's conclusions as they relate to *peer* influence, as they underscored the need to distinguish between peer influence and *school* influence as a whole, which includes teacher influence. In short, McDill and Rigsby (1973) did not demonstrate that nonselected peers have an impact, and neither did McDill et al. (1967)

in a previous study that employed similar teacher–student combination scales to measure school value climates. It is possible, also, that the impact of Bennington College's politically liberal normative climate, measured by Newcomb (1943), is attributable to teacher influence and not to peer influence (or at least not to peer influence alone).

The best-known study to conceptualize school value climates in terms of the press of school peer societies was J. S. Coleman's (1961) study *The Adolescent Society*. Coleman hypothesized that the antiacademic values of high school peer societies held back students' educational achievements. However, when he attempted to show that schools with the least intellectual value climates most discouraged studying and college going, the evidence was mixed. Moreover, since his results were not based on a before-and-after design, he could not demonstrate conclusively that school value climates made an impact.

In sum, evidence is mixed regarding the influence of nonselected peers. Most peer influence exists in practice as the mutual influence of close friends. Back (1951) has shown that the stronger the bond between two people, the more they will attempt to influence each other and the greater the likelihood that their influence attempts will be successful (see E. Katz & Lazarsfeld, 1955). This means that the nature of peer influence depends on which peers students select as their close friends and on how they select them.

SELECTION AND INFLUENCE VARIABLES

The general principle that selection affects influence may now be specified in greater detail. There are several different properties of selection that can affect influence. These include (a) the setting in which selection is made; (b) the principle or principles of selection employed; (c) the number and types of friends selected; and (d) the types of relationships formed. These selection variables will affect the following influence variables: (a) the direction of influence; (b) the magnitude of influence; and (c) whether the influence tends to reinforce or change prior characteristics.

Effects of the Setting on the Other Selection Variables

The chain of causal events begins with the setting. Peers may be selected at school or in nonschool settings. The previous chapters in this book stress school environments and divide these into curricular and extracurricular settings. Curricular settings refer to classrooms, school grades, and tracks, whereas extracurricular settings include school clubs and organizations. The type of setting affects several of the other selection variables: the type of friend selected, the number of friends selected, and the types of relationships formed.

The type of setting affects the type of friend selected by (a) preselecting a pool of peers available in that setting; (b) establishing patterns of proximity and contact; and (c) prescribing task and reward structures that condition opportunities and preferences for friendship choice. These three aspects of the setting may have separate effects on selection, as follows.

First, the type of friends available depends on whether the setting is a school setting, such as a classroom or a school club, or a nonschool setting, such as a street corner, bowling alley, home, or church. Type of friends will differ in similar settings—for example, a school club can be a group of debaters or athletes and a classroom can be an accelerated math class or a shop class. Also, a setting may be homogeneous or heterogeneous, containing people quite similar to each other or a diverse pool of potential friends. The similarity among the persons present in a setting depends on a variety of preselection factors, such as neighborhood segregation and schools' age grading and ability grouping (Hallinan, 1978). Also, people self-select themselves into settings where others are similar to themselves by choosing settings that satisfy their tastes and interests.

The second type of setting effect—the establishment of patterns of proximity—occurs because patterns of contact are dependent on spatial arrangements, the shared use of space or equipment, and communication required to carry out tasks. Some settings encourage widespread contact, some lead to repeated selective contacts with the same few peers, and others erect barriers to contact.

The third type of setting effect—prescribed task and reward structure—affects the number of friends chosen and the principles used to select them. Rewarding group performance rather than individual efforts tends to increase friendship formation and friendship stability (Hallinan & Tuma, 1978). Similarity between two students may be more important as a criterion of friendship when *relative* rather than *absolute* performance is rewarded (Hallinan, 1978).

Research in this section illustrates how school settings can affect the direction of friendship choice. Epstein (Chapter 5) shows that participatory classroom settings result in a wider range of choices than do traditional classrooms. Slavin and Hansell (Chapter 6) report that team learning enhances the likelihood of cross-racial choices. Hansell and Karweit (Chapter 9) illustrate how tracking influences contact, choice, and content of interactions. Karweit (Chapter 8) focuses on how extracurricular settings affect contact and selection.

The setting can influence not only the *type* of friend chosen but also the *number* of friends. Settings that encourage large numbers of contacts, that define activities and participants as desirable, that are considered appropriate places to seek friends, that establish cooperative task relationships, and that bring together interdependent, similar, and compatible people will produce the greatest number of positive peer relationships.

The setting can also affect the type of relationship formed. For example, compared to traditional classrooms, the participatory and team learning settings studied in other chapters led to an increased number of mutual-choice friendships.

In sum, one selection variable—the setting—can influence the other selection variables. It is also likely that the other selection variables can influence each other: For example, the type of friend selected can influence the type of relationship formed. However, the one detailed example described here, the effect of the setting, suffices to illustrate the interplay of selection variables.

Effects of the Setting and Selection on Change and Reinforcement in the Influence Process

After the selection variables have been determined through the actions of sociometric choosers and through the mutual effects of the selection variables on each other, they contribute to the determination of the influence variables. Some effects of the selection variables on the influence variables are analyzed in detail in the following discussion.

The first influence variable considered is whether social influence leads the person influenced to change traits or reinforces the person's existing traits. Both effects have been observed in research on peer influence. Wallace's (1966) study of college students' attitudes toward grades concluded that peer influence had changed their attitudes; conversely, Kelley and Volkart's (1952) study of Boy Scouts showed that those who felt closest to the organization and most like other scouts were most resistant to outside attempts to change their attitudes away from those endorsed by the group. In other words, influence can act to *anchor* friends' characteristics, not just to change them.

If peers or friends are initially unlike, they will experience pressures toward uniformity that can change their characteristics to make them more alike; conversely, peers who are initially alike will pressure each other not to change. Thus, whether influence takes the form of change or reinforcement depends on whether friends are initially similar or different. When friends are alike, there is no need for mutual influence to take the form of pressure to adopt each other's traits. Therefore, there is no pressure to change. To the contrary, pressures toward uniformity are pressures to remain uniform. Therefore, existing characteristics are anchored by interpersonal influence. In contrast, whenever relationships are heterogeneous at the start, pressures toward uniformity take the form of pressures to change.

These effects were observed in married couples. Newcomb, Koenig, Flacks, and Warwick (1967) studied (a) husband–wife similarities in political party preference reported for Bennington College alumnae (the wives), and (b) changes in these wives' political party preferences over 20 years. In marriages where husband and wife differed at marriage in party preference, 78% of the wives changed party, but where husband and wife held the same preference at marriage, 76% of the wives kept their original party preferences for the full 20 years. Since most women in the Bennington studies had changed political views earlier, during college, the persistence of party preference among women in homophilic relationships stands out in contrast. Regardless of prior changes, the development of homophilic relationships can serve as a potent anchor.

For friends at school, whether peer influence results in change or reinforcement depends on the degree of homophilic choice—that is, the degree to which students have chosen friends just like themselves. It is possible to wind up with friends who are like oneself either by chance, or by virtue of a homogeneous pool of friends in one's interaction setting, or because homophily has been employed as a principle of choice. Therefore, the change-versus-reinforcement influence variable depends mainly on two selection variables: the setting and the principle of friendship selection. Unless the pool of potential friends in each setting is already highly selective, the principle of friendship selection is crucial, and the direction that influence takes—change or reinforcement—depends on the degree to which homophilic choice is the prime criterion of friendship selection.

Research findings strongly suggest that homophilic selection is the most important basis for friendship, dating, and marital choice. Newcomb (1961) showed that college students living in the same house ultimately came to choose as friends those who held similar values; likewise, Precker (1952) found shared values to be an important basis of college student friendship choice. Byrne and his associates found that interpersonal attraction "is a positive linear function of the proportion of attitude statements" on which pairs agree (cited in Berscheid & Walster, 1969, pp. 90–91). And J. Cohen (1977) found that newly formed friendship groups were homogeneous on a broad variety of values, attitudes, and behaviors. It is well known also that spouses tend to be quite alike in religion, race, social class, education, and even intelligence (see Berscheid & Walster, 1969). The inverse hypothesis, that spouses will tend to be opposite and complementary in personality, has been disconfirmed by numerous studies (reviewed by Berscheid & Walster, 1969). In sum, the principle of homophilic selection is one of the best-confirmed laws in sociology. Hallinan (1978) lists sex, race, age, academic ability, SES, attitudes toward schoolwork, attitudes toward authority, shared school activities and sports, and educational and occupational aspirations as characteristics on which similarity is frequently judged.

Homophilic selection begins to work even before initial contact because settings help to segregate people so that each person meets others with similar characteristics. In the case of schools, Hallinan (1978) notes that parents of similar ethnicity and SES are likely to be found in the same school districts; schools then segregate students by age and ability grouping; and, finally, students who choose the same courses and extracurricular activities have common interests. Upon initial acquaintance, Kerckhoff and Davis (1962) suggest, people use common demographic characteristics, such as SES, as a filter, particularly in screening potential dating choices. Once a relationship is under way, its persistence depends on sharing values (Newcomb, 1961). In this volume, Epstein shows in Chapter 11 that students become more similar to their friends over a year's time on academic and nonacademic measures.

The principle of homophilic selection is not only applied to single, isolated attitudes, values, and demographic characteristics but also typically used to select friends similar on a wide variety of characteristics at once. J. Cohen (1977), in a study of newly formed high school peer groups, found that boys' groups were more homogeneous than the school as a whole on all 20 attitudinal and behavioral measures employed, and girls' groups were more homogeneous than the school as a whole on 19 of the 20 items. Among items indicating strong homophily were drinking, smoking, dating frequency, church attendance, desire to join additional clubs at school, number of evenings per week spent at home, and desire to be remembered as a brilliant student. At first glance, it would seem surprising that adolescents could choose friends who are like themselves in so many ways at once.

One reason such broad-based homophilic choice occurs is because student characteristics are not independent. Those students who drink the most, for example, also tend to smoke the most, spend the least time at home, date the most, and study least; they are least likely to plan to attend college or to want to be remembered as brilliant students. Therefore, when choosing a friend on the basis of the person's likeness to oneself, a high school student will usually be choosing someone similar in many ways.

Each cluster of intercorrelated traits defines a recognizable type of student. For example, Buff (1970) has listed "greasers," "dupers," and "hippies" as three common high school types. Likewise, Newcomb et al. (1967) discovered several types at Bennington College, including "scholars," "wild ones," "the social group," and "creative individualists." B. Clark (1962) conceptualized three high school types—the "fun," "academic," and "delinquent" groups; J. Cohen (1979a) went on to show that these three types correspond to actual clusters of intercorrelated behavioral and attitudinal measures. Because these social types are well known to high school students (not just to sociologists) and because each type occurs repeatedly (in view of the pattern of intercorrelations among the traits that define the types), students can make broadly homophilic choices simply by choosing friends of the same type as themselves. J. Cohen (1971) found that high school friendships were homogeneous with regard to social type. At the college level, Newcomb et al. (1967) found that all but one of the social types at Bennington overchose peers of the same type. Thus, when peers choose friends of the same social type, their friendships became homophilic on a large number of traits at once without their even being aware of all the dimensions upon which they and their friends are matched.

However, despite the widespread tendency toward homophilic selection, heterophilic selection is even more likely. Each individual possesses many different values, attitudes, interests, behavior patterns, personality traits, and demographic characteristics. It would be virtually impossible to find an entire friendship group or even two people that matched perfectly. In practice, sociometric selections tend to be made from a limited circle of acquaintances; the best match available may be far from perfect. Under these circumstances, the odds against a close match seem astronomical. The intercorrelation of traits is a help, as noted above, because it reduces the number of traits that need to be matched to a smaller number of independent dimensions or factors than if each trait occurred independently. However, there is virtually never a manageable small number of dimensions that can account for all the variance in a large list of traits. J. Cohen's (1979a) study of high school types found that the two leading dimensions or factors that substructured 47 traits accounted for less than 40% of the variance and that additional factors contributed little extra. While these two dimensions and their association with well-known types undoubtedly simplified students' quests for similar friends, it is clear that choice on the basis of social type could not come close to producing perfect homophily. Moreover, the intercorrelation of traits creates problems of homophilic choice for students who have unusual combinations of traits, some of which are part of a given social type but others of which are opposite to the trait characteristic of that type. In this case, the odds of finding a perfect match are less than if all traits occurred independently of each other.

Because a perfect match is all but impossible, people make choices that are homophilic on the dimensions that are most important to them. Byrne's (1961a) subjects were more attracted to people who agreed with them on important issues than to those who agreed on unimportant issues. And according to Newcomb (1961), the relevance of an attitude to potential friends conditions the degree to which similarity affects liking. Berscheid and Walster (1969), reviewing this literature, see the principle established by Byrne and Newcomb as a limitation to the rule that associates similarity and attraction. The double implication of this limitation is (a) that some forms of similarity are too unimportant to result in sociometric choice, and, obversely (b) that along dimensions of lesser importance, heterogeneity is fully compatible with a close relationship.

Although heterogeneity along unimportant dimensions might be presupposed to be irrelevant to the influence process, this presupposition is contradicted by the facts. Dimensions that are unimportant for selection purposes can be important influence items. J. Cohen (1971), for example, actually found a negative relationship between the importance of an item for the selection of homophilic cliquemates and the degree of conformity observed on the item. Put somewhat differently, it is largely on the traits considered unimportant for purposes of homophilic selection where pressures toward uniformity are most effective in producing change. When traits not central in the homophilic selection process later became the focus of pressures toward uniformity, the pressures will affect friends who started out heterogeneous on these traits. The result of these pressures will be change rather than reinforcement.

Heterogeneous peer relationships are also created when friendships are formed on bases of selection other than homophily. Hallinan (1978) lists a number of other bases for friendship selection. First, she notes that propinquity facilitates interaction purely on the basis of chance. Moreover, Berscheid and Walster (1969) argue that propinquity facilitates the acquisition of interpersonal information and thereby intensifies sentiment; where sentiments are positive (and positive sentiments are more usual than negative), interpersonal attraction is intensified. One might add to this that propinquity decreases the costs (i.e., the inconvenience) of a relationship. Second, Hallinan (1978) lists status differences as an alternate basis of choice. Rather than choosing status equals, people are often attracted to status superiors. Blau (1964) points out that associating with a high-status person can raise one's own status. A third alternative to homphilic choice is reciprocity of liking. Berscheid and Walster (1969) reason that if one person likes another, the other is likely to find the relationship rewarding and reciprocate the first person's friendship. Newcomb (1961) has observed that reciprocity of liking is used as a basis of choice relatively early in the acquaintance process, before people know each other very well. Because insufficient information is available for homophilic choice based on common values, people base their choices on more accessible information, reciprocating the known attraction of others. Fourth, choices may be based on physical characteristics. Physical attraction is stressed as a basis of interpersonal choice by Walster, Aronson, Abrahams, and Rottmann (1966) and Byrne (1971). Whenever other bases of choice besides homophily are employed, heterogeneous relationships are created. Consequently, as already noted, uniformity pressures tend to induce change.

Even when homophily is the basis of choice, successful homophilic selection is by no means guaranteed. As Newcomb (1961) has emphasized, insufficient interpersonal information can lead to unsuccessful matching even when matching is desired. J. Cohen (1977) has replicated Newcomb's (1961) finding that homophily increases as acquaintance grows. Additionally, Cohen (1979b) explained an observed decline in social class homophily among Elmtown's youths in their friendship and dating relationships by pointing to the concomitant decline in clarity in the Elmtown class structure. By the time "correct" social class information could be discerned, relationships had already formed on other characteristics and it was too late for the principle of class homophily to serve as a filter in the screening process.

Cohen (1979b), on the basis of Kennedy's (1944) finding that national origins had declined as a basis of homophilic mating choice and his own finding that social class homophily had declined in importance, concluded that, on any item, the level of homophily may vary from relationship to relationship, from locality to locality, and from time to time. As levels of homophily vary, so does the extent to which pressures toward uniformity produce anchorage or change in attitudes and behaviors.

Other Effects of Selection Variables upon Influence Variables

It has been shown in this discussion and in the other chapters in this section that the setting and the principle of friendship choice affect the degree of homophily in a relationship. We suggest, and Epstein shows in the next section, that the degree of homophily in turn affects whether uniformity pressures will result in change or reinforcement. Thus, selection variables affect influence variables. In addition to the setting, each of the other selection variables can affect the kinds of influence that occurs among friends. The effects of type of friend, number of friends, and type of relationship on peer influence are outlined briefly in the following paragraphs.

The *type of friend* selected is important because some types are more influential than others. Gibb (1954), for example, notes that a person's degree of leadership is positively related to IQ, confidence level, and sociability. Lippitt, Polansky, Redl, and Rosen (1960) found that camp boys who excelled in campcraft exerted more influence than those who did not, which implies that expert friends will be most influential and that friends will be most influential in the areas of their expertise. Katz and Lazarsfeld's study (1955) supports this hypothesis. They found that different types of people exert opinion leadership in different areas of life. Young girls most influenced others' opinions on movies and fashions; wives in large families were most influential in marketing; and high-status people, older people, and males were most influential in the area of public affairs. The more interested a person was in each of these areas of life, the more influence that person exerted in that area, provided that the person being influenced also held an interest in the same area.

Some types of friends will exert influence in one direction, while other types will exert a different influence. Wallace (1966), for example, found that the more nonfreshmen and the more fraternity–sorority members in a freshman's interpersonal environment, the greater the reduction in the importance the freshman attached to college grades. As another example, the higher a high school friend's SES or IQ, the more positive is that friend's influence on educational and occupational aspirations (see, for example, Duncan et al., 1968).

Another selection variable is the *number of friendships* formed. Having more than one friend (or more than one peer group) can produce conflicting influences. The different pressures from different people or groups may offset each other. Such conflict can free a person from one friend's influence and result in greater autonomy. Alternatively, several influential peers can reinforce each other; Asch (1960) has shown that such reinforcement increases the magnitude of influence.

The *type of relationship* formed may also affect the influence process. Different types of relationships, include (a) mutual relationships versus one-sided relationships; (b) group versus dyadic relationships; (c) strongly bonded versus weakly bonded relationships; and (d) stable versus short-term relationships. Newcomb (1961) found that mutual-choice relationships are characterized by a greater intensity of liking than are unreciprocated choices. We would expect more influence from these relationships. Moreover, mutual liking should lead to mutual influence. In contrast, if choice is one way, the person least interested in the relationship tends to be more powerful and the person *most* interested tends to be most dependent and most influenced (see Emerson, 1964). Similarly, a friendship based on equality should lead to mutual influence, whereas an unequal relationship will be unequal in the amount of influence exerted. Also, Wallace (1966) has hypothesized that unified groups of peers exert more influence than the same number of peers acting individually. However, when J. Cohen (1971) compared group influence to dyadic influence on a number of behavioral and attitudinal scale items, he found little influence of either kind, and he found group influence no greater than dyadic influence.

We would expect the effectiveness of peer influence to depend on the way that peer relations are structured, but no positive evidence is available to support this supposition. Additionally, it would appear that the stronger the friendship bond, the greater the influence; evidence supporting this point has been reviewed earlier (Back, 1951; Katz & Lazarsfeld, 1955). The Wallace (1966) study only partially supported this principle. We would also expect that the most stable, long-lasting friendships would be the most significant and foster the greater influence. However, Cohen (1977) found that stable cliques displayed no more conformity than dying cliques. Moreover, Cohen (1981) found that new friends have just as much influence as old friends on educational aspirations. No evidence shows any connection between stability of relationship and magnitude of peer influence. Overall, then, previous data only partially support the hypothesis that the type of relationship created in the selection process affects the nature of subsequent influence.

CONCLUSION

The chapters in this section of the volume illuminate the selection process and, as a consequence, the influence process as well. Because selection and influence are so closely connected in life, it is difficult to study one in isolation from the other. The research in this volume helps to identify the variables that allow us to conceptualize the effects of selection on influence and provides empirical support for the existence of some of the connections. This commentary assembles empirical evidence that confirms the link between selection and influence, and provides a framework for codifying the research findings in this volume and future research.

IV

SCHOOL ORGANIZATION
AND THE INFLUENCE PROCESS

JOYCE LEVY EPSTEIN

The Influence of Friends on Achievement and Affective Outcomes

An important task for research on peer groups is the separation of the *selection* of friends from the *influence* of friends. The challenge arises because cross-sectional studies of the influence of friends cannot take into account the similarities of students that existed prior to selection. These studies attribute all similarity of friends to the influence of one friend on another. Logically, a single measure of similarity cannot be an unbiased indicator of influence (Cohen, 1977; Duncan, Haller and Portes, 1968; Hallinan, 1978; Kandel, 1978).

If students select their friends from a pool of students who are already similar to themselves on many characteristics, then the apparent influence is really a function of prior socialization by families, schools, earlier peers, demographic characteristics, geographic boundaries, and other factors. For example, students in a college preparatory school or track cannot be said to have influenced their friends to attend college if all had college plans before they selected each other as friends. Of course, students can influence each other to maintain similar plans, attitudes, and behaviors. Cross-sectional studies of peer influence have used causal models that establish a temporal order of variables, but these studies have typically lacked the individual, demographic, and contextual data that are needed to specify their models adequately.

Many researchers assert that peers do influence each other on many important behaviors, including aspirations, achievements, values and attitudes, social skills, and appropriate sex roles (Hartup, 1978; D. W. Johnson, 1981a). Others have made clear that how much friends influence each other has been overestimated

177

FRIENDS IN SCHOOL
Patterns of Selection and Influence in Secondary Schools

because of the missing data on friends' similarities prior to selection (J. Cohen, 1977; Kandel, 1978). In this chapter, longitudinal data are used to take into account the similarities in attitudes and behaviors of students and their friends that were present at the Time 1 survey. Then we chart the influence of the students' differently structured friendship groups on these attitudes and behaviors 1 year later at Time 2.

Many studies show that children and adolescents pick friends similar to themselves on selected characteristics, such as sex, race, achievement, age, and interests. In this study, we want to know what happens to varied student attitudes and behaviors over time when the students *do* and *do not* select friends who are initially similar on these characteristics. The analyses presented in this chapter improve our understanding of the influence of friends in several ways. First, patterns of influence on diverse behaviors are examined, including achievement and nonacademic outcomes. Second, patterns of influence in contrasting school environments are examined to follow up the report in Chapter 5 that patterns of selection are influenced by school and classroom organizations. Third, the patterns of influence of reciprocated, unreciprocated, and stable friends on diverse outcomes are studied. Fourth, family and peer influences are contrasted on diverse outcomes. Finally, results from longitudinal and cross-sectional data are compared to illustrate the differences in influence and attributed influence of early and current friends. Developmental patterns from early to late adolescence are reported and illustrate how influence is the result of the dynamics of friendship choices and change.

DATA

The data used in this chapter come from a survey of students in Grades 6, 7, 9, and 12 in middle and high schools, and from a survey conducted 1 year earlier when the students were in Grades 5, 6, 8, and 11. These data are described in Chapter 5 and in greater detail in McPartland and Epstein (1977), Epstein and McPartland (1979), and Epstein (1980, 1981). Several features of the data are important for studying influence. Friends' reports about their own college plans, attitudes toward school, and all other outcome measures, and school reports about all students' achievements are used instead of students' perceptions of friends' characteristics. Perceptual reports by students about their friends tend to inflate the similarity and the importance of the friends (Davies & Kandell, 1981; Davitz, 1955).

These data limit our attention to the students and their most direct or proximate influences—their close friends and the educational environment in which they interact. Two questions are addressed: Do students influence each other's affective and academic behaviors? Do the patterns of influence differ in high-participatory versus low-participatory schools and in differently structured friendship groups?

The assumption is that the positive affect that exists between a student and his or her best friends permits influence to occur. There are several theories about how influence occurs (see, for example, Chapter 12 by Miller and Chapter 13 by Hallinan, this volume), but these data cannot be used for formal tests of competing theories. Instead, we aim to extend an understanding of the *patterns* of influence, so that new questions about theories of influence will be based on developmental and environmental information. We examine the common assumption that more influence occurs among students whose friendships are reciprocated or stable over 1 year. We ask whether students who choose no friends in school have different patterns of change in school outcomes than students who choose close friends. These questions introduce some important complexities to studies of peer influence that should affect how theories of influence are framed and tested in the future.

The structure of a student's friendship group is identified on the basis of the student's scores on initial Time 1 measures. Four friendship group structures are identified: LL (low student, low friends); LH (low student, high friends); HL (high student, low friends); and HH (high student, high friends). The first letter of the category tells whether the student's own score on a measure at Time 1 was above or below the mean score, and the second letter tells whether the average of the student's friends' scores on the same measure at Time 1 was above or below the mean. For example, a student and his or her friends could be LH in achievement and HL in self-reliance. The different characteristics of a student and friends on various outcomes illustrate how studies of influence may need to account for the students' and friends' scores on particular behaviors and attitudes in order to determine if friends influence those outcomes. Thus, we are examining the effects of differently structured friendship groups at Time 1 on students' outcomes at Time 2. The outcome measures include self-reliance, satisfaction with school life, college plans, report card grades, and standardized achievement scores.

RESULTS

Influence Patterns in Differently Structured Groups

Table 11.1 compares the current (Time 2) scores of students who were initially in differently structured friendship groups. For example, current scores of students initially low with high friends are compared with current scores of students initially low with low friends (LH versus LL). T tests that indicate significantly different scores for the comparison groups are underlined.

Columns 1 and 2 of the table show that, overall, high-scoring friends positively influence affective and academic outcomes. Students who are initially low or high with high-scoring friends have, with two exceptions, significantly higher scores 1 year later than similar students with low-scoring friends. Evidence of generally

TABLE 11.1

t-Test Statistics[a] Comparing Current Scores of Students Initially Low or High on Measures, Whose Friends Were Initially Low or High, for Total Population, by Sex and by Grade[b]

Outcome	Total population		Female		Male		Grade		
	LH vs LL[c]	HH vs HL[c]	LH vs LL	HH vs HL	LH vs LL	HH vs HL		LH vs LL	HH vs HL
1. Self-reliance	2.64[a]	2.79	2.49	3.02	1.03	2.66	6	2.48	0.88
							7	0.23	2.04
							9	0.32	2.50
							12	0.91	3.35
2. Satisfaction with school life	1.65	3.26	1.47	2.01	0.90	2.69	6	0.27	2.23
							7	1.10	1.67
							9	0.31	0.82
							12	0.93	0.59
3. College plans	4.55	2.89	2.55	1.79	3.66	2.26	6	3.07	0.02
							7	0.33	1.73
							9	2.75	1.94
							12	2.94	2.15
4. English report card grades	2.46	7.21	0.94	5.47	1.90	2.65	6	1.24	1.12
							7	1.93	4.31
							9	0.95	5.71
							12	1.71	2.60

							Grade		
5. Math report card grades	0.46	3.38	1.78	2.07	−1.16	2.46	6	1.47	1.34
							7	0.02	2.43
							9	0.78	2.34
							12	1.87	0.94
6. English standardized achievement	5.36	6.38	4.28	4.75	3.63	4.28	6	NA	NA
							7	2.73	4.75
							9	4.71	4.44
							12	0.53	3.62
7. Math standardized achievement	5.47	6.65	6.30	4.22	3.16	5.77	6	NA	NA
							7	4.95	4.04
							9	4.58	6.09
							12	NA	NA

[a] t-test statistics are underlined to indicate significantly different scores of the comparison groups, with 1.96 significant at the .05 level, 2.58 at the .01 level, and 3.29 at the .001 level.

[b] N's for total population for each outcome are: 1. low 1622, high 1705; 2. low 1280, high 1879; 3. low 965, high 840; 4. low 711, high 1310; 5. low 716, high 1086; 6. low 870, high 960; 7. low 951, high 664. N's for females and males are about equal and are available from author. N's by grade level 6/7/9/12 for self-reliance are: low 616/493/365/148, high 511/479/459/256. N's for other outcomes are similar and are available from author.

[c] LL, LH, HL, and HH categorize the initial friendship group structures. The first letter of each pair indicates the students' own initial scores on a measure (L = low; H = high), and the second letter indicates the average of the students' friends' initial scores on the same measure.

positive influence of high-scoring friends appears for males and for females in Columns 3–6. The within-sex comparisons suggest that the influence process works similarly for males and females, with both sexes positively influenced by high-scoring friends on a variety of achievement and affective outcomes. This supports Maccoby and Jacklin's (1974) conclusion that sex differences in vulnerability to peer pressures is not empirically well established. In Columns 7 and 8, results of these analyses by grade level are presented. There are many instances of positive influence by high-scoring friends for initially low-scoring students on different outcomes at all grade levels.

Across the grades, low-scoring students are influenced by high-scoring friends on academically related outcomes, such as achievement test scores and college plans. There are even more indications that initially high-scoring students are influenced by high-scoring friends, especially on affective outcomes. The measure least influenced by friends is attitudes toward school life. This measure of satisfaction with school has been shown to be affected by the students' own daily school experiences (Epstein, 1981).

The LL and HH friendship groups are based on the initial *similarity* of students and their friends; the LH and HL groups are based on initial *differences* in scores on outcome measures of students and their friends. These categorical groups make gross distinctions in levels of scores, but they are useful for studying patterns of influence. If students who are initially low in scores become significantly different over time, and if they are members of differently structured friendship groups (i.e., students in LL versus LH groups), then at least part of the change may be due to the influence of friends on behavior. Our analyses show that students initially in LH groups have significantly higher scores 1 year later than students initially in LL groups—especially on college plans and achievement test scores. Students initially in HH groups have significantly higher scores 1 year later than students in HL groups on every outcome and in almost every grade.

Influence of Friends in High- and Low-Participatory Schools

Differences in patterns of friendship *selection* in high- and low-participatory schools were reported in Chapter 5. A necessary, next question is whether there are differences in the patterns of *influence* in differently organized schools. For example, the wider contacts reported for students in high-participatory schools could result in the weaker influence of any single friend or group of friends. If students have more friends with diverse norms for behavior, the influence of any one group may be offset by influence from other groups or may be easier to resist because of ties to other groups. Or it could be that wider contacts and greater diversity among contacts would lead to more careful selection of best friends and result in greater influence of friends in high-participatory schools.

Table 11.2 presents results of tests of friends' influence on students in differently structured friendship groups in contrasting school environments. In all

TABLE 11.2

t-Test Statistics[a] Comparing Current Scores of Initially High and Low Students[b] in Differently Structured Friendship Groups in Low-, Mid-, and High-Participatory Instructional Programs in Secondary Schools

Outcome	Low-participatory program		Mid-participatory program		High-participatory program	
	LH vs LL	HH vs HL	LH vs LL	HH vs HL	LH vs LL	HH vs HL
1. Self-reliance	1.61	1.14	1.47	1.76	2.04	2.05
2. Satisfaction with school life	2.26	1.07	0.49	2.12	0.13	2.51
3. College plans	2.50	1.07	2.96	2.72	1.82	0.97
4. English report card grades	2.12	3.54	0.96	5.64	1.38	2.96
5. Math report card grades	0.08	3.25	−1.05	2.76	0.65	−1.16
6. English achievement	4.31	2.94	2.71	5.47	2.66	2.55
7. Math achievement	2.47	4.79	5.97	4.11	2.40	2.52

[a] *t*-test statistics are underlined to indicate significantly different scores of the comparison groups, with 1.96 significant at the .05 level, 2.58 at the .01 level, and 3.29 at the .001 level.

[b] N's for the given categories listed by student initial score are: 1. 323/291/615/506/164/158; 2. 351/489/727/1053/199/332; 3. 242/201/544/472/175/165; 4. 255/362/373/730/85/215; 5. 273/285/362/573/80/226; 6. 243/331/496/483/130/144; 7. 240/246/561/319/159/97.

schools, patterns of significant influence are similar on the achievement outcome. Students who are initially high or low in achievement and who have initially high-achieving friends have significantly higher achievement scores 1 year later than high- or low-achieving students who have initially low-achieving friends. However, in high-participatory schools, students initially low or high in self-reliance are influenced by highly self-reliant friends. This is an important effect because self-reliance is an outcome linked to the goals of high-participatory schools and classrooms. Students may be moved toward a school goal by friends and peers who have already adopted the goal in their own behavior. Other patterns are less regular or do not add to the conclusions drawn from Table 11.1 and are therefore unlikely to be due to the contrasting school organizational characteristics.

The effect of friends in high-participatory schools on self-reliance is examined more carefully in Table 11.3 by comparing two groups of students of theoretical interest—students who are initially low in self-reliance who have friends initially high on that measure, and students initially low in self-reliance who have initially low-scoring friends. The school program's emphasis on participation is treated as a continuous measure; schools are scored on a continuum from low- to high-participatory programs. Each of the four outcomes—satisfaction, perceived rewards

TABLE 11.3
Summary of Correlations and Effects of the Formal Organization of Participation on Four Outcome Measures for Students Initially Low in Self-Reliance in Differently Structured Friendship Groups

Dependent measures from four separate equations	Students low in self-reliance					
	With initially higher friends			With initially equal or lower friends		
	Zero order	b^a	(t)	Zero order	b^a	(t)
1. Satisfaction with school life	.088	.047	(1.78)	−.087	−.123	(−2.61)
2. Perceived teacher rewards for self-reliance	.097	.085	(3.04)	.016	.019	(0.37)
3. Change in self-reliance over 1 year	.103	.044	(1.61)	.070	.030	(1.00)
4. Own social status	.045	.066	(2.35)	.055	.052	(1.27)

[a] b = standardized regression coefficient; (t) = associated test statistic. In each equation, these background characteristics were statistically controlled: grade level, sex, race, parents' education, family style, rules in the home, and report card grades.

for self-reliant behavior, change in self-reliance, and perceived social status—is regressed on school program and student background characteristics, including grade, sex, race, parents' education, participation in decisions at home, family rules, and report card grades. Separate analyses are conducted for initially low self-reliant students in differently structured friendship groups. Zero-order correlations and standardized regression coefficients reporting the independent effects of school program on each outcome are presented in Table 11.3.

The results suggest that an emphasis on participation in classroom decisions affects student satisfaction, self-reliance, social status, and perceived rewards for self-reliance of initially low self-reliant students *if* they have initially high self-reliant friends. There are several coefficients of interest. First, students low in self-reliance with low self-reliant friends are significantly less satisfied with school life in high-participatory schools ($b = -.123$), whereas low self-reliant students with high self-reliant friends are just as positive about school life in high- or low-participatory schools ($b = .047$). Initially low self-reliant students with high self-reliant friends perceive teacher rewards for self-reliance ($b = .085$) significantly more in high-participatory schools, whereas low self-reliant students with low self-reliant friends do not perceive differences in teachers' rewards in contrasting schools ($b = .019$). Initially low self-reliant students with high self-reliant friends report that they have significantly higher social status in high-participatory than in low-participatory schools ($b = .066$).

The effects are particularly strong for the perceived rewards that teachers give for self-reliant behavior in the more participatory schools, and for the dissatisfaction with school life of students if neither they nor their friends show behavior that is rewarded by the school organization. It seems that students may be better adjusted to school, better understand the school's goals, and feel more secure themselves if their close friends already fit the school's expectations.

Influence of Reciprocated and Stable Friends in Differently Structured Friendship Groups

It is often assumed that the stronger and longer lasting the relationship of students and their friends, the greater the influence on behavior. Table 11.4 presents the tests of differences in scores of students with reciprocated versus unreciprocated friends in the four types of friendship groups. Then tests are presented of differences in scores of students with stable and unstable friends in each type of group.

The first column of Table 11.4 shows that students in LL groups have significantly higher English achievement scores if they have reciprocated friends. No other outcome is significantly affected by the reciprocity of LL friendships. The second column indicates that reciprocity has significant positive effects for the LH group on self-reliance, English report card grades, and English and math achieve-

TABLE 11.4
Summary of t-Tests[a] on Differences in Student Scores within Type of Friendship Group Due to Reciprocation and Stability of Friendships

	No versus all friends reciprocated[b]				No versus all friends stable			
Outcome	LL	LH	HL	HH	LL	LH	HL	HH
1. Self-reliance	0.13	1.96	1.79	0.87	0.91	2.13	0.68	2.44
2. Satisfaction with school life	−0.05	0.65	−0.52	1.41	0.48	0.90	0.52	2.00
3. College plans	1.20	1.44	2.00	−0.54	−1.23	0.62	0.68	1.10
4. English report card grades	1.77	2.20	2.89	2.33	1.76	0.92	2.08	2.55
5. Math report card grades	0.46	1.35	1.74	0.54	0.47	−0.67	0.10	0.66
6. English achievement	3.11	2.04	−1.28	0.73	0.54	2.11	−1.26	0.13
7. Math achievement	1.06	2.90	1.36	0.66	1.25	2.98	−0.20	0.25

[a] t-test statistics are underlined to indicate significantly different scores of the comparison groups, with 1.96 significant at the .05 level, 2.58 at the .01 level, and 3.29 at the .001 level.

[b] N's for the categories across rows for tests of reciprocation: 1. 394/341/293/340/; 2. 552/302/605/602; 3. 369/237/213/334; 4. 275/209/254/607; 5. 262/222/261/467; 6. 373/211/204/398; 7. 450/188/185/226; and across rows for tests of stability; 1. 469/351/321/383; 2. 615/350/679/663; 3. 431/280/273/364; 4. 321/239/284/649; 5. 317/230/254/510; 6. 428/228/234/441; 7. 521/299/194/252.

ment scores. This group benefits most from reciprocated friendships on a number of outcome measures. For students initially high on each measure (HL or HH groups), reciprocity of friendships makes little difference. Of all outcomes measured in this study, English report card grades are most consistently higher for students with reciprocated friends in all the differently structured friendship groups.

About one-half of a student's initial reciprocated friends are also stable friends, so the populations and the results overlap considerably on the two sides of Table 11.4. There is one notable pattern of differences in scores based on stability of all friends. Students with initially high scores who have stable, high-scoring friends have significantly higher scores than similar students with no stable friends on the affective outcomes of self-reliance and satisfaction with school life. For students with low-scoring friends, stability of friendships make no significant difference—positive or negative—on the outcomes measured.

Differences in influence on student behavior of unreciprocated, reciprocated, and stable friends are presented separately by sex in Table 11.5. The table shows the unstandardized regression coefficients of the effects of average friends' initial scores on a student's current affective and cognitive outcomes, after statistically taking into account the student's own initial score. The student's initial (Time 1) score for each measure is the most powerful predictor of a current score at Time 2.

TABLE 11.5
Unstandardized Coefficients for Regressions of Student Affective and Cognitive Scores on Average Unreciprocated, Reciprocated, and Stable Friends' Scores and Student Initial Scores, by Sex[a]

Dependent measures from seven equations	Female			Male		
	Unreciprocated friends	Reciprocated friends	Stable friends	Unreciprocated friends	Reciprocated friends	Stable friends
1. Self-reliance	.0210*[b]	.0184*	.0296*	.0142*	.0203*	.0318*
2. Satisfaction with school life	.0004	.0005	.0001	.0006	.0014*	.0011*
3. College plans	.0009*	.0010*	.0011*	.0016*	.0014*	.0021*
4. English report card grades	.0013*	.0018*	.0004	.0010*	.0012*	.0016*
5. Math report card grades	.0001	.0014*	.0005	.0011*	−.0005	.0001
6. English achievement	.0100*	.0081*	.0103*	.0079*	.0088*	.0093*
7. Math achievement	.0094	.0163*	.0196*	.0048	.0114*	.0123*

[a]N's for the categories across rows are for females: 1. 443/791/475; 2. 643/1233/707; 3. 636/1226/716; 4. 436/789/480; 5. 387/654/432; 6. 434/776/469; 7. 337/667/384; for males: 1. 522/498/328; 2. 760/810/518; 3. 743/798/524; 4. 517/488/321; 5. 474/461/307; 6. 492/487/323; 7. 418/432/273.

[b]Asterisks indicate that the regression coefficients are more than twice their standard errors.

By statistically controlling the student's Time 1 score, we are, in effect, holding constant the prior accumulated influence of friends and other individual characteristics on the Time 1 score. The regression coefficients, then, report the *continuing influence* from Time 1 to Time 2 of earlier friends' behaviors on the student's later behavior. Separate coefficients are shown for unreciprocated, reciprocated, and stable friendship pairs. An asterisk indicates a significant influence of early friends on the student's current score on each outcome. Unstandardized regression coefficients permit comparisons across differently structured groups and male and female groups on each outcome. These coefficients cannot be used to compare outcomes within type of friendship, but they can be used in these comparisons to indicate direction and strength of effect. For example, for females, high-scoring unreciprocated friends had positive effects on four of the seven outcomes measured, and high-scoring reciprocated friends had positive effects on six of the seven outcomes.

On measures of self-reliance, college plans, English report card grades, and English achievement, males and females, on the average, benefit from earlier membership in high-scoring friendship groups, whether or not the friends reciprocate or endure. Two of the three other outcomes for females (math report cards and math achievement) and the two outcomes for males (satisfaction and math achievement) show the significant influence of reciprocated, high-scoring friends.

There are instances where the effects on student outcomes are stronger for students with reciprocated and/or stable friends than for students with unreciprocated friends. This is true for males on all outcomes except math report card grades. Thus, the nature of friendships—unreciprocated, reciprocated, or stable—has an effect on the extent of friends' influence on many different outcomes, especially for males. It will be observed that reciprocity and stability in friendship groups has more effect on satisfaction with school life for males, whereas reciprocity appears to be important for math achievement and report card grades of females. While it is tempting to explain these patterns with references to differences in male and female behaviors in school, or responsiveness of males and females to group pressures, we will resist ad hoc explanations in favor of the more logical conclusion that the process of influence by friends across outcomes for males and females is generally equivalent. The differences noted here should serve as clues for more detailed studies.

Some Friends versus No Friends

Table 11.6 reports the results of tests comparing scores of students who chose no friends on the initial survey with students in differently structured friendship groups. First, scores of students who selected no friends are compared with scores of students who selected low-scoring friends. In this comparison—no friends versus low friends—students who chose some friends (even low-scoring friends) are at an advantage on measures of academic skills over those who chose no friends. Interestingly, the third column of test statistics indicates that initially

TABLE 11.6

Summary of t-Test Statistics[a] Comparing Scores on Outcomes of Students Selecting No Friends and Some Friends, by Type of Friendship Group and Students' Initial Scores[b]

Outcome	No friends versus low-scoring friends if student is initially		No friends by low scorer versus low-scoring stable friends	No friends versus high-scoring friends if student is initially		No friends by high scorer versus high-scoring stable friends
	Low	High		Low	High	
1. Self-reliance	1.68	0.74	−1.68	0.41	1.58	2.78
2. Satisfaction with school life	0.03	−1.59	−0.72	1.31	0.11	1.52
3. College plans	1.04	0.69	−3.54	2.66	1.57	1.83
4. English report card	0.74	2.80	1.74	2.91	2.76	3.50
5. Math report card	0.20	−0.65	0.41	0.57	2.06	1.73
6. English achievement	3.58	3.11	2.07	7.91	4.20	2.64
7. Math achievement	−0.62	2.37	2.55	8.08	1.78	0.91

[a] t-test statistics are underlined to indicate significantly different scores of the comparison groups, with 1.96 significant at the .05 level, 2.58 at the .01 level, and 3.29 at the .001 level.

[b] N's for the given categories going across rows are: 1. 849/690/632/725/758/312; 2. 1257/1063/979/617/1180/242; 3. 860/519/265/623/673/235; 4. 624/631/258/529/1147/365; 5. 572/577/210/474/935/298; 6. 808/478/296/550/798/262; 7. 901/362/279/492/460/121.

low-scoring students who select no friends may have higher scores on self-reliance and college plans than students who select and keep low-scoring friends.

The right side of the table reports results of tests comparing scores of students who chose no friend versus those who selected initially high-scoring friends. Initially low- and high-scoring students who selected high-scoring friends are better off 1 year later on measures of college plans, report card grades, and achievement than are students who chose no friends. Initially low-scoring students are especially assisted on standardized achievement test scores by high-scoring friends in comparison with students with no friends. The last column of the table shows that high-scoring students in high-scoring, stable friendship groups have higher scores on most of the measures than do high-scoring students with no friends, with significantly higher scores on self-reliance, English report card grades, and English achievement. Although the measures are far from perfect, there are indications that students who select no best friends at school are at a disadvantage on many outcomes compared to students who have friends who can serve as positive influences.

The results in Tables 11.4, 11.5, and 11.6 raise some interesting questions about the important characteristics of children's friendship groups and their influence. It is clear that reciprocity and stability are not always needed for positive influence to occur. Although some mutual and stable choices are clearly advantageous, others either may have no special effect on an outcome over unreciprocated friends or may be disadvantageous for student development over the long term. For example, low-scoring students with no friends scored higher in self-reliance and college plans than did students with stable, low-scoring friends.

The lack of many consistent and strong effects of reciprocation and stability may be due, in part, to the measures used and, in part, to the changing nature of children's friendships. New friends may be "exchangeable" with old friends, and school interactions in the classroom may be frequent whether or not mutual choices of friends are made. It is possible, too, that many students' friends who are not considered reciprocated in these data are actually reciprocated friends, but our limited measure of choice of best friends is masking the true extent of mutual social relations. Low-scoring students may have one high-scoring influential friend who affects behavior even though the average score of the friendship group is low.

Kandel (1978) documented two important effects: Students selected friends who were similar before the selection was made, and students who remained friends and reciprocated their friendship became slightly more like one another, especially on their patterns of drug (marijuana) use. In that study, however, there were few dramatic differences between stable friends and newly selected friends. On most measures new friends were more homophilic than were stable, unreciprocated friends.

We know very little about whether, when, or why reciprocated or stable choices are beneficial for student development. Other research also notes the uncertain importance of reciprocity on influence. Kandel and Lesser (1970), for example, point out the importance for student attitudes and behaviors of the person selected "best friend overall," regardless of the reciprocity of the selection. Leinhardt (1972), Hallinan (1976a), and J. Cohen (1977) note that the short-term nature of student alliances makes stability of friendships an uneasy measure. The assumption has been that mutuality and stability are ideal conditions of friendships, but the analyses reported here raise important questions about that assumption for future research.

Influence of Friends and Families

There has been much debate on the relative importance of family and friends on student behavior. On the one hand, it is argued that peers increase their influence on each other during adolescence. However, there has been little empirical support for beliefs about decline of influence of the family (see Elder, 1971; Kandel & Lesser, 1970). Estimates of the relative influence of parents and peers on youngsters' behavior differ across studies because of different measures, methods, and populations.

Douvan and Adelson (1966) showed that adolescents' agreements with parents or peers depend on the particular ideas and behaviors in question. Although it is enticing to pit family and peer influences against each other, not enough has been studied about the influences of both groups on different outcomes. Many have suggested that youngsters' strong ties to parents do not necessarily mean weak ties to peers (Clausen, 1968; Douvan & Adelson, 1966; Elder, 1971; J. Keats, Biddle, Keats, Bank, Hauge, Rafaei, & Valentin, 1981; Brittaim, 1971; Magnusson et al., 1975).

Socialization practices of families, schools, peers, and close friends can play a major role in the development of dependability, internalization of achievement norms, and other qualities that steer students in their personal development and life course. Magnusson et al. (1975) suggest that parental support and influence is directly tied to peer and friends' support and influence. If parents do not support their youngsters' peer interactions, there may be less interaction of the child with other youngsters.

Our data permit an examination of the influence of early friends, current friends, and family on several academic and affective outcomes. Family SES has been the variable most frequently used in previous studies. It is used here for comparison with earlier work, but see Epstein (1980, 1983) for a more complete representation of the influence of family socialization practices on student behavior.

Table 11.7 presents the F statistics associated with tests of the increase in percentage of variance explained when early friends, current friends, and family are added, separately and in combination, to an equation that regresses current scores on students' initial scores on the affective and cognitive measures at each grade level. Five separate additions to the equation are tested: early friends, current friends, family SES, early and current friends with family SES statistically controlled, and family SES with early and current friends statistically

TABLE 11.7

F Statistics for Significance of Increase in Explained Variance Due to the Addition to the Regression Equation of Early and Current Friends and Family SES, by Grade[a]

Outcome and variable added to equation	Grade			
	6	7	9	12
1. Self-reliance				
Early friends[b]	7.71*[c]	1.92	4.87	16.44*
Current friends[b]	54.07	27.73	44.20	0.56
Family SES	10.17	25.84	55.56	7.70
Friends net of family	25.45	9.68	13.92	7.88
Family net of friends	3.21	17.24	38.02	6.68
2. Satisfaction with school life				
Early friends	4.86*	6.13*	0.11	3.78
Current friends	22.67	15.27	10.94	41.72
Family SES	2.17	1.17	5.21	0.54
Friends net of family	12.57	9.32	5.01	20.58
Family net of friends	1.86	0.22	4.20	0.10
3. College plans				
Early friends	6.01	5.46	16.44*	13.91*
Current friends	29.87	42.28	57.04	74.80
Family SES	82.17	82.64	80.83	23.87
Friends net of family	7.41	9.87	18.45	18.54
Family net of friends	48.29	57.62	51.56	17.94
4. English report card grades				
Early friends	6.48	29.62*	15.90*	15.17*
Current friends	87.82	136.65	94.13	9.38
Family SES	36.60	41.75	28.32	0.46
Friends net of family	36.36	62.40	42.91	9.99
Family net of friends	20.60	21.76	17.22	0.01
5. Math report card grades				
Early friends	4.68*	0.77	1.74	13.26*
Current friends	113.94	40.83	89.67	1.24
Family SES	8.27	7.50	6.35	0.30
Friends net of family	56.74	18.84	44.15	6.88
Family net of friends	4.97	4.51	5.07	0.74
6. Standardized achievement[d]				
Early friends		23.67*	25.13*	24.54*
Current friends		73.72	43.42	41.60
Family SES		25.55	30.31	19.81
Friends net of family		32.29	19.42	18.02
Family net of friends		10.10	15.65	10.22

[a]N's by grade (6/7/9/12) for each outcome are: 1. 1138/995/855/407; 2. 1174/1002/859/411; 3. 1173/1007/866/411; 4. 1135/988/836/409; 5. 997/937/827/295; 6. NA/1015/839/333.

[b]F statistics of 3.84 or more are significant at .05 level; 6.64 at .01 level.

[c]Asterisk indicates that the F statistic remains significant for the contribution of early friends *after* the addition of current friends to the equation, at or beyond the .10 level.

[d]For this table, we use math achievement for Grades 7 and 9 and English achievement for Grade 12, which did not have a math achievement test. Grade 6 was not tested.

controlled. These analyses take into account statistically the history of influence of friends on students' initial scores, and focus on the continued influences on students' later behaviors.

Early friends make a significant contribution to the explained variance in students' current scores on all outcomes for more than one grade level. The greatest influence of early friends is on measures of English report card grades and standardized achievement, with sizable contributions noted also for college plans at the high school level. Moreover, for each outcome for at least two grade levels the contribution of early friends remains significant even after the characteristics of the students' current friends are taken into account (see asterisks in Table 11.7).

As expected, with students' initial scores held constant, current friends' contribution to the explained variance of students' current scores is more significant than the contribution of earlier friends. Indeed, for every grade and every outcome (with three exceptions in Grade 12), students' current friendship group characteristics on that outcome make substantial, significant contributions to the equations made by students' earlier, Time 1 friends. These concurrent conditions of selection and influence create the same unsolvable problems for interpretation as in other cross-sectional studies of friendship groups. Without the longitudinal tests described earlier that indicate the continued influence of early friends, we would know only that students select friends whose attitudes and behavior are similar to their own.

Next in Table 11.7 are the F statistics associated with tests of the increase in the contribution of family SES to the explained variance in student outcomes. Family SES makes significant, sizable contributions to the explained variance of all outcomes, with the exception of satisfaction with school life across the grades and report card grades for students in Grade 12.

The last two entries for each outcome in Table 11.7 report the F statistic for the independent contributions to explained variance of friends and family SES. First, friends are added to the equation after family SES; second, family SES is added to the equation after friends have been accounted for. Family SES is an equal or more important influence than friends on college plans and, in three of four grades, on self-reliance. Family SES contributes significantly, but substantially less than the characteristics of students' friends to the explained variances of the other affective and academic outcomes.

Interestingly, only the measure of college plans shows a systematic pattern of increasing significant contributions of friends from the middle to the high school years. Parents' SES is clearly an important variable in the years when students are thinking about preparing for college attendance. For example, decisions must be made about courses and about plans to apply to college before Grade 12. The family's ability to pay for college is a very strong influence during those years. Indeed, the F statistic associated with family's contribution to explained variance of college plans is the most significant contribution of this family measure to any student outcome across the middle and high school years. Davies and Kandel

(1981) also report that parental influence on aspirations persists throughout adolescence.

The results of tests of the contributions of early and current friends suggest a dynamic model of friendship selection and influence. The earlier tables in this chapter emphasized that the *type* of selection made (low- or high-scoring friends on specific measures) can affect students' own scores 1 year later. Table 11.7 offers information on the continuity of early friends' influence on students' behavior. There is evidence of a refinement of the selection process as new friends are made or as different friends assume the position of best friends. New selections of best friends are likely to be based on revised attitudes and behavior, so that each set of current friends are more similar to the student who is making the selection than was an earlier set of friends. Newcomb (1961) was aware of these dynamics in studies of college students. He suggested that early agreements among selected friends lead to new interactions on which disagreements may be observed. We note the process may be most volatile for younger children. When friends who are similar in some respect observe important differences, they may attempt to influence and change each other or they may dissolve the friendship. New groups of friends will be based on earlier *and* new reasons for selection. Newly formed, more similar groups find new differences among members, and the process of refining choices or influencing others continues. While we have some evidence that this process stabilizes over time—older students have somewhat more stable best friends—there is no evidence that the process ever stabilizes completely. Rather, we assume that the dynamic selection and influence processes continue into adulthood.

For some outcomes, the influence of students' friendship groups is as great or greater than the influence of the family. This conclusion is only temporarily informative. The measures used for friends' characteristics were outcome specific, but the measure used for family is a single measure of SES, indicated by parents' education. At best, the use of SES provides conservative estimates of family influence on student behaviors. Research shows that family socialization practices, such as decision-making style, affect development of nonacademic attitudes and behavior more than family SES does (Epstein, 1980, 1983). It will be important to use measures of specific family contexts in the next studies of the relative influence on behavior of family and friends.

Friends' influence is behavior specific. Friendship groups will be high on one measure and low on another, reflecting the averages of the members' strengths and weaknesses. It may be that observed influence on a specific measure is due to the high score of only one friend, while for a different outcome it is the high score of a different friend that has an influence. The interrelationships of an individual's own placement on a given measure with the multiple possible combinations of influence of three or more friends and across one or more membership groups are complex indeed. Studies that aim to explain the influence process will have to deal with these complexities in the design of data collection and plan for analyses.

Scores of Students in Differently Structured Groups

Multiple outcome measures. Table 11.8 presents the means and standard deviations of Time 2 scores for students who were initially in differently structured friendship groups. In every case, for high- and low-scoring students, the average Time 2 score for students with initially (Time 1) high-scoring friends is higher than the average for students with low-scoring friends. All but one of the comparisons (math report card grades for initially low-scoring students with high- versus low-scoring friends) yields significant t-tests at or beyond the .01 level. As would be expected, on the average, the highest scores of all are obtained by high-scoring students with high-scoring friends; the lowest scores are obtained by initially low-scoring students with low-scoring friends. Of course, there is considerable overlap in the scores for individuals, but it is interesting that the higher mean scores of students with high-scoring friends are accompanied by slightly lower standard deviations.

Figure 11.1 shows the average scores at Time 1 and Time 2 for students in the four types of friendship groups. The patterns are totally consistent. There is a clear regression toward the mean for the total population, but within the subsets of high- and low-scoring students, there is an indication of an accentuation of scores (Feldman & Weiler, 1976). That is, the mean scores of the groups within subsets diverge slightly. In each case, the initially low-scoring students with high-scoring friends move *more* toward the mean than the low-scoring students with

TABLE 11.8
Means and Standard Deviations of Current Outcome Measures for Students Initially High or Low Whose Friends Were Initially High or Low[a]

		LH versus LL			HH versus HL	
Outcome		Mean	SD		Mean	SD
1. Self-reliance	LH	10.07	(3.00)	HH	12.58	(2.87)
	LL	9.60	(2.83)	HL	12.05	(2.87)
2. Satisfaction with school life	LH	1.22	(1.29)	HH	2.49	(1.57)
	LL	1.11	(1.18)	HL	2.25	(1.56)
3. College plans	LH	.39	(0.49)	HH	.80	(0.40)
	LL	.25	(0.43)	HL	.72	(0.45)
4. English report card grades	LH	3.48	(0.85)	HH	4.21	(0.81)
	LL	3.31	(0.89)	HL	3.85	(0.89)
5. Math report card grades	LH	3.47	(0.97)	HH	4.06	(0.88)
	LL	3.44	(1.02)	HL	3.87	(0.94)
6. Standardized achievement, English	LH	39.80	(16.13)	HH	71.40	(16.27)
	LL	33.04	(18.41)	HL	64.21	(16.68)
7. Standardized achievement, math	LH	42.57	(20.62)	HH	78.77	(15.26)
	LL	32.37	(21.14)	HL	70.37	(16.46)

[a]See Table 11.1 for N's for the comparison groups.

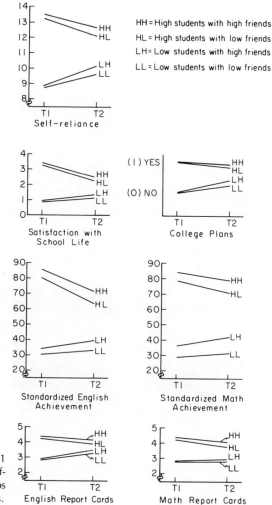

FIGURE 11.1. Mean scores at Time 1 and Time 2 for students in initially differently structured friendship groups on academic and affective outcomes.

low-scoring friends, and initially high-scoring students with high-scoring friends move *less* toward the mean than the high-scoring students with low-scoring friends.

Different influence processes are suggested by these results for the four types of friendship groups: The low-scoring (LL) students move toward the mean but change less (maintenance); the LH students change more (positive influence); the high-scoring (HH) students move toward the mean but change less (maintenance); and the HL students change more (negative influence). The combination of maintenance for similar groups and influence for dissimilar groups produces the general pattern of more positive behavior for students with high-scoring friends.

College plans.   The influence of friends on student aspirations has received the most attention in previous sociological research on peer influence (C. N. Alexander & Campbell, 1964; Alwin & Otto, 1977; J. Cohen, 1981; McDill & Coleman, 1965; Picou & Carter, 1976), so we highlight the longitudinal patterns of the influence of friends on college plans. Table 11.9 presents the mean scores of current college plans for students who did or did not initially plan to attend college and who had no, some, or all friends with definite plans to attend college. Having some or all friends with college plans makes a dramatic difference in the *change* toward college plans for students in Grades 6, 9, and 12. For students in Grades 7, 9, and 12 who initially planned to attend college, those with some or all friends with initial college plans were more likely to *maintain* their own plans. The data confirm that the time between Grades 11 and 12 is an important decision-making period and that peer influence on college plans can be especially important during this period for students who have no definite plans.

These patterns corroborate the results of earlier tables that suggest that at all grade levels the structure of the group of best friends can have important consequences for students' later attitudes, behavior, and decisions. Moreover, the timing of measurements across the years from childhood to adolescence is important. We see in the earlier tables a developmental pattern of increasing influence of friends on college plans in the high school years and, in Table 11.9, different

TABLE 11.9
Mean Current College Plans of Students Having No Friends, Some Friends, and All Friends with Plans to Attend College, by Students' Initial College Plans and by Grade[a]

Own plans Time 1	Friends with college plans		
	None	Some	All
Grade 6			
No	.266	.301	.424
Yes	.742	.737	.724
Grade 7			
No	.323	.370	.342
Yes	.676	.698	.784
Grade 9			
No	.174	.279	.333
Yes	.685	.721	.804
Grade 12			
No	.190	.471	.452
Yes	.833	.864	.898

[a] N's by grade across rows are: 6—no 199/242/139; yes 132/236/155; 7—no 167/138/111; yes 108/116/97; 9—no 172/93/72; yes 73/86/143; 12—no 63/17/42; yes 24/44/108.

influence of initial plans on later plans by the time students are in Grade 12. Without the developmental patterns, there would be distorted or incomplete reports about friends' influence on outcomes that change over time in importance.

SUMMARY AND DISCUSSION

It has not always been clear in previous research on students and their friends whether the similarities noted among them were due to the purposeful selection of friends already like themselves, to the demography of a school or community, to the institutional procedures that produce similar results in students regardless of their interactions, or to the real influence of one friend on another over time. Studies (J. Cohen, 1977; Kandel, 1978) have raised questions about the similarity and influence of friends and have shown the importance of longitudinal data for accurately representing the degree of influence on students' behaviors. This chapter, with longitudinal and developmental data in contrasting school settings, contributes new information to the discussion. We report 10 important results from analyses of the influence of friends across the middle and high school grades on students' academic and nonacademic outcomes:

1. Low- or high-scoring students with initially high-scoring friends have higher scores 1 year later than similar students with initially low-scoring friends.
2. For students with initially low scores, the effect of high-scoring friends on improved students' scores is strongest for achievement test scores and for college plans, for males and for females, in most middle and high school grades.
3. In high-participatory schools, students' self-reliance scores are influenced by having initially high self-reliant friends.
4. Students low in self-reliance who have high self-reliant friends perceive rewards for self-reliance more clearly in high-participatory schools.
5. Students low in achievement and self-reliance improve their scores on the measures if their high-scoring friends reciprocate their friendship choice and if those friendships are stable for at least 1 year.
6. High-scoring unreciprocated friends can be about as influential as reciprocated or stable friends for males and females on most outcomes. A pattern of increased influence of high-scoring reciprocated and stable friends is more prominent for males than for females. Future research can show whether these patterns have more to do with the nature of the measure of best friends or with reciprocated or unreciprocated friendships.
7. Students who pick no friends are at some disadvantage in making positive changes in their scores, especially when compared to students who select high-scoring friends.
8. Early friends show significant, continued influence on many outcomes across several grade levels, even after students' current friends are taken into account.

9. Peers and family influences differ across outcomes, with family SES most important for college plans and peer influence prominent on other measures.
10. Though evidence of measurable influence of high-scoring friends on student outcomes is apparent, the gap in scores between initially low-scoring students and high-scoring students is substantial. It will require more than peer influence, encouragement, modeling, or any other peer influence process to close the gap in scores of students who start out low and high on academic and social behaviors. Schools and families have responsibilities to provide educational programs to improve students' scores on important outcomes.

Positive Influence of Friends

The results of the analyses of the influence of differently structured friendship groups suggest that students with initially low or initially high scores on varied outcomes can be influenced in positive ways by friends who have high scores on the same academic or nonacademic outcomes. The influence of friends is the result of a dynamic process of selection, interaction, influence, and reselection that produces increasingly similar friends. Blau (1974) suggests that individuals move toward homophily, and J. Cohen (1977) found evidence of the same process. Boys' new friendship groups were more similar than old groups on 10 of 14 measures, and girls new groups were more similar on 8 of 14 measures. It may be that, as a student's personality and self-knowledge become better defined, new friends are selected and old friends are kept who are most like the selector on some important behaviors. Cohen's discussion of the link between selection and influence in Chapter 10 of this volume is supported by the patterns of results in this chapter.

The results show that the adolescent peer group is not necessarily a force antagonistic to the school's goals of achievement and academic success. Keeves (1972) reports that Australian elementary students are influenced by their friends in attitudes toward math and science, even after initial attitudes and achievements and family influences are taken into account. We see strong evidence that students both low *and* high in achievement are positively and cumulatively influenced on achievement by high-achieving friends, even when stringent controls are placed on students' own initial scores. The selection of "good influencers" appears to have some academic payoff. Duck, Miell, and Gaebler (1980) suggest that educators give attention to the patterns of social interaction in classrooms and how they relate to achievement. The results reported here extend their suggestion because there are many outcomes, including academic and social behaviors, that can be influenced by the way peer groups and friendship groups are organized in schools and classrooms.

The data did not permit detailed specification of the mechanisms that determine influence. We assume that modeling or emulation of attitudes and behavior takes place, but we also believe that best friends define and communicate expectations for each other's behavior and compare themselves to one another and to other groups (Kelley, 1952; Woelfel & Haller, 1971). Mead (1934) attributes influence to interaction with and signals from significant others. These may be direct or indirect signals. In direct communications, friends who are high scorers may define particularly important behaviors. In indirect communications, students may model their own behavior on a friend's, even if the friend does not reciprocate the choice. Informational exchange, social reinforcement, observational learning, and social expectations all may operate in school settings to influence behavior.

Miller (Chapter 12) and Hallinan (Chapter 13) discuss the need for information and trust or acceptance of friends as basic features of the peer influence process. Research is needed on the process of gathering and using information. It may be that normative influence applies more often among reciprocated friends because the sanctions on behaviors are direct; comparative influence may apply more often under unreciprocated conditions because the sanctions on behaviors are indirect or internal, and the influencer is more distant from the individual. With more detailed longitudinal sociometric and behavioral measures, one could study the processes that underlie the patterns of influence noted in this study.

Using Longitudinal Data

We have assumed here that a measure at Time 1 represents a starting point for charting the influence of friends on each other. However, students' friendships do not originate with the arbitrary Time 1 measurement. Rather, the friendship group at Time 1 reflects even earlier processes of interaction and selection, and incorporates the knowledge gained about people before they are selected as best friends. If we take seriously the links between selection and influence, the *selection* process at any one point in time is, in part, a result of the selection *and* influence processes up to that point in time. There is no question that studies of influence require longitudinal data to provide information on the initial qualities and scores of students and of their friends. Other longitudinal data on concurrent and earlier experiences in school, family, and other socializing environments that influence particular outcomes are also necessary. Substantively, new studies of influence must be linked to facts about selection.

Empirical studies of influence have been few because of the absence of detailed, longitudinal data needed to document influence. However, longitudinal data do not always help researchers clarify when an effect is influence. For example, in a dyad or a group, the *maintenance* of commonly held attitudes and goals may be an example of the groups' stabilizing influence on the behavior of all its members (see, for example, Feldman & Weiler's, 1976, discussion of accentuation and retention). The continuation of previously similar behavior is an effect of group interaction and a form of influence. After behavior that was different among group members becomes similar, maintenance takes over as the process of group influence for particular behaviors. We saw in our data on students' college plans that there is a time between Grade 9 and Grade 12—probably in Grade 11—when maintenance is clearer for students who previously had college plans and change is clearer for students who previously had no plans to attend college.

It is only with longitudinal data that research can begin to understand the process of maintenance and change, when particular behaviors become important to students, when students are open to influence, or when they resist change in order to maintain attitudes or behaviors. For example, it will be important to identify developmental patterns of change and maintenance in various attitudes and behaviors that become increasingly important to adolescents—smoking, drug and alcohol use, dating, dress styles, study habits, and occupational interests.

Bain and Anderson (1974) suggest that students who have strong desires to fit in a group will change behavior more readily. Those who are comfortable in a group may try to maintain many behaviors. Schmuck (1970) notes how the climate of settings is part of the influence process, as it defines the preferred behaviors of those who share the environment. We saw in our data that students whose friends were self-reliant in a school environment that promotes self-reliance were apt to become more self-reliant 1 year later and were more likely to recognize the school's rewards for self-reliant behavior.

The longitudinal analyses in this chapter show that selection and influence are linked. The selection of friends defines the nature and extent of influence that is likely to occur; continued selection determines how patterns of influence persist; and new selections establish new potentials for influence. The findings provide only a lean understanding of the important connections among selection, influence, developmental processes, and environmental factors.

NORMAN MILLER 12

Peer Relations in Desegregated Schools

Though advocates differ in the number and specificity of goals for school desegregation, most people who are directly concerned with school desegregation cite improved academic performance and increased interracial acceptance as important concerns. Academic performance is the most salient outcome variable, perhaps because it has been studied most frequently, because it appears to be most directly related to the manifest function of schools, or because the courts (*Crawford* v. *Board of Education of the City of Los Angeles*, 130 Cal. Rptr. 724, 1976) have viewed it as instrumental to minority social mobility.

THEORETICAL ACCOUNTS OF ACADEMIC IMPROVEMENT

The Social Science Statement appended to the plaintiff's case in the 1954 Brown decision (*Brown* v. *Board of Education* 347 U.S. 483, 495, 1954) provided the beginnings of a conceptual model of the interrelation among theoretical variables relevant to desegregation goals. The goals of reducing prejudice and improving academic performance are prominent; however, the notion of an impaired self-concept among minority children seemed most central, not only as an impetus for pursuing school desegregation, but also as a variable affecting the outcome of schooling. A segregated society and segregated schooling, with their implicit rejection of blacks as a social group, were thought to undermine the development of

201

FRIENDS IN SCHOOL
Patterns of Selection and Influence in Secondary Schools

positive self-attitudes of blacks. In the model developed in the Social Science Statement, this self-doubt and lack of confidence lowered the minority child's expectations and resulted in poorer academic performance. This, in turn, impaired motivation and added to a feeling of defeatism. Hostility and prejudice of whites were seen as further exacerbating these effects. Thus, as Stephan (1978) points out, in its broad conceptualization the model is circular; one can start with any of the major variables in it and proceed in a circular, causal path.

When one turns to examine in detail the theory of how school desegregation might improve academic performance, the gaps in the model become apparent. Some parts of the Social Science Statement relied on analogy. Klineberg (1935) concluded many years ago that the IQ scores of blacks who moved from southern (segregated) to northern (unsegregated) states improved as a function of the length of time they resided in the north. He argued, also, that these differences were not attributable to the selective migration of brighter blacks to northern states. By analogy then, the Social Science Statement assumed that shifting black children from segregated to desegregated schools would produce commensurate gains in academic achievement. Unfortunately, such analogizing provides little insight into the processes underlying the expected improvement.

Other parts of the document suggest a motivational explanation of academic achievement gains. Rejection and hostility from whites, hostility on the part of blacks toward whites, low expectations for success, and low aspirations were seen as impairing the minority child's attention to and pursuit of behaviors instrumental to high academic achievement.

The belief that black children have impaired self-concepts, though pivotal to the theory in the Social Science Statement, has not been confirmed in the latest reviews of empirical work (Epps, 1975; Porter & Washington, 1979; St. John, 1975; Stephan, 1978; Wylie, 1979). In fact, black self-esteem usually exceeds that of whites. There are several explanations for this disconfirmation. First, the notion of impaired self-concepts rested largely on projective data, and in particular on Clark's doll-choice study, in which children were shown black and white dolls and asked which one "do you like," "is nice," or "is most like you" (Clark & Clark, 1939). A preference for the white doll was interpreted as rejection of black people and, ergo, rejection of self when the child being tested was black. The assumptions that underlie studies using these procedures, as well as the interpretation of their outcomes, have been seriously questioned (Brand, Ruiz, & Padilla, 1974; Stephan & Rosenfield, 1979). For instance, children may simply reject toys that seem unfamiliar or peculiar; until quite recently, black dolls were not commercially available. A summary of the now voluminous doll-choice literature shows that the choices of black children do not depart from chance (Banks, 1976), suggesting no significant differences in their preferences for either black or white dolls.

On the other hand, the recent data on which the reviews of black self-esteem are based are mostly paper-and-pencil self-reports. Is the fact that black self-esteem typically exceeds that of whites merely the product of self-defensive or self-presentational motivation? Perhaps, but Shrauger and Osberg (1981) argue that the validity of self-report personality assessments stands high among assessment alternatives. Nevertheless, some researchers believe that living in a racist culture inevitably has consequences for the personalities of out-group members (Cook, 1979; Miller, 1979). Consequently, it may make sense conceptually to separate minority children's self-esteem from their concept of how the dominant group appraises their racial–ethnic subgroup.

At any rate, taken at face value, current research argues against the view that impaired self-concepts among minority children need attention (and can be remedied by school desegregation). However, this does not invalidate the psychological processes underlying the theoretical model implicit in the Social Science Statement. If research shows any effect of desegregated schools on black self-esteem, it is that self-esteem is lower *after* desegregation (Porter & Washington, 1979; St. John, 1975). When coupled with the common finding of racial–ethnic resegregation within desegregated schools after implementation of desegregation programs, a decrease in the self-esteem of minority children can be interpreted as a consequence of social rejection. Lowered self-esteem may interfere with academic motivation and mastery. This process is compatible with the dynamics implicit in the model developed in the Social Science Statement. The emphasis here is on the debilitating effects of social rejection and not on the opposing process whereby academic performance is improved.

I. Katz (1964) also emphasized the role of social threat as an inhibitor of performance in his review of evidence related to the intellectual performance of blacks. However, he spells out how an opposing process might operate. Building on the notions that (*a*) people respond to the standards of those with whom they desire to associate; (*b*) achievement standards tend to be higher in (formerly) segregated white schools than in segregated minority schools; and (*c*) black children desire the friendship of white age-mates, he concluded that they should adopt the scholastic norms of the high status majority group. In support of this expectation, he cites a study by Dittes and Kelley (1956) in which private and public adherence to group norms were highest among those who experienced a fairly high degree of acceptance from the group and could anticipate further acceptance. Little adherence to group norms was found among those who experienced little acceptance.

Throughout the 1960s, these ideas formed a widely accepted model of how school desegregation might benefit minority children—namely, the lateral transmission of values model. The scholastic performance of white children, which exceeds that found in general among blacks, presumably reflects greater acceptance or internalization of scholastic achievement norms. Such internalization on the part of any single child cannot, of course, establish a classroom climate that promotes academic excellence as a standard or norm. Thus, among the basic assumptions of this model is the notion that white children must be numerically preponderant in the classroom. If not, there is little reason to expect principles of normative influence to apply in a beneficial way.

Findings from the Coleman report (J. S. Coleman, Campbell, Hobson, McPartland, Mood, Weinfeld and York, 1966) and the U.S. Commission on Civil Rights (1967) were interpreted as supporting this basic model. In particular, Coleman *et al.* found that black children who attended classes that contained more than 50% white children scored higher on achievement tests than did their counterparts in predominantly black classes. Similarly, in the report of the U.S. Commission on Civil Rights (1967), high school blacks in classes that were more than half white scored higher on verbal achievement.

If both the characteristics of the white peers of minority children and their interpersonal relations with them are important influences on minority achievement, any of several underlying processes might be responsible. One process stresses the consequences of long-term exposure to normative influence. Eventually, such exposure could result in modification of the personality of the minority child. In this view, those characteristics of the minority child's personality that are related to achievement motivation, as broadly conceived, are changed as a result of attending a desegregated school. This might include such specific aspects of personality as tolerance for deferred gratification, level of aspiration, field independence, and internal locus of control. Changes in character or personality gradually occur in response to the stronger achievement orientation of the middle-class white children who, because of their numerical preponderance, create a normative climate in which these personality structures as well as high academic achievement are modal. Only after these personality changes occur, however, can one expect to see improvement in minority academic performance. Thus, in this view, changes in certain aspects of personality are important antecedents of academic competence.

Coleman *et al.* (1966) and Crain and Weisman (1972) found that black children who attended desegregated schools had a more internal orientation than those who attended segregated schools. (A sense of internal control refers to the belief that one marches to the beat of one's own drum as opposed to seeing oneself as a mere leaf being tossed by the fickle wind of fate.) Self-selection, however, provides an equally plausible explanation of their results. Furthermore, in Crain and Weisman's data, the personality traits that presumably underlie high academic performance were found only among those blacks who had attended desegregated elementary schools, yet this group did not show academic superiority. In contrast, stronger academic performance was found among those blacks who had attended desegregated high schools (and segregated elementary schools), yet this group lacked the requisite personality traits. Nevertheless, both studies were interpreted as supporting a personality mediational version of the normative influence or lateral transmission of values model.

Another version of normative influence parallels this model but does not require personality change as an antecedent to improved academic performance. Instead, majority influence might operate directly by making clear to the minority students that certain behaviors are important, valued, and appropriate. In this case, whether or not sustained modification of achievement behavior eventually results in changes in personality is irrelevant. Thus, whereas the first version views personality change as causally prior to improved scholastic behavior, the second does not.

D. Campbell (1961), M. Deutsch and Gerard (1955), and Kelley (1952) all noted some time ago that social groups provide information not only on what is important but also on how to achieve it. The students in each of two sixth-grade classrooms at different schools may believe it is important to score highly on math tests, but they may differ dramatically in the means by which they achieve high math scores. In one class, youngsters might individually master the material by studying independently or in study groups after school. In the other class, the children might develop elaborate procedures for covertly passing answers during tests from the smartest three or four students to others throughout the class. This example distinguishes sharply between a widely accepted norm—namely, obtaining good grades—and the means used to achieve it. Thus, it distinguishes between *normative influence*—information on appropriate or valued behavior—and *informational influence* (or *locomotion influence*)—information about how to achieve the goal. Although a conceptual distinction can be drawn between these two processes, they do not operate independently. Typically, groups provide information *and* induce conformity to expected values and behaviors.

The social influence processes discussed here depend on peer acceptance of minority children by the numerically dominant white majority. Without evidence of acceptance from white students, it is unlikely that black students will seek acceptance from them. If mutual acceptance does not occur, there is little reason to expect successful normative influence to occur.

EMPIRICAL TESTS

Gerard and Miller (1975) collected data in Riverside, California, to test the personality modification version of the lateral transmission of values hypothesis. Approximately 1800 children were premeasured prior to the closing of ghetto schools and the implementation of a busing program. They were then tracked with post measures that were administered yearly over the next 5 years. The assessments included personality, social acceptance, and academic achievement measures.

These data showed that peer popularity has many important correlates. Westman and Miller (1978) provide a striking illustration of this point. Two oppositely extreme subsamples based on sociometric popularity and unpopularity were selected from each of three racial–ethnic groups—white, black, and Mexican-American. Sex ratios were balanced within each group. The sociometric data consisted of three choices made by each child for seating partner (friendship), schoolwork partner, and playground teammate. The subsamples of 108 popular and 108 unpopular elementary school children were selected on the basis of the total number of nominations that each child received. Popularity within each dimension of sociometric choice was standardized within ethnic groups. In almost all cases, only those children who differed by more than one standard deviation from the mean of their ethnic group were selected for inclusion in the two subsamples.

A set of 19 dependent measures was arbitrarily subdivided into three broad categories: performance, situational, and personality indices. Data from measures administered both 1 and 3 years after implementation of the district-wide desegregation program was examined in the study. All scales were scored so that high scores reflected positive qualities.

Performance data included verbal achievement, classroom grades, and intelligence. Verbal achievement was assessed by several state-mandated tests. Classroom grades provided two indicators of performance, one for mathematical achievement and one for verbal ability (reading, writing, spelling, and composition). Intelligence was assessed by the Wechsler Intelligence Scale for Children, Raven's Progressive Matrices test, and the Peabody Picture Vocabulary test. Raven and Peabody scores were combined and restandardized. (See Gerard & Miller, 1975, for a detailed description of all variables.)

Situational measures consisted of evaluative ratings made by the students, teachers, interviewers, and parents on a series of bipolar scales. Teachers' ratings were based on a set of 13 personality-trait adjectives that represented intellectual competence and motivation as revealed by factor analysis of a larger item pool. These were good memory, quick, intelligent, able to communicate, persevering, interesting, curious, self-confident, deep, organized, independent, strong willed, and formed.

The interviewers' ratings consisted of a subset of five scales from a larger collection adapted from Meyers *et al.* (1964). Ratings were obtained twice during each year of data collection and were combined to form a single summary score for a particular year. Cooperation with the examiner, interest in tasks, effort displayed, attention, and lovability were the favorable endpoint labels.

Parental ratings were furnished by either both parents jointly (post measure in year 1) or by the mother alone (post measure in year 3). Anderson's (1968) adjective checklist identified the favorable pole for most scales. Those for the first post measure were: healthy, not fearful, sociable, not demanding, quick, obedient, not prone to anger, strong willed, helping, not difficult to discipline, self-confident, relaxed, independent, quiet, likes school, not prone to tantrums, patient, happy-go-lucky, energetic, bold, assertive, extrovert, and persevering. In year 3, the following items were added: good natured, cheerful, responsible, not jealous, and trusting.

Self-report and behavioral indices of general personality traits, field dependence, and achievement motivation were included in the group labeled as personality measures. The general personality measures were selected from various standard tests, such as those of Cattell (1965), A. L. Edwards (1953), and Sarason, Davidson, Lighthall, Waite, and Ruebush (1960). Each of these five paper-and-pencil measures was composed of 15 items. Two scales tapped anxiety (general and school related), two assessed self-worth or esteem (other's attitudes toward the self and self-attitudes), and one assessed a need for school achievement.

Field independence or psychological differentiation represents the tendency to perceive one's environment in an analytic as opposed to a more global, passive manner. The measure of field dependence was the "man and frame test," a variant of Witkin, Lewis, Machover, Meisner, and Wagner's (1954) "rod and frame" instrument. In this task, the subject peered into a wooden box in which the silhouette of a man surrounded by a square frame appeared. The angular tilt of each was independently varied from the rear by the examiner. The subject was instructed to align the man with the true vertical, disregarding the position of the frame. Three blocks of four trials, each with different initial settings of the man and frame and with the subject's chair in an upright position or tilted to the left or to the right, yielded a summary score of total errors toward the frame.

Several personality measures theoretically related to achievement motivation were examined: level of aspiration, goal-setting behavior, delay of gratification, and internal–external control. Level of aspiration was determined by a ringtoss task patterned after McClelland, Atkinson, Clark, and Lowell (1953). Scoring was derived from the subject's estimation of success on 9 tosses across each of 11 trials.

The realism of the subject's goal-setting behavior on the ringtoss game was determined in two ways. The first involved absolute goal discrepancies—discrepancies between the subject's expectations of success on any given trial and his or her actual performance on the preceding trial. The second index was the number of unusual shifts made—increased expectations after failure or decreased expectations following successful performance. Summary scores were computed for each measure.

The measure for voluntary delay of gratification was adapted from Mischel (1958) and required the subject to respond to a series of hypothetical choices between a small, immediate reward and a larger but deferred outcome.

Two measures assessed internal–external control of beliefs. The first was a modification of the Intellectual Achievement Responsibility (IAR) scale (Crandall, Kathkovsky, & Preston, 1962), on which the subject attributes a series of negative outcomes to either him- or herself or to some external factor. Half of the internal responses referred to a lack of ability, the others to a lack of effort. The second locus of control index was composed of eight items derived from Bialer's (1961) Fate Control Scale.

One question we can raise with these data is how children's characteristics are related to their acceptance or rejection as friends. The results depicted in Figure 12.1 for seating choice subsamples are characteristic of those found with the other popularity criteria. The figure is organized with measures of achievement and personality characteristics arrayed horizontally. Their identification and the level of significance for popularity main effects and interactions are indicated at the bottom of the diagram. Mean scores for each measure for the high- and low-

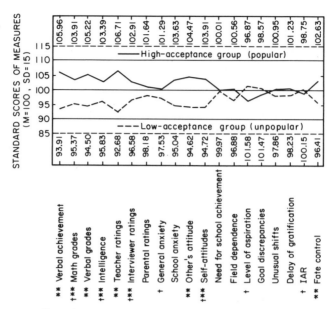

FIGURE 12.1. Profiles of popular and unpopular elementary school students. Profiles are based on the tri-ethnic subsamples of students identified as popular or unpopular seating partners. Profiles for popular or unpopular work partners or teammates were almost identical to the one shown here. (*$p < .05$ main effect for popularity; **$p < .01$ main effect for popularity; †$p < .05$ interaction including popularity.)

acceptance groups, expressed in standard-score form, are presented in the upper and lower portions of the figure, respectively, and plotted graphically in the center. The vertical axis represents the favorability of the scores, increasing as the scores increase. The overall profile for the popular children shows higher scores than the profile for the unpopular children on most measures. The divergence between profiles is most pronounced among the performance measures for verbal scores, among situational measures for teacher ratings, and among the personality measures for anxiety, two measures of self-esteem, and fate control. These associations are striking. They show how popular and unpopular children differ in achievement and personality characteristics.

Other analyses conducted to test the lateral transmission of values model were disappointing. An extensive and varied array of analyses show that changes in personality or lack of such changes do not causally account for or mediate the academic gains or losses of minority children. Indeed, there were few personality changes of any substance to discuss (Miller, 1975).

The data were analyzed using Joreskog's (1973) procedures for developing and evaluating causal models with structural equations. In both cross-sectional and longitudinal analyses, personality variables do not independently affect the academic performance of children attending desegregated schools. In longitudinal analyses, the data raise questions about the second version of the normative influence model—namely, the notion that social acceptance by white peers functions directly to mediate educational gains. The direction of effects in our own data is opposite to that posited by the lateral transmission of values model. Although we find white peer acceptance to be related to the academic performance of minority children, it is a consequence and not an antecedent of their academic performance (Maruyama & Miller, 1982; McGarvey, 1977).

These outcomes led us to reexamine the single other published study that provides strong support for the lateral transmission of values model—namely, R. Lewis and St. John's (1974) path analysis of longitudinal data. Although the Coleman *et al.* data and the U.S. Commission on Civil Rights report a relation between peer acceptance and black academic performance, their data are cross-sectional and cannot be used to identify cause and effect. In our reanalysis of Lewis and St. John (Maruyama & Miller, 1979), we applied Joreskog's (1973) LISREL procedures, which use maximum likelihood estimators instead of the more typical least squares techniques used by Lewis and St. John in their report. They concluded that "the social process that best explains the beneficial effect of acceptance by white peers on black achievement is probably the lateral transmission of achievement-oriented norms and/or skills [p. 89]." Our reanalysis, with more rigorous analytic techniques, contradicted this interpretation. We found that the causal effect of peer popularity on report card grades as well as reading achievement was nonsignificant, and, in confirmation of our own Riverside data, the popularity or acceptance of black children was *caused by* their level of scholastic achievement.

For a dominant group to exert normative influence upon a minority child, that child must want to belong to or feel accepted by the dominant group. If not, there is little reason to accept their standards. In the studies reviewed in the preceding discussion, a minority child's acceptance was operationally defined as sociometric popularity among whites. One might question whether such sociometric measures are valid. However, in other studies we have examined the link between such sociometric choices and actual cross-racial interaction patterns assessed by observers in the classroom and on the playground and have confirmed the validity of defining social acceptance with sociometric measures (Rogers & Miller, 1980).

There is one other possibility, however. One could argue that acceptance from white children is not the critical factor. Instead, what matters is simply whether the minority child *wants* to be accepted. According to this line of thought, all that is necessary for the normative influence processes described previously to operate is that the minority child be motivated to be accepted. Indeed, many years ago, in discussing self-hatred among the Jews, Lewin (1948) pointed out that socially rejected out-groups often adopt or internalize the attitude and values of the dominant group even though they are rejected by them. This suggests an alternate operationalization in which sociometric data are tabulated to reflect the extent of a minority child's *choice of* white children as work or play partners, rather than the extent to which the minority child is *chosen by* white children. We are currently testing the effects with this alternate operationalization.

In summary, then, we conclude that there is little empirical support for explaining gains in academic achievement by minority children using normative influence processes.

TEACHER EFFECTS

Another aspect of social acceptance rests not on peers but on teachers and other authority figures. Our data from Riverside confirmed the important role that the teacher plays in moderating desegregation outcomes. Although minority children showed no overall academic gains after desegregation, this general outcome masks two distinct processes occurring in different classrooms. Minority children in the classrooms of biased teachers showed academic deterioration on state-administered achievement tests, whereas their counterparts in the classes of unbiased teachers showed academic gains after desegregation.

Fraser (1980) identified the difference in the behaviors of these two types of teachers. Unprejudiced teachers in desegregated classrooms provide more opportunities for positive interaction between white and minority children by making more use of aspects of minority culture in the classroom, by giving minority students more specific duties, by structuring more contact with white students (e.g., via seating plans), by using class discussion to foster cross-racial interaction, and by providing with their own behavior a positive example of interaction with minority children.

The two types of teachers also differ in their attitudes and beliefs. Those low in discrimination tend not to believe in a single performance standard for all children, and thus they provide more opportunity for successful experiences in learning for all children. In many ways, unprejudiced teachers seem to correspond to the type of teacher that Brophy (1979) identifies as effective in low socioeconomic settings—namely teachers who work to get the most out of students, and who are warm and encouraging rather than businesslike and demanding. In contrast, the prejudiced teachers run fairly rigid classrooms and indicate having made few changes in order to accommodate to desegregation. Their classrooms have a more rigorous, businesslike atmosphere that is focused on academic rather than social or emotional objectives. It is teacher dominated and highly structured, with fewer opportunities for student interactions, cross-racial or otherwise.

It seems likely that the differences between these two types of teachers produce effects not only on the academic performance of the minority children in their classes but also on the amount and quality of cross-racial interaction among students. The classroom behaviors of the unprejudiced teacher appear to correspond to the warm, accepting, and supportive environment that has been identified as a meaningful predictor of cross-racial association (R. Lewis & St. John, 1974; Serow & Solomon, 1979) and positive relations between white and minority classmates (Patchen, Davidson, Hoffman, & Brown, 1977). In our data, too, we find that these two types of teachers produce different patterns of cross-racial social interaction. White children in the classes of unprejudiced teachers were more likely to nominate minority children for their friendship choices than were those in the classes of prejudiced teachers (Gerard, Jackson, & Conolley, 1975). One might argue that these same basic differences in the academic outcomes produced by prejudiced and unprejudiced teachers would befall the minority child whether the classrooms were desegregated or segregated. However, the differences are theoretically important because they emphasize the importance of social threat rather than academic achievement norms as the more critical variable in the desegregated classrooms. In retrospect, it is rather curious that, though Katz had provided important experimental evidence in his own research on the debilitating effects of social threat on intellectual functioning, he seemed to place equal if not greater emphasis on the role of normative influence processes, despite the fact that his own research did not directly evaluate them.

One last piece of evidence, however, adds further confirmation to Katz's laboratory work. As one might anticipate, it is upsetting for a child to leave a familiar school environment where social relations with peers have become well established. Members of one's own racial–ethnic group can provide a network of social support. In Riverside, because of the relatively small percentages of minority children, it was sometimes the case that a desegregated child would find no other members of his or her own racial–ethnic group in the classroom. Rogers and Miller (1980) show that the absence of a social support group consisting of other children of one's own racial–ethnic background is indeed threatening and detrimental to adjustment and academic performance.

EFFECTS OF SCHOOL SETTINGS ON CROSS-RACIAL INTERACTION

In the preceding discussion of the role of peer relations in influencing academic outcomes of minority children in desegregated settings, the conceptual emphasis was correlational. Are acceptance measures taken at Time 1 (immediately after desegregation) positively correlated with scholastic achievement at Time 2, or instead, is scholastic achievement at Time 1 correlated with subsequent popularity? Having argued that empirical data thus far supports only the latter process, we now turn to intergroup relations as a goal in its own right rather than viewing it as a determinant of achievement. Thus, we shift from correlational analyses to the examination of intergroup acceptance at various points in time following desegregation.

Earlier research showed that, although children were relatively accepting toward those belonging to other racial–ethnic groups at the outset, racial–ethnic encapsulation increased in successive years following desegregation (Gerard & Miller, 1975). More recently, in observational studies of classes in desegregated

Los Angeles schools, we have confirmed the finding of resegregation within class-rooms following implementation of a desegregation program (Rogers & Miller, 1980, 1981).

Direct observations of the interactions of sixth-grade children on the play-ground and in the classroom (during unstructured activities) were coded by a triracial team of five observers into 13 categories of prosocial and antagonistic behaviors. Interobserver agreement of observations made 5 days a week over an 8-week period ranged from .69 to .93, with a mean of .76.

The results show that the setting influenced the quality and quantity of inter-racial behavior in three of the four groups. As shown in Figure 12.2, white girls exhibited extreme racial encapsulation in both settings. In contrast, black girls sought out whites as targets for their antagonism, but only during recess. White boys directed more of their prosocial behavior toward black boys during recess, whereas in the classroom, they directed it primarily toward other white boys. Black boys directed more of their prosocial behavior toward white boys in the classroom than on the playground. In general, and particularly among girls, we found evidence of strong racial–ethnic cleavage. Failure to establish the condi-tions necessary for equal-status contact is often given as the reason for failure to find cross-racial acceptance. In one of these studies, however, most of the minor-ity children in the class were intellectually gifted. Thus, the intellectual dif-ferences that some would argue ordinarily preclude the possibility of equal-status contact between black and white children (and thereby undermine any possibility of cross-racial acceptance) were not a relevant factor.

In a study of another desegregated school setting conducive to equal-status contact, Schofield (1981) reports results in the classroom that are similar to our own. E. G. Cohen (1980a) also reports strong effects of ethnic encapsulation. What accounts for the sex differences in cross-racial acceptance that we and others find? One explanation is that the characteristics of male and female friend-ship networks differ at this age. Boys tend to interact in larger social units and display a greater propensity to accept newcomers than do girls (Hallinan, 1980). Alternatively, as suggested by Schofield (1981), greater racial encapsulation of

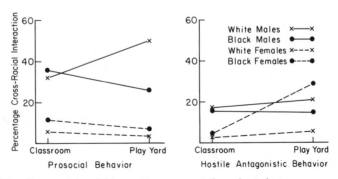

FIGURE 12.2. Cross-racial social interaction among sixth-grade students.

girls may be due to differences in the kinds of attributes that girls and boys value most at this age. Girls may be particularly concerned with physical attractiveness, whereas boys may focus on success at sports. If so, we would expect girls to make a significant number of cross-racial comparisons on attributes having to do with beauty, whereas boys would make comparisons on athletic characteristics.

For boys, these comparisons are not likely to lead to a perception of white superiority. Even accounting for the typical ethnocentric biases in evaluation (Hinkle & Schopler, 1979), the average differences between white and black males on these consensually valued attributes are such that the whites are unlikely to be perceived as superior.

For girls, however, if the standards of beauty are those associated with white features and skin color, comparisons on physical attractiveness could contribute to perceptions of white superiority, especially among the white girls. In our own work (Maruyama & Miller, 1981), we confirmed that physical attractiveness does not benefit black schoolchildren the way it seems to benefit white children.

The sex differences in cross-racial interaction occur most strongly outside the classroom. Boys, especially white boys, engage in more cross-racial interaction at recess than in the classroom; girls engage in very little cross-racial interaction in either setting. At recess, girls participate in physical games to a lesser extent than do boys, and the games they do play (e.g., jump rope, hopscotch, tetherball) generally require interaction with only one or two other children. The games boys play at recess (e.g., basketball, softball) generally require more participants on a team than the number of same-race classmates available. Thus, black and white boys need each other to form complete teams.

Another important difference between the games boys and girls typically play at recess has to do with the goal structure of the games. Boys' team sports have mixed reward structures in which cooperation is one important ingredient (Slavin, 1978). In a game of basketball or softball, each team member is expected to contribute his best effort to achieve a goal shared by all team members. Given the typical within-race individual differences in athletic skill and the fact that distributions of athletic ability overlap, when teams are chosen they are normally mixed in their racial composition. Thus, in accord with the analysis of Sherif, Harvey, White, Hood, and Sherif (1961), which argues that teammates should become more attracted toward one another across time, cross-racial social acceptance will also increase. And because different teams are chosen at each new occasion, the cooperative experience with cross-race peers becomes broad and general rather than being confined to specific others, thereby promoting a more generalized cross-racial acceptance (Slavin & Madden, 1979).

These observations of sex differences in racial encapsulation and in playground activities, along with other considerations, led us to develop a cooperative games intervention for girls, which has been evaluated and shown to be successful (e.g., Rogers, Miller, & Hennigan, 1981). In its approach to the problem of how to improve intergroup acceptance within the desegregated school, it parallels the procedures and tasks of numerous other interventions that employ cooperative goal structures (e.g., Aronson, 1978; Cook, 1979; DeVries & Edwards, 1973; D. W. Johnson & R. T. Johnson, 1981; Sharon & Hertz-Lazarowitz, 1980; Slavin, 1978).

The sex differences in cross-racial acceptance that we and others find are particularly interesting because they add new information to the normative influence processes discussed earlier. Despite the fact that children attend school in order to develop their cognitive abilities and master particular curricular skills, norms about these aspects of schooling may be less salient to them than other norms for social behaviors, such as those outside the classroom that are concerned with beauty or sports.

COOPERATIVE LEARNING STRATEGIES AND
PEER ACCEPTANCE AND INFLUENCE

Although many researchers believe that cooperative activity is important in the desegregated setting and that it promotes intergroup acceptance, they have not systematically determined the variables that account for its effectiveness. Furthermore, many of the specific procedures developed to structure cooperation into the daily school program (e.g., Aronson, 1978; DeVries & Edwards, 1973; D. W. Johnson & R. T. Johnson, 1981; Sharon & Hertz-Lazarowitz, 1980; Slavin, 1978) contain elements that may interfere with the development of cross-racial acceptance, despite the fact that the advocates of such procedures specifically cite increased intergroup acceptance as a by-product, if not the manifest goal achieved by their use. In addition, many cooperative procedures fail to change the features in desegregated school settings that work against the goal of improving intergroup acceptance.

Some explicit examples will make these contentions clearer. For instance, DeVries and Edwards (1973) (in the Teams-Games-Tournament procedure) and Slavin (1978) (in the Student Teams–Achievement Divisions procedure) use a mixed model of cooperation that combines within-group cooperation with between-group competition. In a meta analysis that compares cooperative to mixed-goal structures (namely, the cooperative–competitive described above) as well as to pure competitive and individualistic goal structures (D. W. Johnson, Johnson, & Maruyama, 1982), the cooperative structures produced greater cross-racial attraction than mixed-goal structures.

Another characteristic that seems relevant is the extent to which the teacher, in classroom actions, explicitly responds to race or ethnicity as a characteristic that guides her own behavior. In the classroom implementation of most cooperative learning procedures, the teacher explicitly uses race or ethnicity (as well as sex) as the basis for assigning children to the work groups. It is hard to imagine that the children are unaware of this criterion for assignment to teams. In this sense, the teacher emphasizes these social category distinctions to the children; they are presented (albeit inadvertently) by a powerful model as important cues for guiding action. Thus, it is possible that social category boundaries, which are known to function as barriers to interpersonal acceptance (e.g., Wilder, 1976), are being strengthened by the implementation procedure used to create cooperative interaction. Ideally, the situation should be structured so that students' feel that team membership is due to the students' unique personal attributes (thereby individuating the in-group and out-group members), rather than the result of category-based assignment (sex, ethnicity, or skin color), which may function to deindividuate the students.

Another aspect of typical implementation procedures is the absence of choice or the perception of choice. Typically, the teacher assigns children to teams. Postchoice justification processes are among the strongest of all findings in social psychology. Ideally, procedures of team formation should enable students to choose or to contribute to the choice of team members, so the team is a result of mutual choice rather than teacher assignment. The principle of choice can be extended to the cooperative activity as well. Thus, the improvement in cross-race or cross-ethnic social acceptance produced by cooperative task activity should be further enhanced to the extent that the children see the cooperative learning procedure as one they have selected themselves rather than as one externally imposed on them by the teacher.

A functional analysis of *why* cooperation leads to greater interracial or interethnic acceptance is also needed. A cooperative task or reward structure may induce more self-disclosure between participants, more physical proximity or contact, more affectively positive exchanges, and a greater opportunity to note differences between self and others and to observe that those differences contribute positively to a common goal. It may be that the most critical feature of the cooperative task and reward interventions is the extent to which cooperation enables participants to individuate one another and thereby ignore, if not destroy (or loosen), other beliefs or stereotypes about out-group members.

If mutual self-disclosure is increased by structured cooperative interaction, its benefits may rest simultaneously upon two distinct processes. People may like others better after having self-disclosed to them (a justification effect: "I've given this person something valuable. He must deserve it."), and they may like those who self-disclose to them (a reinforcement effect: "This person has just given me something unique. He must like me."). Balance theory can, of course, also be applied to explain the manner in which self-disclosure functions to promote liking. We lack concrete data on whether cooperatively structured interactions increase cross-ethnic self-disclosure above the level normally found between children at any particular age level.

The question of which among these variables is most critical for the generalization of increased interethnic acceptance of out-group members in settings other than the classroom team has not been addressed. Nor has the issue of which plays a more critical role in maintaining out-group rejection—informational cognitive schemas or precognitive perceptual–emotional schemas of the sort that Leventhal (1980) refers to.

Dependency and helping are other interactional features produced by structured cooperative interaction. The more powerful (popular, brighter) child brings more resources to the interaction and consequently is "needed by" his or her teammates. He or she also "needs" the other children who are on his or her team. Even the least powerful child is "needed by" the other children because of the structural characteristics of the cooperative learning procedures. Do these dependencies promote trust, or do they interfere with trust by becoming a cost in relationships? Perhaps more importantly, do the long-term effects differ when dependencies exist among members within the boundaries of a group-based identity (as in the case with TGT or Jigsaw) as opposed to when dependencies exist between individuals?

Brewer's (1981) analysis points to two reasons that trust develops in a group when students are dependent on each other. First, trust results when combined actions lead to group gain: "When self and others are included within a common boundary, or social unit, psychological distance is reduced; and this may have the effect of increasing orientations toward mutual and joint outcomes rather than individual gain [p. 356]." Second, trust results when group membership makes it possible to bring to bear sanctions by the group for violations of trust or reciprocity that an individual actor may not be able to impose. In other words, violations may be viewed as transgressions against group norms or goals and thereby be subject to group (as opposed to individual) sanctions. The resulting increase in cross-racial or cross-ethnic trust within the context of a new social category (e.g., the "fast spellers" team) as opposed to separate individuals (e.g., a black girl and a white girl) may be mediated by the lack of (or constraint on) power differences between the actors in the group context. As already suggested, power differences are diminished when the interaction occurs within the group context because the less powerful members can rely on a coalition of other less powerful members to exert control over the actions of the most (or more) powerful members who are seen as threatening group solidarity.

Although structured cooperative interaction increases cross-racial acceptance among the participants, relatively little is known about how or why it does so or what causes such acceptance to generalize to new out-group others. Future research on these issues will increase understanding of the processes underlying peer influence.

CONCLUSION

There are three major points in this chapter about peer and friendship relations in desegregated classrooms. First, in accounting for the scholastic development of minority children, the level of social threat that white children and teachers create in classrooms probably plays a more important role than do normative influence processes that are concerned with the transmission of academic achievement values.

Second, the goal of promoting cross-racial tolerance, respect, and acceptance cannot be achieved by benign or passive desegregation procedures. Merely creating the circumstances for cross-racial contact by putting students of different racial–ethnic backgrounds in the same classroom or on the same playground is not sufficient. If segregation is to be successful in improving intergroup relations, specific programs that are demonstrably effective must be interjected into the school setting. And as suggested by Slavin and Madden's (1979) analyses, in-service teacher training programs designed to increase teachers' sensitivity to interracial issues are probably not the most effective programs. Instead, programs should directly involve the children. Those that attempt to infuse cooperative goal structures into class and school activities (as opposed to competitive or individualistic goal structures) seem to hold the most promise.

Finally, analyses of the specific programs and procedures currently used to introduce cooperative interaction in classrooms suggest that they contain elements that may be counterproductive for breaking down stereotypes and social rejection of out-group members.

MAUREEN T. HALLINAN 13

Commentary:
New Directions for Research
on Peer Influence

Questions concerning the influence on students of friends and peers have long been of interest to sociologists and educators. Numerous empirical studies may be found in the literature on peer effects on students' norms, values, and attitudes, as well as on their academic achievement and educational aspirations and attainment. These studies include both case histories and surveys, and many have the attractive feature of being longitudinal in design. Indeed, the study of the peer influence process is one of the more extensive if not comprehensive areas of research on students in schools.

In considering a future agenda for research on peer effects, it is necessary first to summarize the already known theoretical and empirical information about peer influences. This task includes examining the empirical evidence related to peer effects, identifying the theoretical propositions that explain the results, and outlining questions that existing theory and research leave unanswered. The second task is to reconceptualize the peer influence process in order to explain empirical findings better and to pose new research questions. These tasks set the agenda for this chapter. The first section reviews selected studies on peer influences, summarizes empirical findings and theoretical explanations, and poses some unanswered questions. The second section develops a conceptualization of the peer influence process from which new hypotheses for future research can be generated.

219

FRIENDS IN SCHOOL
Patterns of Selection and Influence in Secondary Schools

SELECTED FINDINGS ON PEER INFLUENCES

Most research on peer effects falls into one of two categories: studies of the effects of context on student outcomes and studies of proximate influences on students by their peers. This distinction is not a rigorous one, because one of the mechanisms often posited to explain contextual influences is interpersonal interaction processes. Nevertheless, it is a useful distinction for summarizing the research on peer influence. A comprehensive review of the literature will not be attempted; rather, major findings in these two areas of peer effects research will be presented.

Contextual Influences

A large body of literature examines the effects of school context on student outcomes. Typically, school context is measured as racial or socioeconomic composition. These variables are generally related to student achievement and aspirations. Empirical support generally is found for the existence of contextual effects, although the magnitude of the effects is usually small.

Several studies report an effect of school racial composition on academic achievement. The research shows a small positive effect of percentage of whites in the school (D. Cohen, Pettigrew, & Riley, 1972, St. John & Smith, 1969) and in the class (McPartland, 1968; McPartland & York, 1967) on the achievement of blacks. The higher the SES of the black student, the greater the effect appears to be (McPartland & York, 1967). A few studies show an effect of school racial composition on student aspirations. The aspirations of blacks from all-black schools are found to be higher than those who have studied in desegregated schools (St. John & Smith, 1969), with the results appearing stronger for girls than for boys (Armor, 1972). Moreover, the more blacks in the school, the higher white aspirations are found to be.

Research on the effects of socioeconomic composition on achievement generally finds that high-SES schools have a small positive effect on the academic achievement of students (Turner, 1964; Wilson, 1963). The effect is greater for high-SES students and those whose parents have high educational attainment (Hauser, 1971) and for students in classrooms with mostly white classmates (McPartland & York, 1967). SES composition also appears to have a positive effect on student aspirations (Armor, 1972; McDill & Coleman, 1963; Sewell & Armer, 1966; Spady, 1970b). Controlling for student SES and grades, students in high-SES schools are found to have higher educational aspirations than those in low-SES schools (Armor, 1972; Nelson, 1972).

These contextual analyses have been criticized (Hauser, 1970, 1974), and contextual effects disappear in some reanalyses of existing data (Hauser, Sewell and Alwin, 1976). Nevertheless, researchers continue to argue that their data show effects of racial or SES composition in schools and classrooms. Also, a few studies report effects of other contextual variables, such as educational climate (McDill & Rigsby, 1973) and average ability of students (K. L. Alexander & Eckland, 1975; Meyer, 1970) on achievement and aspirations.

Two theoretical rationales are generally offered to explain these contextual effects. The first rationale argues that direct effects of context operate through normative reference group processes. Spady (1973) states that reference group theory can account for contextual effects in three ways. The first way is through normative group influences—the response of students to the norms, values, and standards that characterize their environment. Several case studies that document the presence of distinctive student subcultures in schools support this argument (cf. J. S. Coleman, 1961; Cusick, 1973; Gordon, 1957). A second mechanism is role models. While normative group influences *define* desirable behaviors, role models *illustrate* the behavior and show how group norms can be met. Third, contextual effects may operate through comparative group influences. Students compare themselves to their school peers and adjust their aspirations and achievement to correspond to their relative position in the class. J. Davis (1966) refers to this process as the "frog pond effect." Most studies of contextual effects on achievement and aspirations rely on these theoretical frameworks in a post hoc manner to explain their findings.

An alternative theoretical perspective on contextual effects is that contextual variables operate indirectly through interpersonal mechanisms, such as friendships. The values and standards that characterize a school or class are communicated to a student through interactions with individuals in that environment. Support for this perspective is found in studies showing that an effect of racial and SES composition on achievement and aspirations is conditioned by whether a black child has at least one close white friend (Campbell & Alexander, 1965). Some studies claim that both reference group processes and interpersonal mechanisms operate simultaneously and that both account for contextual effects (Armor, 1972; McPartland & York, 1967; Meyer, 1970).

While both reference group and role modeling processes and interpersonal influence mechanisms provide reasonable post hoc explanations for some of the research findings on contextual effects, the theories have little power to predict peer influence. They cannot answer salient questions about the peer influence process, such as when one would expect normative or comparative reference group processes and role modeling to occur.

A major weakness of these theories is that they are too general. They fail to specify conditions that affect the influence process, such as individual characteristics of students or situational characteristics that make some students more vulnerable to influence than others. The theories assume that ascribed or achieved characteristics of students have no effect on the likelihood of their being influenced. The lack of specificity of the theories may explain the small magnitude of the observed contextual effects on student outcomes. Analytical models guided by these theoretical formulations are likely to omit important characteristics of students and schools that modify the influence process.

Proximate Peer Influences

An even larger body of research compares attitudes and behaviors of students to those of their peers and infers peer influences from observed similarities. This research generally relies on interpersonal influence models to explain peer effects.

Many of the studies of proximate peer effects are found in the status attainment literature. In the Wisconsin social-psychological model of status attainment (cf. Sewell & Hauser, 1980), three sources of significant-other influence are posited: teacher encouragement, parental encouragement, and friends' plans regarding college. Of these three variables, friends' plans have the strongest effect on educational attainment and mediate the effect of sons' SES status on school performance (Sewell & Hauser, 1972, 1975). If friends expect to go to college, students are more likely to attain a college education regardless of their SES. An effect of peers' college plans on student educational aspirations is also reported, although the effect is less than that of mother's expectations (Kandel, 1978) or parental expectations (McDill & Coleman, 1965). Peer influences and aspirations are reported to increase over time from freshman to senior year (McDill & Coleman, 1963) and to increase with the strength of the friendship ties between students and peers (Kandel, 1978).

One criticism of these studies on peer influence is that they fail to separate selection and influence factors. Most studies attribute similarities among peers to peer influences and ignore selection factors. There is some empirical evidence that these studies overestimate peer influences on aspirations because selection factors have not been taken into account. For example, J. Cohen (1977) examines the relative effects of homophilic selection, group pressure to conform, and departure from the group by deviates on student homogeneity of a sample of high school friendship groups. The results show that conformity pressures or influences contribute slightly to group homogeneity, whereas homophily has a large effect. On the other hand, peer influences do not disappear in some studies when selection factors are taken into account. Controlling for social status, C. N. Alexander and Campbell (1964) found significant peer effects on college aspirations and attendance. Duncan, Haller and Portes (1968) demonstrate that some of the similarity between the educational and occupational aspirations of students and their best friends comes from mutual influence rather than from selection. In Chapter 11 of this volume, Epstein reports peer influences on both academic and nonacademic outcomes, controlling for salient selection characteristics. Placing rigid controls for peer selection on the data on which the Wisconsin model was originally tested, Williams (1981) found significant peer effects on educational attainment that likely underrepresented the influence of peers.

Another weakness of some studies of proximate peer effects on educational outcomes is that they do not distinguish between friends and other peers. In fact, peers are often defined as a student's best friends. This limits the studies conceptually because qualitative and quantitative differences in student interactions between friends and nonfriends are likely to affect the domain and strength of the influence. Moreover, the degree of sentiment that students experience toward their friends probably affects their ability to influence them. Different processes may govern the influence of friends and nonfriends. Friends may influence a student by stimulating feelings of affection, loyalty, or fear of rejection; friends and nonfriends may evoke esteem or appeal to a student's need to conform. Separating the influence of friends from that of other peers is necessary to explicate the peer influence process.

Several studies, mostly case histories based on observations in schools, examine proximate peer effects on noncognitive outcomes, including attitudes, self-concept, values, and behaviors. The studies attempt to determine the existence and nature of peer influences, rather than their magnitude. Early case histories show that students form cliques primarily on the basis of similar characteristics, such as social status or shared interests, and that once formed, the groups exercise considerable control over members' behaviors (Hollingshead, 1949; Gordon, 1957; Whyte, 1967). Other studies point to the existence of a student subculture that affects pupils' attitudes and behaviors (J. S. Coleman, 1961; Cusick, 1973). Student cliques are seen to govern and control members' behaviors in ways that are often antiacademic (J. S. Coleman, 1959; Cusick, 1973). Further, student values and behaviors vary across cliques within a school, which implies that the content of peer influences varies within the larger context of a student subculture. Evidence of peer influences is also found in field experiments, such as the classic studies of Bennington College students (Newcomb, 1961) and of children's groups in camp (Sherif & Sherif, 1953). Finally, the literature on small groups documents peer influences on conformity, persuasion, attitude change, interpersonal influence, and group conflict.

In general, the studies of peer influences on noncognitive outcomes conclude that both friendship groups and reference groups strongly influence student attitudes and behaviors, and the influences on noncognitive outcomes may be stronger than those on educational outcomes reported in the status attainment literature. An underlying assumption of the literature on peer effects is that the processes governing peer influences are relatively similar regardless of the type of outcome being considered, but empirical results suggest that mechanisms governing the influence process may differ depending on whether the outcome is cognitive or noncognitive.

Another generalization that can be drawn from this literature is that, even when a well-defined student culture is found in a school, subgroups of students can develop counternorms that insulate them from the influence of the dominant value climate. This finding challenges another assumption sometimes found in studies on peer effects—namely, that students belong to a single peer group or that schools can be characterized by a dominant normative or value climate that acts as the major peer influence on students. To the contrary, the research indicates that a school climate may have a number of distinct components (J. S. Coleman, 1961; B. Clark, 1962; Cusick, 1973). Moreover, students are probably exposed to and influenced by different and possibly conflicting values, especially in a school that has more than one recognizable normative system. On the other hand, a student's friendship or reference group may act as a barrier to influences from other peers. How a student reacts to various peer pressures and how a friendship group insulates a student from other influences are important considerations that a comprehensive theory of the peer influence process should address.

Finally, the studies on proximate peer effects on cognitive and noncognitive outcomes reveal a contradiction in the research on peer effects. Case studies of peer influences suggest that efforts of adults to channel student values, norms, and behaviors toward academic interests have generally been unsuccessful. Student norms appear to be nonacademic, if not antiacademic. The status attainment studies, on the other hand, show that friends' college plans have a positive effect on educational aspirations, as strong as parents' expectations (Hauser, 1972; Picou & Carter, 1976). The question of the extent to which peer influences support the learning process requires careful attention and well-designed research. It may be that the relative impact of parental, teacher, and peer influences varies by characteristics of the school and the student body. Identifying factors that affect the nature of peer influences on academic outcomes is one of the central tasks for future research.

In summary, the empirical literature on proximate peer effects on cognitive and noncognitive outcomes raises several questions that have not been adequately dealt with by reference group theory, role modeling, or interpersonal influence models. Among these are:

> Do different social-psychological processes govern peer influences on cognitive and noncognitive outcomes?
> Can the influence of friends insulate a student from other peer influences?
> How do some students respond to conflicting norms and value systems within a school or class?
> How do some students resist the influence of peers?
> Under what conditions does a normative system based on nonacademic values influence a student?

A reconceptualization of the peer influence process is needed to answer these and related questions about peer effects.

THE PROCESS OF PEER INFLUENCE

This section presents a conceptualization of the peer influence process based on Parson's theory of influence (Bauer, 1963; J. S. Coleman, 1963; Parsons, 1963a, 1963b; Sorensen, 1968) as well as on reference group theory and role theory. Conceptual propositions and hypotheses for future research on peer effects may be derived from the proposed framework.

Influence can be defined as any factor that affects the formation of a person's attitudes and opinions by acting directly on his or her beliefs. As such, influence is only one of many ways by which interactions produce results. Other ways include inducement, in which rewards are promised for compliance, and deterrence, in which sanctions are threatened for noncompliance. Both of these kinds of interactions are based on social power. Another, coercion, depends on physical power. What distinguishes influence from these forms of interaction is the presentation of a rationale to persuade persons to change their beliefs.

Parson's theory pertains to intentional influence as opposed to unintentional persuasion. In defining influence narrowly, Parsons ignores the kinds of attitude or opinion formation that occur through social comparison and reference group processes. On the other hand, the literature on peer effects implicitly assumes that influence is unintentional persuasion and does not address situations in which direct convincing is attempted. Both aspects of influence need to be considered and their underlying mechanisms specified to understand peer effects. Because Parson's theory can be applied more broadly than he states in his initial formulation and because it can provide insights into occasions of unintentional influence, I will rely primarily on his theoretical framework to conceptualize the peer influence process.

In the Parsonian model, influence is assumed to occur through the following mechanism: Individuals need knowledge to help them adapt to and interact in their environment. They choose to or are in a situation in which they have to rely on others to obtain the needed information. When individuals accept information from others, influence occurs. The condition for influence, then, is the willingness of the individual to accept information from another.

The extent of a person's willingness to accept information from another is determined by the extent to which individuals believe they will not be deceived when they accept the information. To be vulnerable to influence, a person must be willing to trust either the person transmitting the information or the normative system that the transmitter is articulating. Individuals will trust another person when they believe that they aspire to the same goals and when they perceive that the chances of being deceived are small. This occurs when the individual and the transmitter are in a relationship of solidarity, such as friendship. When an individual and the person from whom information is received are not in a relationship of solidarity or are not pursuing the same ends, the individual will be open to influence only if the normative system that governs the actions of the person transmitting the information can be trusted. Here, even in the absence of knowledge about the transmitter, the individual will accept the information presented.

Thus, the amount of trust elicited in a potentially influential interaction depends on how much knowledge the individual has either of the person transmitting the information or of the normative system that governs that person's behavior. Maximum influence will occur when the individual who needs information trusts either the informative or the normative system. Influence will be at a minimum if the individual has little or no knowledge of either the transmitter or the normative system and, consequently, no reason to trust them.

Vulnerability to Influence

The primary condition for either intended or unintended influence is that individuals need or perceive that they need information. The greater the need for information, the greater the vulnerability to influence. The extent of the need for information is determined by several factors—the newness of a situation, the necessity to take some action, the visibility of the action to significant others, and the salience of the opinion of significant others regarding the action. When a person is unfamiliar with a situation either cognitively or experientially, guidelines governing appropriate attitudes and behaviors are sought. The less familiar the individual is with the situation, the greater the need for information. If the situation requires that the individual take action, the need for information becomes more pressing. The risk of acting in the absence of information is to make a mistake and suffer whatever negative consequences are associated with error. If the action and possible mistake will appear publicly and be subject to evaluation by significant others, then the individual may be less willing to act in the absence of information. Moreover, if the opinion of and positive evaluation of the group is important to individuals, they may be less willing to risk a mistake by acting before obtaining the information.

A second condition for influence is that the person who needs the information must, or chooses to, rely on another to obtain it. When an individual turns to another for information, that person is put in a position of influence. The influence may be intended or unintended—individuals may ask for advice, or they may simply observe the actions of others and model their own behavior accordingly. The greater the willingness to rely on others for information, the greater the vulnerability of the individual to influence. A person is apt to rely on others if the desired information is not available elsewhere, if the need for immediate action precludes the possibility of searching for the information oneself, or if one believes that the information obtained from another will be more accurate than information that he or she could gather in another way.

In some situations, the needed information pertains to group values, norms, beliefs, and attitudes. Here, reliance on others for the information is essential. In other situations, an individual may believe that information received directly from others is more accurate than that obtained by observation, making one's willingness to accept advice from others greater. If individuals are required to act before having the opportunity to obtain the information for themselves, they have to learn what they need to know from others or risk acting inappropriately. The greater the negative consequences of an incorrect or inappropriate action, the greater the willingness to rely on others. The impact of these factors on an individual's need for information and willingness to rely on others determines the vulnerability of the individual to influence.

School settings provide numerous occasions that require students to use information or knowledge that they do not already possess. For example, a new freshman entering high school must learn a dress code; make decisions about appropriate leisure time activities, including use of drugs and alcohol; and learn acceptable study habits and performance criteria. Many of the decisions the pupil faces involve actions that are required almost immediately after school begins and that must be performed in public before significant others. The student may obtain the needed information by observing peers (unintended influence), by seeking advice (intended influence), or by searching for information from other sources. However, because some actions may be called for before the opportunity to observe or obtain the information directly is presented, reliance on others becomes essential. The amount of information to be learned and the need to perform in public shortly after entering the new situation make new students particularly vulnerable to influence from others, especially peers.

Another example is the situation in which students must make decisions about which courses to enroll in at the beginning of a school semester. They need information about course difficulty, work load, characteristics of the teachers, and grading procedures. Some of this information may be obtained from school records or from teachers, but students who have taken the courses previously are often the best source of information. The necessity of having the information and the difficulty of obtaining it themselves make students vulnerable to influence from peers. Knowledge passed on informally from one student to another has been referred to as part of the hidden curriculum and is believed to be a major influence on students' choices of academic programs.

In these examples and in most school situations, conditions peculiar to school life increase the vulnerability of students to peer influence. Students are surrounded by peers in school and interact almost exclusively with them. Opinions are usually voiced and behaviors performed in the presence of peers. The public nature of behavior in school leads to frequent peer evaluation. The importance of peer approval and respect is intensified by the power of peers to include students in their friendship networks or to socially exclude or ostracize them. Students are generally unwilling to act in such a way as to evoke the disapproval of peers. To win peer approval, they are likely to seek their advice or to model their behaviors on that of their peers. Moreover, peers are an easy source of relevant information. Thus, institutional characteristics of schools increase the vulnerability of students to peer influence.

Trust in the Individual Transmitting Information

Even when conditions promoting an individual's reliance on others for information are present, the opinions or advice of others will be accepted only under circumstances of trust. Parsons argues that the individual must trust either the person providing the information or the normative system that is being transmitted. Individuals will trust the transmitter of the information if they believe that the likelihood of deception is small. This would happen if the transmitter had little reason to deceive or if the transmitter would suffer negative consequences from deception or positive consequences for truthfulness. When individuals share the same goals, then truthfulness in the transmittal of information is expected. When goals are conflicting and shared information decreases the chances of the transmitter's achieving desired ends, such as in a competition, then deception is more likely. Individuals seeking information judge the subjective ability of the transmitter to communicate correct information and base their willingness to trust the person on that judgment.

A special case of shared goals occurs in what Parsons (1963a, 1963b) refers to as a relationship of solidarity, or what may be described as a friendship relationship. A friendship is built on a set of exchanges that benefit both members of the dyad. Deception in a friendship could seriously jeopardize these exchanges and threaten the mutual benefits that accrue to both members. Thus, truthfulness in communication between friends is seen as advantageous, if not essential, which makes an individual more likely to trust a friend than another acquaintance.

Students in school are faced with the decision of whom to trust in seeking information to guide their beliefs and behaviors. In addition to several adult sources of information, including parents, teachers, and other school personnel, they have a large body of schoolmates to rely on. In some cases, advice from adults and fellow students is congruent, making no choice necessary between the two sources of information. In other cases, information obtained from adults is contradictory to that received from peers. Here, the individual must decide which source of information to trust. The literature on status attainment suggests that students generally accept advice from parents or teachers, implying that they believe adults have their best interests in mind. However, occasions arise when students feel that the generation gap prevents adults from understanding a particular situation, leading them to have greater trust in peers. In this case, students' trust is based on the belief that peers share their goals and can best help them attain them.

When students are confronted by different value systems and normative climates in a school, they are again faced with decisions of whom to trust. Students are most likely to trust advice or information obtained from friends, because they share the same goals and are least likely to deceive them. A student's friendship group may act like a buffer against contradictory or conflicting sources of information from other peers. That friends are a primary source of influence in schools is demonstrated in the literature on school effects and in Epstein's research reported in Chapter 11 of this volume. The role of friends as a major source of influence is based primarily on an individual's readiness to trust information received from them.

In the absence of a friendship group, individuals seeking knowledge and confronted by conflicting sources of information and advice are likely to trust the person or group whose goals most closely resemble their own. Judgments about similarity of goals are based on the attitudes and opinions expressed by the students' peers as well as on their observable behaviors. Peers who reveal shared interests and concerns are more likely to evoke trust than those whose goals are conflicting or not discernable.

School and classroom characteristics can affect the extent to which a student trusts another peer to transmit correct information. The chapters in this volume show how the organization of schools and classrooms affects the likelihood that students interact, become acquaintances, and form friendships. Organizational constraints make it more likely that certain students become friends than others, increasing the chance of influence between these students. Teachers' pedagogical techniques and practices determine the extent to which students share academic goals. If teachers provide opportunities for certain students to work together through cooperative assignments, joint projects, and tutoring relationships, they increase the bases for trust among these students. The reward structure of a classroom affects the advantages and disadvantages to a student of sharing information about schoolwork with classmates. When a reward structure fosters competition, individuals' goals for academic success may be in conflict with those of their peers. This could decrease the students' willingness to trust peers in providing information related to academic goals. Future research on peer influence should specify the school and classroom variables that affect trust and influence.

Trust in the Normative System

In some circumstances, an individual may not be willing to trust a person who is communicating information. The individual may not know the person well enough to evaluate the chance of being deceived, or individuals may judge that they are not pursuing the same ends as the person transmitting the information. This may be the case when persons are not in a relationship of solidarity or friendship. When an individual does not trust the information giver, influence can occur only if the person is willing to trust the normative system that governs the statements made by the informant. For example, individuals are influenced by physicians, even if they do not know them, because they are willing to trust the Hippocratic oath that they believe governs doctors' statements.

In order to trust a normative system, it must first be known. The better defined and more clearly articulated the set of norms governing a person's behavior, the easier it is to come to know the system and recognize it in operation. In addition, the greater the number of people who trust the normative system, the greater the likelihood that it is fair and equitable. Finally, the more serious the penalty to be paid for behavior that violates the norms, the more likely that the person communicating the information is governed by the norms.

Students generally believe that teachers' actions are governed by a normative system that requires that they act to promote the students' welfare. A set of professional ethics directs teachers to guide students in such a way as to cause them no harm. Pupils may also perceive one or more student normative systems in their school that they are willing to trust. Which normative systems evoke students' trust depends on their familiarity with the norms, their judgment of the congruence between their goals and those defined by the normative system, and the opinions and advice of their friends and other peers. Once they accept a normative system, they will trust peers who transmit information that is consistent with that system, even if the transmitter is not well known personally. For this reason, students are influenced by group leaders and by other popular peers; they may not trust the individual as much as the effective enforcement of the normative system governing the individual's statements and behaviors.

Unintended Influence

Parson's framework states that influence occurs when an individual needs information and is willing to trust another person or a normative system to obtain it. In discussing the implications of this conceptualization for the peer influence process, the focus has been primarily on intended influence. From the perspective of the person seeking information, however, it is not relevant whether intent to influence is present. The same conditions that govern vulnerability to intended influence affect a person's likelihood of responding to unintended influence—the greater the need for information and the greater the willingness to trust either the persons providing the information (whether or not they are aware of providing it) or the normative system governing the opinions and behaviors of persons being observed, the more vulnerable the individual is to being influenced.

The Parsonian framework augments rather than contradicts role modeling and normative and comparative reference group explanations of the peer influence process. The major limitations of these other theories of peer influence is that they lack predictive power. Previous empirical work on peer effects has relied on the theories simply as post hoc explanations of the findings. Applying Parson's conceptualization to the research on peer effects suggests *when* these processes may be expected to occur. When the conditions for influence are present, the individual is susceptible both to intended influences from other persons and to unintended influences through modeling and reference group processes. Variation in the conditions for influence results in differences in students' vulnerability to influence, willingness to trust peers as models or references, and willingness to trust a normative system that supports observed behavior.

CONCLUSION

The literature on peer effects is currently guided by loosely connected propositions derived from normative and comparative reference group theory, and by notions about role modeling, and unspecified interpersonal mechanisms. These conceptual frameworks fail to explain peer effects in a satisfactory manner; moreover, they lack predictive power. Consequently, despite extensive research in this area, several important questions regarding peer effects remain unanswered.

This chapter outlined a conceptualization of the peer influence process that is consistent with previous empirical findings and that explains certain contradictions in the literature on peer influences. Parson's theory of intended influence was used to describe the dynamics of influence and to identify several factors that affect a person's vulnerability to influence and likelihood of being influenced. This conceptualization should have considerable heuristic value in terms of generating new propositions about peer influences. The test of its utility will be its power to organize existing peer influence studies and stimulate new research.

V

CONCLUSION

JOYCE LEVY EPSTEIN

School Environment and Student Friendships: Issues, Implications, and Interventions

Three conclusions should be drawn from the chapters of this volume. First, the environments in which peer interactions occur affect the nature and extent of peer contact and the friendship selection and influence processes. Second, the ages and developmental stages of students affect peer relations and patterns of selection and influence. Third, if the important developmental and environmental characteristics that affect interaction are taken into account in studies of peer and friendship relations, then the results of the research can be useful in educational practice.

1. *The environment affects peer contacts, choices of friends, and patterns of influence.* The research and commentaries in this volume focus on how patterns of contact and interactions are affected by different aspects of the school environment. These aspects include school offerings, such as academic tracks and extracurricular programs; school conditions, such as the size of the student population or its racial composition; and strategies of classroom instruction, such as the extent of student participation in classrooms, the way rewards are dispensed to individuals or groups for academic improvement, or the way tasks are designed and assigned to students. The results of the studies highlight the effects of school and classroom environments on peer association, friendship selection, and influence, and they imply that the characteristics of other environments in which youngsters work and play also will affect their interpersonal relations.

235

FRIENDS IN SCHOOL
Patterns of Selection and Influence in Secondary Schools

Characteristics of the school environment can be changed in order to alter patterns of contact and interaction among other students. School environments change naturally in ways that affect patterns of contact. For example, high schools generally demand more decisions from students about their elective courses than do junior high schools. Elective courses put students in contact with other students who have similar interests in subject areas. Or school environments can be changed by design. For example, a junior high school may institute a program of minicourses in which students choose elective courses for a short time in the school year. This kind of organizational change increases student participation in the procedures used to group students in their academic classes and can alter patterns of contact among students. School environments can be changed by design to introduce programs that use peer groups for academic purposes. For example, peer tutoring, math tournaments, or students' political parties may be instituted in high schools to create new patterns of peer association and new purposes for peer interaction. The research in this volume suggests that, across or within schools, the organization of school programs, classroom instruction, and the demographic characteristics of the groups of students in school and classroom activities lead students to different patterns of selection of friends and to different opportunities for influence.

2. *The ages of students and their stages of development affect peer relations.* The results of several studies and commentaries suggest that patterns of peer interaction vary across the years from childhood to adolescence. Although it has often been assumed that such concepts as exchange, reward, and status are equally useful in studies of children's and adults' friendships, these terms have different meanings across the years of development. This is an important perspective for theory-based research, for the design of new studies, and for the interpretation of data on peer relations through adolescence.

The discussion across chapters suggests that we are far from ready to explain youngsters' friendship selections or influence with a single theory. It is still important to collect data to examine developmental patterns of selection and influence of friends in terms of several sociological and developmental theories, to see how the patterns of youngsters' behaviors fit or depart from the patterns expected by the various theories of friendship. With a considerable store of information added to the contributions of this volume, researchers will be able to generate more appropriate theories of interpersonal attraction and selection in youngsters.

3. *The results of research that account for environment and development may be useful for educational practice.* Later in this chapter, we discuss the implications of the research on peer and friendship groups for educational practice and describe several interventions currently used by teachers that alter the structure of peer and friendship groups in schools and classrooms.

Selman and Jacquette (1978) discuss the need to reconcile social psychology and developmental psychology in studies of peer associations. They use a good example to make the point: Lewin Lippitt and White (1939) reported that students benefited from participation in democratically organized groups. Piaget's studies suggest that there are developmental changes in students' preferences for leadership styles from autocratic to democratic over the years from childhood to adolescence. Selman and Jacquette suggest that the results of Lewin *et al.* take on a different meaning when placed in a developmental framework.

Our research suggests that, even if the clinical, social, and developmental psychological approaches were integrated, the studies of peer and friendship groups and their socialization processes still would be incomplete unless attention were given also to the social organization of the environments in which the peer relations occur. For example, productive group behavior is also a function of the rewards dispensed for cooperative–competitive efforts, of the extent of official approval of the students' behavior, and of the degree to which students participate in deciding how leadership is defined and allocated. Productive group behavior is influenced, too, by the number of students assigned to work together, the characteristics they bring with them to the task, and how important the tasks are to them. These factors operate differently for children of different ages. Studies across age groups, in clearly defined, contrasting environments are needed to reach informed conclusions about the productivity, satisfaction, and peer relations of youngsters working in groups under different styles and levels of autocratic and democratic leadership.

Because environmental and developmental characteristics are important, researchers must pay attention simultaneously to typically sociological variables (such as the demographic characteristics of the population of students or the reward structures and the grouping practices in classrooms), to typically psychological variables (such as student self-concept, values, levels of cognitive and social maturity, and concepts of friendship), and to typically social-psychological variables (such as intergroup relations, leadership, and social perception). Of course, not all studies can measure all variables, but researchers must clearly indicate how the environment and student development are measured in their studies or why either set of characteristics is omitted from the research.

Three topics drawn from the results and conclusions across chapters should affect the design and conduct of future research. These are the positive and negative consequences of friendship, the effects on children of frequent changing of friends, and the importance of children's multiple friendship groups for research on selection and influence.

POSITIVE AND NEGATIVE
CONSEQUENCES OF FRIENDSHIP

Most research on peer and friendship groups assumes that *more* friendly relations or friendships are better than fewer, and that *any* peer ties and friendship choices made or received are better than none. This oversimplifies the important, debatable issues of the positive and negative functions of friendships. Although most agree that social relationships among students in school are inevitable and generally beneficial, it is not clear that strong binding friendships are the most important goals for all youngsters, nor is it agreed that educational programs should reward social behavior in school activities.

Positive Functions and Consequences

Many researchers have concluded that social ties are needed to develop positive social skills and that reciprocal and stable relations promote positive mental health and personal development (Asher, Oden, Gottman, 1977; Asher & Renshaw, 1981; Corsaro, 1981; Douvan & Gold, 1966; Fine 1981; Hartup, 1978; Magnusson Duner, and Zetterblom, 1975 McCall, 1970). These researchers found that poor social skills were related to other behavior problems—withdrawal from school, discipline problems in school, delinquency out of school, and poor health.

The causal order of these relationships, however, is not well established in research. Students' poor social skills and lack of friends may cause students to be disruptive or delinquent in school in order to gain the attention of their peers and teachers. Or disruptive students may be removed from the classroom, punished or ridiculed, and made unavailable or undesirable as friends. They may not learn the needed social skills to establish social ties. Similarly, poor social skills and lack of friends may be the cause or the result of physical or mental health problems and school absences. The research in this volume adds another important complication to the problem of clarifying a causal order between social skills and social behavior: Youngsters with poor social relations may be similar to other students in all respects *except* for the environment in which they work. Classroom rules differ about walking around and talking to others, so that in some classes students are called sociable or interactive, whereas in other classes the same students would be considered disruptive.

Young children's friendships are expected to contribute to the development of general social skills, cultural values, sex roles, and assertive or aggressive behavior (Allen, 1981; Fine, 1980; D. W. Johnson, 1981a; La Gaipa, 1981; Savin-Williams, 1980; Youniss, 1980). Social interactions may help students obtain a realistic perception of the self in comparison to others and provide them with norms for behavior in different situations. The positive fit of a person in a group may facilitate group and individual accomplishments.

Older youngsters' friendships fulfill other functions (Asher & Renshaw, 1981). For example, only in their relations with peers can youngsters learn to share interests, disclose and discuss thoughts and feelings, and build and maintain trust. These social skills develop as students gain experience interacting with others and as they increase cognitive skills that enable them to recognize and describe their interests, feelings, expectations, and reactions to others.

There is some disagreement over when and why social skills develop. The advanced social skills that characterize mature, mutual exchanges of information and of feelings may be gained through trial and error, with increasingly more advanced skills accumulating over the years of childhood and adolescence. Or they may develop at a particular stage in conjunction with the development of cognitive skills that enable students to understand the abstract principles of social relations. There is disagreement, too, over how many friends are needed to ensure positive social development. La Gaipa (1979) suggests that at least one close friend may be all that is required for someone to develop positive social behaviors, but it may be that such skills as group leadership and decision making, or conflict resolution and compromise, require experiences in large friendship groups.

The logical associations among social skills, behavior, and inclusion or exclusion by friends need to be studied across the elementary and high school years, and explained in terms of the environment in which the relationships occur and the ages of the students.

Negative Functions and Consequences

The expectations for positive consequences of friendships and peer relations are countered by assertions that social relationships require such conforming and compliant behaviors that they restrict or inhibit individuality, freedom of expression, and personal development.

The demand for conformity in a group can be detrimental for individual development. Conformity to group norms and excessive following behavior may reduce individuality, self-esteem, independent thinking, and leadership behavior—skills that typically increase across the years of adolescence. Pressures for conformity and against individuality can affect youngsters' decisions about their current and future behaviors, aspirations, and career paths (J. D. Campbell, 1964; Douvan & Adelson, 1966; La Gaipa, 1981). Epstein shows in Chapter 11 that there are some disadvantages for students who have no friends in school, but also that students who have low-scoring friends and who keep those friends over time may be at a greater disadvantage in the development of particular skills and attitudes than students who have no friends. For example, students who had no friends scored higher in self-reliance 1 year later than students who had stable, low-scoring friends.

Too much emphasis on friendship can result in rejection, stereotypes, cruelty, jealousy, and resentment if a student's social skills are not developed or if the desired friends are not obtained (Maas, 1968, Putallaz & Gottman, 1981; D. Reisman, 1950; Rubin, 1980). Students may learn negative behavior in order to maintain friends. Douvan and Adelson (1966) point to some of the negative social skills used by friends to resolve conflicts to preserve friendships. Students may believe they must offer falsehoods, hypocrisies, and distortions instead of truthful reactions in order to keep a friend. These social skills can be less healthy for the individuals involved than losing or changing friends.

Group membership can have positive or negative consequences. Douvan and

Adelson (1966) and D. Campbell (1961) discuss how youngsters may be punished more readily for mischievous behavior if they are in groups, and excused from punishment for the same mischief if they act as individuals.

The poor social skills of some students show other students how they do *not* want to act. Thus, the rejection or isolation of some students can serve a positive function for the others. Patchen, Hoffman and Brown (1980) suggest that avoidance behavior and unfriendly contacts may be as important for research on social and academic development as are friendly contacts. In different ways, positive and negative group experiences can solidify friendship and loyalty among the members. When schools put students into groups, they are establishing boundaries that keep students separate by ability, grade level, age, sex, or race. Thus, selection of friends and exchangeability across boundaries are reduced, but in-group friendships are strengthened and exchangeability within boundaries is increased.

It is debatable whether social skills enhance or restrict personal freedom, originality, and mental health. It is also debatable whether the gains in particular social skills are offset by losses in other skills. Because children's social skills are in formation and are flexible, schools and other environments need to provide opportunities for both unique personal development and for conforming, cooperative effort. How to provide at each grade level an optimal mix of freedom (for individual growth) and conformity (for social integration) is a challenge for educational practice and an important issue for research.

There is some question about whether students see friends as positive influences. By adolescence, students have learned that true friends are hard to find. La Gaipa (1979) reports that about two-thirds of the adolescents in a Russian study were doubtful about ever finding genuine friendship. In a survey of adolescents in the United States, 61% of the females and 47% of the males said they were lonely (reported in Bernikow, 1982). But the data from the varied samples of students in this volume show that adolescents keep looking for and choosing friends. In addition to questions about general positive and negative effects of friendships and peer relations, an important question is raised across chapters about the advantages and disadvantages of changing friends.

BENEFITS OR DISADVANTAGES OF CHANGING FRIENDS

The results in these chapters contribute to a controversy about the importance in adolescence of maintaining secure, reciprocated, stable friendships versus choosing new friends. Research has tended to stress the importance of group affiliation and friendships and of particular forms of association, such as stable and reciprocated friendships. However, data suggest that these forms of friendship are not needed for friends to influence each other's behavior. Indeed, school assignments and experiences sometimes make maintenance or reciprocation difficult (as when students move from their small elementary school to a larger middle school or from a junior high to a larger high school, where many new students may become friends) or even impossible (such as when busing plans are instituted that send students to diverse schools, when magnet schools or programs separate students who previously attended the same schools, and when students leave high school for work or college).

Students have many opportunities to test their cognitive and social compatability with other children. As a result of their interactions, they make, break, or keep friendships with great frequency, often switching back and forth from old friends to new ones. Epstein's chapters suggest that reciprocity and stability of friendships may not be necessary conditions (and sometimes may be negative conditions) for children's friendships. Others also suggest that conflict and change may have positive consequences in friendship groups (D. W. Johnson, 1981a; La Gaipa, 1981). Dealing with conflict may develop students' conflict resolution skills. However, if conflicts cannot be resolved, interpersonal conflicts may lead to the dissolution of friendships and to the need to select new friends. The tensions and disagreements among friends often provide the dynamics for building better relationships and more advanced social skills. Students who change friends may be constructing more elaborate social systems and personal understandings of their own and others' thoughts and actions. New friends open new opportunities for influence and can promote the positive development of social and self-awareness.

Changing friends is easy in school settings where, for many purposes, friends are interchangeable. If one student is not available to work with another, a third student is substituted as a lab mate or project partner. Some school and classroom organizational features make students more interchangeable and encourage a wide range of contacts from which friends are selected. Other school and classroom organizations reduce the exchangeability of students by emphasizing status differences and separating groups of students into curricular or ability tracks or into groups within classrooms.

The organization of the school and class limits or extends students' contacts and the potential selection of friends through the kinds of assignments that teachers make (e.g., a play or dramatic reading, a group mural or individual illustrations, a committee or individual project), through the procedures for classwork (e.g., cooperative, competitive, or tutorial structures), and in the extra opportunities for interaction that occur before, during, and after the academic program in the schoolday. These factors, and other organizational components discussed throughout the volume, can affect the stability and reciprocity of friendships from one week to the next and from one school year to the next. We are only beginning to gather the needed information on how the organization of school and classroom programs affects the rate of change in students' friendships. How important is security in friendships at different ages, and for what social or academic outcomes? For what kinds of outcomes are stable and reciprocated friends most benefical or least important? At what grade levels? In what kinds of school and classroom environments?

Related questions can be raised about the importance of similarity in friends' characteristics. Some assert that similarity of friends serves positive functions, such as establishing a shared social identity, reducing interpersonal conflict, and increasing each student's approval of the other. Tuma and Hallinan (1979) suggest that similarity provides status for each member in the group because their attitudes and behaviors cluster around group norms. However, Lazarsfeld and Merton's (1954) research on populations in housing projects raises questions of whether and when too much homophily can be dysfunctional for an organization, institution, or individual friendship group. Certainly, in studies of influence, the dissimilarity of friends is a critical part of the influence process. And the awareness of new dissimilarities among friends may lead back to the process of changing friends in order to select students who are more similar to oneself in important characteristics.

Changing friends is not a simple question for research—children belong to many groups and have different intensities of friendships across the multiple memberships. Students' contacts and interactions in multiple peer and friendship groups in all important socializing environments must be considered to understand how attitudes and behaviors will be influenced.

MULTIPLE GROUP MEMBERSHIPS

The research in this volume focuses on students' friends in school but, like most previous research, looks at the selection of one group of friends for each student or of a group of friends at two different points in time. However, students belong simultaneously to many groups in school and out.

Schlecty (1976) reminds us that no single group commands all the time or loyalty of any individual. Lippitt (1968) suggests that students may adjust to and participate in more than 10 membership groups in an average day, and this estimate does not include all the classroom groups and subgroups to which students are assigned. Dunphy (1963) notes that different, equally important groups may be encountered on weekdays and weekends. Neighborhood friends (Berg & Medrich, discussed in Rubin, 1980), siblings and cousins in families (Cicirelli, 1978; Isherwood & Hammah, 1981), members in clubs and teams in and out of school (Fine, 1980, 1981), camp friends, and colleagues in part-time work environments (Hamilton, 1981) may be important influences on adolescents at particular ages and for particular outcomes. For some students, these nonschool peer and friendship groups are—or become—more important than school groups.

Multiple memberships of persons may define the multiple, sometimes contradictory aspects of personalities (Duck, Miell, & Gaebler, 1980). Certainly after infancy, when children begin to make social contacts outside the family, the multiple groups to which they belong can simultaneously influence their behavior.

Maehr (1978) and Granovetter (1982, in press) suggest that the switching of social roles in a group can alter the way a task is conducted. A student who is a member of many groups and has different roles within them (e.g., leader in one, follower in another, strategist in another, conciliator in another) may develop more varied social skills than a student who is confined, by personal choice or by school organization, to few groups or to groups in which the student has the same role.

One issue for research on multiple peer groups is the importance of concordant and discordant norms for behavior across socializing contexts (Epstein, 1983; Hartup, 1978). Multiple membership groups or networks that have similar emphases may have an especially strong influence on an individual because of the repeated support of an attitude or behavior across settings. For example, parents and peers may give students the same messages (e.g., the importance of good grades, attending college, smoking, or not smoking). If the varied groups to which students belong have similar goals for behavior, then the desired behavior may be clear, but it becomes difficult to determine which group or groups are actively influencing the students' behavior. If the norms of groups of friends, families, teachers, clubs, and schools differ, then questions arise about which goals for behavior the student adopts and which group or groups have greater influence, or any influence, and on which outcomes. If norms for behavior differ, students may be forced to pick among friends, to decide which friends to influence, and which ones to be influenced by. Students may have to compromise or resolve conflicts within and across their membership groups and may be forced to order their own priorities concerning their attitudes, behaviors, and goals.

The multiple groups to which people belong may use multiple tactics to maintain or change individual behavior. Studies of multiple memberships are needed to provide information on what similarities within and across groups and what strategies for influence affect achievement and attitudes most strongly from childhood to adolescence in varied settings. Measurement of multiple influences is needed in order to understand in which arena influence occurs most often and on which outcomes. For example, if students are socialized similarly at home, they will be similar to each other without ever actively influencing each other's behaviors. Even apparent changes in behavior may be due to independent, simultaneous influence by families or by teachers on students who happen to remain friends. For example, if two friends improve in achievement, it may be due to the teacher's work with each student and not to their influence on each other. Multiple socializing contexts and multiple group memberships complicate the separation of selection and influence processes. Yet, it is the researchers' obligation to address these issues with new data that measure up to the increasingly sophisticated questions about selection and influence.

New studies of multiple group memberships will have to look carefully at the importance of weak ties in children's friendships (Granovetter, 1973, 1982, in press). Strong ties include close friends and closely knit dyads, triads, and small groups. Weak ties are acquaintances and friends of friends—people who share settings without necessarily interacting directly with each other. In schools, weak ties may be classmates or schoolmates who rarely interact or who come into contact only for brief periods of time. Hansell (1982) and Slavin and Hansell (Chapter 6, this volume) discuss strong and weak ties that may result from cooperative team learning in classrooms; other chapters suggest how strong and weak ties may be built or destroyed by the organizational features of schools and classrooms.

Granovetter (in press) suggests that persons who have no weak ties are deprived of extra and diverse information and perspectives because they interact and share information and ideas with a few close friends only. In schools, all children have innumerable weak ties. Indeed, weak ties are created by school settings because children are aware of but do not necessarily interact with all the other students in their grade or even with all the other students in their classroom. How aware students are of the behavior or attitudes of the children who are weak ties and how accurately they perceive weak ties may be a function of the students' perceptiveness, stage of cognitive development, and the school's emphasis on meeting and working with many other students.

It is not clear what benefits or problems in social or personal development result from membership in more or fewer groups (Coser, 1975; Laumann, 1973). The multiple membership groups and reference groups must be identified, and the data collected appropriately, even innovatively. Woelfel and Haller (1971) identified specific influences for particular outcomes—a useful technique for future research on peer influence. Student diaries or logs of time spent with other students, interviews or specific surveys of memberships, and videotape scans of school areas could help identify the multiple groups in which students interact.

More complete research on students' multiple friendship and peer groups may be the single most important new direction for studies of peer and friendship selection and influence. Future studies may be intensive, conducted within a school or in a small number of contrasting school environments, or extensive, to get general patterns of association of students in large and small groups. Our research suggests that such studies will be especially useful if they include measures of the organization of the school, classrooms, and out-of-school environments in which student interactions occur and if they follow the students' groups across grade levels. Even modest longitudinal studies could produce important new knowledge if they include good measures of environments, multiple groups, and multiple academic and social outcomes. Some students belong to many groups, others to few. We have little information about students' ties across groups or about the accumulated, converging, or diverging influences of the varied groups on students' actions, attitudes, and behaviors.

These are a few of the important issues that the chapters in this volume raised for future work—the positive and negative consequences of peer association, the function of changing friends, the extension of selection and influence studies to multiple friendship groups. Even though many questions remain, some important implications for current educational practice can be drawn from the research reported here.

IMPLICATIONS FOR PRACTICE

Many school policies are based on the suppression of peer relations in class-rooms. Even in elementary schools, the use of academic peer groups has been feared by teachers as a potentially negative force in the classroom. The fear is that if students work with other students they will be noisy, disruptive, and inattentive to the school's and the teacher's rules, and that there will be a general breakdown of the teacher's authority over the instructional program and classroom behavior (Hartup, 1978; Hurn, 1978; Jackson, 1968; Schlecty, 1976; Schmuck, 1978).

The evidence and perspectives in this volume suggest that it is just as possible that peer and friendship groups can be positive forces in the classroom and can be used to greater advantage in school settings to advance the goals of the school, the teachers, and the students. Indeed, by avoiding the use of peer groups for academic purposes, teachers are restricting the educational resources that could help them accomplish particular educational goals.

The decision to use or not use peer groups should be based on the teacher's knowledge of organizational structure and group processes and on the desired outcome of the educational activity. If there is a social skills component to a goal set for students, or if interaction will make the learning more efficient or effective, then the use of groups—friends, teams, pairs, tutors, large groups—is a reasonable choice. Teachers must choose how to organize the group to accomplish the desired goals. This involves the design of the tasks, decision-making structures, rewards for group and individual behavior, and decisions about the group composition. For example, the development of leadership and debate skills, tolerance and empathy, and experience in democratic procedures require pairs or groups of students to work together. But the groups may be small or large, and they may be heterogeneous or homogeneous in ability or in other student characteristics, such as race, sex, social class, and grade level.

Some teachers have used pairs and groups of students extensively to conduct their classes. Some teachers use tutorial structures for drill and practice in skills or to orient a new student to the school. Others form ad hoc or formal groups to complete particular projects or to work on advanced or remedial skills. Schmuck (1978) discusses different types of groups that are used in schools—guidance groups for social skills, instructional groups for cognitive skills, and action or governance groups for leadership and problem-solving skills. There also are judicial committees, and service, interest, and activity clubs. Interestingly, these groups are not usually formed in order to develop particular social skills and are rarely evaluated in terms of their effects on student social or academic skills.

Schools have tended to stress the convenience of grouping students without emphasizing the productive use of groups for academic purposes. The *organization* of the students' groups, teams, or pairs is as important as the *use* of peers in academic settings for the accomplishment of particular goals. Teachers who understand the organization of groups in school and classroom settings will be able to decide how and when to use groups, which students to put into the groups, when to allow free choice of team or group members, when to assign group membership, and how to reward the individual and group efforts. Most teachers would quickly select an academic intervention to solve an academic problem. For example, they select a different level textbook for students who need harder or easier material. But the same kind of well-known and well-understood solutions are not readily available for solving problems of student social relations or for organizing student social relations to solve academic problems.

Teachers and administrators need to recognize their power to determine patterns of peer interaction and friendship choice. The way that educators define *success* promotes conformity or originality; the way they reward or punish social behavior and acknowledge or ignore students' varied abilities and contributions to the class can affect how students perceive each other and whom they consider worthy models for behavior or candidates for friends. The school and classroom organization and the expectations for academic and social success determine the characteristics on which students will be similar or different, and how important these similarities or differences are to the students in their interactions.

The school organization and the teacher's classroom organization defines whether and how students are separated from each other. The organization and teacher's practices limit or extend the social distance between students (Laumann, 1973) by the way that academic and extracurricular activities are conducted and by the way that students are rewarded for social or individual behavior. Tasks, obligations, and responsibilities of students can be accompanied by valued rewards in order to reduce distances between students who might be very different on certain criteria. Rewards can be built into classroom organization for inclusiveness rather than exclusiveness in groups, for cooperative and tolerant behaviors, for cross-race interactions, and for appreciation of multiple talents. How large groups, small groups, or pairs are rewarded for working together is part of the teachers' or schools' decisions about what kinds of peer associations will be expected and encouraged.

The importance of peer and friendship groups in educational practice becomes clear with an intriguing example. In "Southie" High School, a Boston secondary school that was desegregated under court order, the black students who entered the school were more likely to have college plans than were the white students who had been in the school prior to desegregation. In time, more white students took the appropriate college preparatory courses, even as tracking was eliminated as a formal structure for separating students. College admissions increased dramatically (Kozberg, 1980). The school changed as a result of the new students' experiences in previous schools and the influence of the new students on the original population. The change in students' behaviors could have been the result of a comparative influence process in which white students observed but did not interact with black students and decided that they too could succeed in college preparatory courses. Or the changes in white students' behavior could have been the result of direct influence of black students who discussed goals and plans with white classmates and convinced them to take college preparatory classes.

These changes could have been the result of particular programs that the school or individual teachers instituted to create conditions for direct or indirect exchanges of information among black and white students. A different history would have been written if the school and teachers had created structures that kept black and white students separate, that did not accommodate students' requirements for college preparatory courses, or that permitted the continuous harassment of black and white students in school settings.

It is possible for a school to change its educational philosophy to encourage new patterns and new purposes in peer influence. One could imagine a school in which few or no students had college plans because the local industry recruited high school graduates from the community. If in this school (as in many industrial communities) the jobs for high school graduates became scarce because of changing economic conditions, the school might revise its ideas about the importance of postsecondary education for its students. Courses, requirements, and extracurricular activities could be initiated to encourage more students to continue their schooling. The reorganization of the school program would in itself be a message to the students that would influence their behavior. However, our research suggests that different patterns of peer contacts will result from the way the school groups its students, rewards them, and includes them in decision making as individuals and as groups, and from the way students are given information and asked to share it with other students. Thus, these school features could reshape peer interaction and friendship selection, and could influence how many and which students adopt the school's new philosophy and redirect their own goals toward higher education.

The school's influence on student contact, selection, and influence is especially interesting and important at points of transition in the educational program— when students change educational levels or enter new schools, when new students enter any school, when new programs are instituted, and when new populations are created by such social programs as desegregation and mainstreaming.

Finally, our research suggests that students can be positively influenced by friends who are high in achievement, aspirations, and self-reliance. Over time, low-scoring students improved their achievement, increased their college plans, and behaved more independently if they had higher-scoring friends. Because interaction with "good influences" makes a difference in positive development, an important question is whether schools should encourage and organize these kinds of potentially advantageous interactions among students. If so, what organizational strategies are available to help schools design their programs? Some friendship groups develop norms for behavior that support and advance school goals; other groups may work against school goals. Research is needed on how different school organizations create more or fewer of these types of groups, and with what results on different kinds of academic and social behaviors.

The selection of friends is not a random process. Schools cannot assign friends, but they can alter the grouping patterns and the structures of tasks, rewards, and decision making for students to increase student access to and interaction with high-scoring students on important outcomes. The opportunities for interaction establish the potential for friendships and for influence. It should be recognized that reorganizing the use of groups in school to influence student behavior carries some risks. For example, if low-scoring students are rejected by the others or cannot perform adequately in their interactions with high-scoring students, they may experience decreased social status and self-esteem. There is no guarantee, either, that low-scoring students will accept high-scoring students as friends. However, there are also serious risks in continuing classroom organizations that keep students separate in fixed tracks and groups. Low-scoring students may also develop low self-esteem if they are assigned to the permanent low group and never interact with high-scoring students or share rewards for group efforts that recognize the valued contributions of all students.

Peer interaction is real, whether teachers accept it, organize it, avoid it, or fear it. Even in the most highly authoritarian, teacher-directed settings, there is a tremendous amount of peer interaction—silently and noisily in the class, before and after class, on the way to and from school. In some schools, teachers and administrators have worked to put the power of peer groups to positive use. They use peer and friendship groups to extend the teachers' resources—to enable students to learn academic skills by assisting one another after the class receives formal instruction from the teacher. They use peer and friendship groups to extend students' social, leadership, and decision-making skills, which require interaction among students and groups. For academic and social skills, peer interaction can be managed so that the teacher can do more educationally than through teacher–student interaction alone.

Although all agree that friendships cannot be assigned, demanded, institutionalized, or legislated, the organization of schools and of classrooms can affect student friendship choices. The extent of interaction with few or many other students is a function of the opportunities or limitations built into the school and classroom environments. Schools can arrange for interactions among students in ways that foster the development of friendships among large or small groups of students. Specific interventions have been introduced to create different social environments in classrooms.

INTERVENTIONS

Two major types of interventions have been applied in schools to put peer groups to use for the academic and social goals of schooling. One approach is psychological—a friendship therapy or coaching model—designed to correct or enhance students' social skills. The second approach is sociological—an organizational reform model—designed to use the structures and conditions of schools and classrooms to create opportunities for student interaction and the development of social skills as part of the regular instructional program.

The psychology-based coaching interventions train children who have poor peer relations to improve their social skills. The assumption is that students will use their improved social skills to make friends. This technique has been used with highly deviant children in out-of-school treatment settings and with children who have been rejected by peers in school. The lack of social skills is treated as a learning problem, and the training program takes the student through role play, discussions, and other activities to help the student learn the concepts and acts of friendship and the procedures for making friends. (See Selman's research and applications at the Judge Baker Guidance Clinic [Selman, 1976; Selman, Jacquette, and Bruss-Sanders, 1979] and research by Asher *et al.*, 1977; Gottman, Gonso, & Schuler, 1976; Oden & Asher, 1977; Putallaz & Gottman, 1981 for examples and discussions of coaching studies.)

The sociology-based interventions alter the organization of the instructional program in order to use peer and friendship groups to advance learning and development. It is suggested in several chapters of this volume that the structure of learning tasks, rewards to students, and students' share of authority in decision making in classrooms and grouping practices can change how students interact with each other, the kinds of social skills they are required to develop and use, and the patterns of selection and influence that occur. The organizational changes can be made without changing the curriculum that teachers must cover in specific academic subjects. The varied conditions for social relations affect how students choose friends and what friends they choose.

Certainly both types of interventions can contribute to better social relations among students. Both skill training and classroom opportunity structures can decrease the number of students who are isolated from friendship groups or rejected by other students. There are differences, however, in the two approaches that could be important for educational practice.

Skill Training and Coaching Approaches

Skill training, based on a deficit model of behavior, requires that children who lack social skills be identified and treated to help them obtain and use social skills. The identification of students must be based on clear criteria and must be accurate, so that students will not be inappropriately identified or labeled in ways that further jeopardize their poor social standing. Finally, the coaching treatment must help students without hurting their self-confidence and must result in some measurable success that justifies the time and expense related to the treatment.

The coaching programs are based on shaping and modeling behavior of making friends and being friendly, and they provide practice in social exchange. Some have been described as successful in improving the skills of students who need training, at least for the short term (Asher & Renshaw, 1981; Chandler, 1973; Furman, Rahe, & Hartup, 1979; Gottman, Gonso, & Rasmussen, 1975; Oden & Asher, 1977; Putallaz & Gottman, 1981; Selman, 1976). However, Asher *et al.* (1977) suggest that most coaching studies show only short-term results. After the direct rewards for social behaviors are withdrawn, the youngsters often revert to their earlier patterns of poor social behavior and continue to be isolated from others.

Reliable instruments and personnel needed to conduct coaching interventions are not readily available in most schools. Teachers do not usually measure children's social skills in any formal way, nor are they likely to revise their educational program to enable many students to receive special training in social skills during academic class time. Coaching strategies would rely on guidance personnel or other special staff (often scarce luxuries in schools) to identify and treat youngsters.

Social Organization Approach

There are requirements also for successful use of the organizational approach. Changing the basic structure of classrooms for the purpose of instruction requires the teacher to manage the classroom as a social system. This means that the teacher must understand the manipulable or alterable features of classroom and instructional organization that affect student interactions and that can be used for academic purposes. The teacher must be aware of the goals that have been set for groups of students and for individuals and must find comfortable ways of using the classroom structures to attain particular goals.

The purposeful formation of groups for social exchange and influence was part of Moreno's (1934/1953) early research. He arranged groups so that low- and high-status children would come into contact, expecting that interaction would increase social acceptance of low-status students by high-status students. Some groups participated in human relations training to encourage social acceptance. Since that time, research has shown that, in addition to contact and interaction, other factors will maximize the likelihood of student acceptance and appreciation of others—having the students work on an important common task, recognizing their equal status on some important criterion, and providing some likelihood of success and rewards for all participants (Blanchard, Weigel, & Cook, 1975; E. G. Cohen, 1980a). These three factors were not part of the earlier designs and are still in need of research to define their part in the process of acquaintance and acceptance.

Some interventions have been designed specifically to use the social behavior of peer and friendship groups to improve student achievement or other school-related outcomes, such as interpersonal skills, friendly behaviors, and friendship choices. These interventions include the Teams-Games-Tournament (TGT) technique devised by DeVries and Edwards (1973); Student Teams–Achievement Divisions (STAD) devised by Slavin (1979); Jigsaw devised by Aronson (1978), and Team Assisted Individualization (TAI) devised by Slavin, Madden, and Leavey (1982). In these interventions, groups of students work together to help each other learn and receive credit for their own and their groups' successful efforts. In TGT and STAD, teams of students study basic skills in drill and practice activities after the teacher has presented the basic lesson to the class (also see Slavin and Hansell,

Chapter 6, this volume). In Jigsaw, each student in a group learns part of a topic and teaches and discusses that part with the other members in the group. All members learn all parts of the topic from each other, and each is expert in one part. In TAI, individualized instruction is combined with team support for personal improvement as students work at their own level and at their own pace but still contribute to a team learning effort.

These interventions directly reward cooperative behavior and have been researched for their effects on friendship choices, helping behaviors, and other peer relations, as well as on academic gains. In practice, these interventions have been particularly useful in racially and ethnically integrated classrooms and in mainstreamed classrooms to attain goals of better peer relations between students of different backgrounds and attributes. When a teacher faces a problem that involves the social relations among different groups of students—such as race relations, mainstreaming, heterogeneous classes—then interventions can be selected that *use* social relations to solve the social problems.

Peer tutoring is another organizational intervention in which pairs of students—older and younger, high and low ability, black and white, or high and low SES—work together so that one student who needs help receives it from a student who has already mastered the information (Allen, 1976; Boocock, 1978; Furman *et al.*, 1979; Hartup, 1979). Interestingly, peer tutoring has been found to help the learning skills of the tutor as well as of the tutee. The theory is that a student can help the teacher reach a slower student by spending extra time on a lesson with that student and by serving as a role model for the other student. In an important sense, tutoring revises the authority structure of the classroom because the teacher shares authority with the tutor in order to obtain more teaching time for the tutee. The success of student tutoring programs depends on the care with which tutors are selected, trained, and matched with their tutees, and the importance the teacher gives to the program and to the improvement of the tutee's learning.

In each of these techniques, the success of the intervention depends heavily on the teacher's skills at managing the organization of instruction and establishing appropriate goals, tasks, rewards, and levels of participation for the students.

There is some evidence of long-term effects of organizational interventions on peer relations. Slavin (1979) and Ziegler (1981) report follow-up effects of the use of student team learning interventions on students' race relations. Epstein (1980, 1983), reports measurable, continued effects of early school environments on later academic and social behaviors.

E. G. Cohen and Intili (1981) organized a system of learning centers in bilingual classrooms in which students are encouraged to work and talk with each other to improve their academic skills, English-language fluency, and friendly relations. Cohen suggests that power among low-achieving students is based on social and not academic skills, and that any power increases the chances of a student being selected as a friend (E. G. Cohen, 1980b). Thus, one goal of an intervention is to arrange interactions among students so they can work together in ways that require them to observe each other's contributions, talents, and powers. The school and the teachers must reward the multiple talents of students. This model—the opposite of a deficit model—builds on the students' competencies, even though they may differ for each student (E. G. Cohen, 1979). This promising classroom intervention raises many questions about how the instructional program can be organized to use the social and academic powers of students in challenging academic tasks that require and demonstrate multiple skills and talents, and still enable all students to attain and advance the basic skills.

Teachers may be more able to adopt organizational approaches for better use of peers and friends for increasing the learning and social skills of all students. The teacher's focus may still be on the students who are low in social status, but the organizational treatment is offered to all students. Indeed, the heterogeneity of groups of students and the cooperation of high- and low-status students are the bases of the interventions that change the task, reward, and authority structures to encourage peer interaction and friendship selection.

The coaching strategy could be combined with the organizational approach, especially for students who have severe social problems. These students might begin to use newly learned social skills in their interactions within the classroom organization that encourages social exchange and rewards interaction and helping behaviors. If the student seeks attention through deviant behavior because he or she does not know the correct social skills, then the coaching strategy that teaches new skills helps the student understand the behavior that is required for peer acceptance. If the student knows the correct behavior but is too often sent from the room or removed from the group because of deviant behavior, then the organizational strategy that gives opportunities and rewards for the appropriate social behavior may help the student gain experience in successful social exchanges within the classroom.

Student-Originated Interventions

The interventions we have discussed here are under the control of teachers. Teachers and guidance personnel can provide coaching and skill-building activities to train students in skills needed in friendships and peer relations. Teachers and administrators can restructure the school and classroom to provide more opportunities for student interactions in order to improve academic and social skills. These interventions (and others that teachers create) are task oriented; they are used by teachers in an instructional program to alter the patterns of contact and exchange among students.

A third type of intervention is under the control of the students. Observational studies suggest that students organize a social system parallel to the official academic school organization (Ahola & Isherwood, 1981; Cusick, 1973; Larkin, 1979). All activities of the students' social organization are based on active participation of the students in continuous social exchange. Sometimes students use their parallel organization of peers to change the school's organization. For example, groups of students with particular talents or interests can change school course offerings, procedures, extracurricular activities, and events. A group of drama enthusiasts can create a school emphasis on drama where none existed before. From their newly created group, new friendships will emerge and patterns of influence on drama and on other issues will be established. A group of students bent on participating in student government activities can create new rules, change or eliminate rules, and organize committees to work with the principal, counselors, and teachers to change the number and kinds of opportunities for students to participate in school governance, extracurricular, or out-of-school activities. The interests of the students will solidify some friendships and create new friendships as the students work together on school problems that concern them.

Cusick (1973) observed that schools respond to the actions or demands of students in small or large groups that have even rudimentary organization. The groups of students may support and maintain school goals, change school emphases, or work against school authorities. The students' interventions—the resulting groups and their functions—can affect the selection of friends and the topics and patterns of influence. However, there is no systematic research on student-originated interventions to change school or classroom social environments and peer relations.

The theoretical, empirical, and practical discussions in this volume support three major conclusions. First, school policies, classroom practices, and population characteristics are organizational factors that affect students' selections of friends and the influence friends have on each other. Second, patterns of selection and influence change as students gain cognitive and social skills. Third, in practice, teachers tend to overlook the potential of friends in school to influence positively the attainment of academic and social skills. The research, commentaries, and examples of interventions suggest that schools can structure opportunities that support and reward the purposeful interaction of students of different grade levels, races, social classes, ability levels, interests, and talents. Organizational decisions to create opportunities that bring diverse students together or that keep them apart will affect the selection and influence of friends.

References

Abramowitz, S. The effect of school and task structure on teacher interaction, classroom organization and student effects. Paper presented at the annual meeting of the American Educational Research Association, New York, 1977.

Ahola, J. A., & Isherwood, G. B. Social life: A student perspective. In J. L. Epstein (Ed.), *The quality of school life*. Lexington, Mass.: Lexington Books, 1981.

Alexander, C. N., & Campbell, E. Q. Peer influences on adolescent aspirations and attainments. *American Sociological Review*, 1964, 29, 568–575.

Alexander, K. L., Cook, M., & McDill, E. L. Curriculum tracking and educational stratification: Some further evidence. *American Sociological Review*, 1978, 43, 47–66.

Alexander, K. L., & Eckland, B. K. Contextual effects in the high school attainment process. *American Sociological Review*, 1975, 40, 402–416.

Allan, G. A. *A sociology of friendship and kinship*. Boston: Allen & Unwin, 1979.

Allen, V. L. (Eds.). *Children as teachers*. New York: Academic Press, 1976.

Allen, V. L. Self, social group, and social structure: Surmises about the study of children's friendships. In S. R. Asher & J. M. Gottman (Eds.), *The development of children's friendships*. New York: Cambridge Univ. Press, 1981.

Allport, G. *The nature of prejudice*. Cambridge, Mass.: Addison-Wesley, 1954.

Alwin, D., & Otto, L. High school context effects on aspirations. *Sociology of Education*, 1977, 50, 259–273.

Amir, Y. Contact hypothesis of ethnic relations. *Psychological Bulletin*, 1969, 71, 319–343.

Anderson, N. H. Likableness ratings of 555 personality-trait words. *Journal of Personality and Social Psychology*, 1968, 9, 272–277.

Armor, D. J. School and family effects on black and white achievement: A reexamination of the USOE data. In F. Mosteller & D. P. Moynihan (Eds.), *On equality of educational opportunity*. New York: Vintage Books, 1972.

Aronson, E. *The jigsaw classroom*. Beverly Hills, Calif.: Sage, 1978.

Aronson, E., Blaney, N., Sikes, J., Stephan, C., & Snapp, M. The jigsaw route to learning and liking. *Psychology Today*, February, 1975, pp. 43–50.

Asch, S. Effects of group pressures upon the modification and distortion of judgements. In D. Cartwright & A. Zander (Eds.), *Group dynamics: Research and theory* (Vol. 2). New York: Harper, 1960.

Asher, S. R., & Gottman, J. M. (Eds.). *The development of children's friendships.* New York: Cambridge Univ. Press, 1981.

Asher, S. R., Oden, S. L., & Gottman, J. M. Children's friendships in school settings. In L. G. Katz (Ed.), *Current topics in early childhood education.* Norwood, N.J.: Ablex Co., 1977.

Asher, S. R., & Renshaw, P. D. Children without friends: Social knowledge and social skill training. In S. R. Asher & J. M. Gottman (Eds.), *The development of childrens' friendships.* New York: Cambridge Univ. Press, 1981.

Asher, S. R., Singleton, L. C., & Taylor, A. R. Acceptance versus friendship: A longitudinal study of social integration. Paper presented at the annual meeting of the American Educational Research Association, New York, 1982.

Back, K. Influence through social communication. *Journal of Abnormal and Social Psychology*, 1951, *46*, 9–23.

Bain, R. K., & Anderson, J. G. School context and peer influences in educational plans of adolescents. *Review of Education Research*, 1974, *44*, 429–445.

Bales, R. F. *Personality and interpersonal behavior.* New York: Holt, 1970.

Bandura, A. Social learning and the shaping of children's judgements. *Journal of Personality and Social Psychology*, 1969, *11*, 275–283.

Banks, W. C. White preference in blacks: A paradigm in search of a phenomenon. *Psychological Bulletin*, 1976, *83*, 1179–1186.

Barker, R., & Gump, P. *Big school, small school: High school size and student behavior.* Stanford, Calif.: Stanford Univ. Press, 1964.

Barker, R., & Associates. *Habitats, environments and human behavior.* San Francisco: Jossey-Bass, 1978.

Bar-Tal, D. Social outcomes of the schooling process and their taxonomy. In D. Bar-Tal & L. Saxe (Eds.), *Social psychology of education.* Washington, D.C.: Hemisphere Press, 1978.

Bauer, B. Comment on "On the concept of influence." *Public Opinion Quarterly*, 1963, *27*, 82–86.

Beady, C., & Slavin, R. E. Making success available to all students in desegregated schools. *Integrated Education*, 1981, *18*(6), 28–31.

Berndt, T. J. Relations between social cognition, nonsocial cognition, and social behavior: The case of friendship. In L. Ross & J. H. Flavell (Eds.), *Social cognitive development: Frontiers and possible futures.* New York: Cambridge Univ. Press, 1981.

Berndt, T. J. The features and effects of friendship in early adolescence. Unpublished manuscript, Yale University, 1982.

Berndt, T. J. Sharing between friends: Contexts and consequences. In E. Mueller & C. Cooper (Eds.), *Peer relations: Process and outcomes.* New York: Academic Press, forthcoming.

Bernikow, L. Alone. *New York Times Magazine*, August 15, 1982, pp. 24–29.

Berscheid, E., & Walster, E. *Interpersonal attraction.* Reading, Mass.: Addison-Wesley, 1969.

Bialer, I. Conceptualization of success and failure in mentally retarded and normal children. *Journal of Personality*, 1961, *29*, 303–320.

Bianchi, B. D., & Bakeman, R. Sex-typed affiliation preferences observed in pre-schoolers: Traditional and open school differences. *Child Development*, 1977, *48*, 924–929.

Bidwell, C. Schooling and moral socialization. *Interchange*, 1972, *3*, 3–22.

Bidwell, C., & Kasarda, J. Conceptualizing and measuring the effects of school and schooling. *American Journal of Education*, 1980, *88*, 401–430.

Bigelow, B. J. Childrens' friendship expectations: A cognitive developmental study. *Child Development*, 1977, *48*, 246–253.

Bigelow, B. J., & La Gaipa, J. The development of friendship values and choice. In H. C. Foot, A. J. Chapman, & J. Smith (Eds.), *Friendship and social relations in children.* New York: Wiley, 1980.

Blanchard, F. A., Weigel, R. H., & Cook, S. W. The effect of relative competence of group members upon interpersonal attraction in cooperating interacial groups. *Journal of Personality and Social Psychology*, 1975, *32*, 519–530.

Blaney, N. T., Stephan, C., Rosenfield, D., Aronson, E., & Sikes, J. Interdependence in the classroom: A field study. *Journal of Educational Psychology*, 1977, *69*, 121–128.

Blau, P. M. *Exchange and power in social life*. New York: Wiley, 1964.

Blau, P. M. Parameters of social structure. *American Sociological Review*, 1974, *39*, 615–635.

Blau, P. M. *Inequality and heterogeneity: A primitive theory of social structure*. New York: Free Press, 1979.

Boocock, S. S. The social organization of the classroom. *Annual Review of Sociology*, 1978, *4*, 1–28.

Booth, A. Sex and social participation. *American Sociological Review*, 1972, *37*, 183–192.

Bossert, S. T. *Tasks and social relationships in classrooms*. New York: Cambridge Univ. Press, 1979.

Bott, E. *Family and social network* (2nd ed.). New York: Free Press, 1971.

Bowles, S., & Gintis, H. *Schooling in capitalist America*. New York: Basic Books, 1976.

Boyle, R. P. The effect of high school on students' aspirations. *American Journal of Sociology*, 1966, *71*, 628–639. (a)

Boyle, R. P. On neighborhood context and college plans, *American Sociological Review*, 1966, *31*, 706–707. (b)

Brand, E. S., Ruiz, R. A., & Padilla, A. M. Ethnic identification and preference. *Psychological Bulletin*, 1974, *81*, 860–890.

Brewer, M. B. Ethnocentrism and its role in interpersonal trust. In M. B. Brewer & B. E. Collins (Eds.), *Scientific inquiry and the social sciences*. San Francisco: Jossey-Bass, 1981.

Brittain, C. V. Adolescent choices and parent–peer cross-pressures. In J. P. Hill & S. Shelton (Eds.), *Readings in adolescent development and behavior*. Englewood Cliffs, N.J.: Prentice-Hall, 1971.

Brody, G. H. A social learning explanation of moral development. Paper presented at annual meeting of the American Educational Research Association, New York, 1977.

Bronfenbrenner, U. *Two worlds of childhood*. New York: Russell Sage, 1970.

Brookover, W., Beady, C., Hood, P., Schweitzer, O., & Wisenbaker, J. *School social systems and student achievement*. New York: Praeger, 1979.

Brophy, J. E. Teacher behavior and its effects. *Journal of Educational Psychology*, 1979, *71*, 733–750.

Buff, S. Greasers, dupers, and hippies: Three responses to the adult world. In L. Howe (Ed.), *The white majority*. New York: Random House, 1970.

Busk, P. L., Ford, R. C., & Schulman, J. L. Stability of sociometric responses in classrooms. *Journal of Genetic Psychology*, 1973, *123*, 69–84.

Byrne, D. Interpersonal attraction and attitude similarity. *Journal of Abnormal and Social Psychology*, 1961, *62*, 713–715. (a)

Byrne, D. The influence of propinquity and opportunities for interaction on classroom relationships. *Human Relations*, 1961, *14*, 63–69. (b)

Byrne, D. Attitudes in attraction. In L. Berkowitz (Ed.), *Advances in experimental social psychology* (Vol. 4). New York: Academic Press, 1969.

Byrne, D. *The attraction paradigm*. New York: Academic Press, 1971.

Campbell, D. Conformity in psychology's theories of acquired dispositions. In I. Berg & B. Bass (Eds.), *Conformity and deviation*. New York: Harper, 1961.

Campbell, E. Q., & Alexander, C. N. Structural effects and interpersonal relationships. *American Journal of Sociology*, 1965, *71*, 284–289.

Campbell, J. D. Peer relations in childhood. In M. L. Hoffman & L. W. Hoffman (Eds.), *Review of child development research* (Vol. 1). New York: Russell Sage, 1964.

Carter, D., DeTine-Carter, S., & Benson, F. Interracial acceptance in the classroom. In H. C. Foot, A. J. Chapman, & J. R. Smith (Eds.), *Friendship and social relations in children*. New York: Wiley, 1980.

Carter, D. E., DeTine, S., Spero, J., & Benson, F. W. Peer acceptance and school-related variables in an integrated junior high. *Journal of Educational Psychology*, 1975, *67*, 267–273.

Cattell, R. B. *The scientific analysis of personality*. Baltimore: Penguin, 1965.

Chandler, M. J. Egocentrism and anti-social behavior: The assessment and training of social perspective taking skills. *Developmental Psychology*, 1973, 9, 326–332.

Charlesworth, R., & Hartup, W. W. Positive social reinforcement in the nursery school peer group. *Child Development*, 1967, 38, 933–1003.

Cicirelli, V. G. Relationship of sibling structure to intellectual abilities and achievement. *Review of Educational Research*, 1978, 48, 365–379.

Clark, B. *Educating the expert society*. San Francisco: Chandler, 1962.

Clark, K., & Clark, N. Development of consciousness of self and the emergence of racial identification in Negro pre-school children. *Journal of Social Psychology*, 1939, 10, 591–599.

Clausen, J. A. *Socialization and society*. Boston: Little, Brown, 1968.

Cohen, D., Pettigrew, T., & Riley, R. Race and the outcome of schooling. In F. Mosteller & D. P. Moynihan (Eds.), *On equality of educational opportunity*. New York: Vintage Books, 1972.

Cohen, E. G. The effects of desegregation on race relations. *Law and Contemporary Problems*, 1975, 39, 271–299.

Cohen, E. G. The desegregated school: Problems in status, power, and interracial climate. Paper presented at the annual meeting of the American Psychological Association, New York, 1979.

Cohen, E. G. Design and redesign of the desegregated school. In W. Stephan & J. Feagin (Eds.), *School desegregation: Past, present and future*. New York: Pilgrim Press, 1980. (a)

Cohen, E. G. A multi-ability approach to the integrated classroom. Paper presented at the annual meeting of the American Psychological Association, Montreal, 1980. (b)

Cohen, E. G., & Intili, J. Interdependence and management in bilingual classrooms-Final report. Unpublished manuscript, Stanford University School of Education, 1981.

Cohen, E. G., Lockheed, M. E., & Lohman, M. The center for interracial cooperation: A field experiment. *Sociology of Education*, 1976, 49, 47–58.

Cohen, J. Adolescent change and peer influence. Unpublished doctoral dissertation, University of Chicago, 1971.

Cohen, J. The impact of the leading crowd on high school change: A re-assessment. *Adolescence*, 1976, 11, 373–381.

Cohen, J. Sources of peer homogeneity. *Sociology of Education*, 1977, 50, 227–241.

Cohen, J. Conformity and norm formation in small groups. *Pacific Sociological Review*, 1978, 21, 441–466.

Cohen, J. High school subcultures and the adult world. *Adolescence*, 1979, 14, 491–502. (a)

Cohen, J. Socio-economic status and high-school friendship choice: Elmstown's youth revisited. *Social Networks*, 1979, 2, 65–74. (b)

Cohen, J. Peer influence on aspirations with initial aspirations controlled. Final project report to the National Science Foundation, 1981.

Coleman, J. C. *Relationships in adolescence*. London: Routledge & Kegan Paul, 1974.

Coleman, J. C. Friendships and the peer group in adolescence. In J. Adelson (Ed.), *Handbook of adolescent psychology*. New York: Wiley, 1980.

Coleman, J. S. Academic achievement and the structure of competition. *Harvard Educational Review*, 1959, 29, 330–351.

Coleman, J. S. *The adolescent society*. New York: Free Press, 1961.

Coleman, J. S. Comment on "On the concept of influence". *Public Opinion Quarterly*, 1963, 27, 63–82.

Coleman, J. S., Campbell, E., Hobson, C., McPartland, J., Mood, A., Weinfeld, F., & York, R. Equality of educational opportunity. U.S. Department of Health, Education, and Welfare. Washington, D.C.: U.S. Government Printing Office, 1966.

Cook, S. W. Motives in a conceptual analysis of attitude-related behavior. In W. J. Arnold & D. Levine (Eds.), *Nebraska Symposium on Motivation* (Vol. 17). Lincoln: Univ. of Nebraska Press, 1969.

Cook, S. W. Interpersonal and attitudinal outcomes of cooperating interracial groups. *Journal of Research and Development in Education*, 1978, 12, 97–113.

Cook, S. W. Social science and school desegregation: Did we mislead the supreme court? *Personality and Social Psychology Bulletin*, 1979, *5*, 420–437.

Cooper, L., Johnson, D. W., Johnson, R., & Wilderson, F. Effects of cooperative, competitive, and individualistic experiences on interpersonal attraction among heterogeneous peers. *Journal of Social Psychology*, 1980, *111*, 243–252.

Corsaro, W. A. Friendship in the nursery school: Social organization in a peer environment. In S. R. Asher & J. M. Gottman (Eds.), *The development of children's friendships*. New York: Cambridge Univ. Press, 1981.

Corwin, R. C. *A sociology of education*. New York: Appleton, 1965.

Coser, R. The complexity of roles as a seedbed of individual autonomy. In L. Coser (Ed.), *The idea of social structure: Essays in honor of Robert Merton*. New York: Hartcourt, 1975.

Crain, R. L., & Weisman, C. S. *Discrimination, personality, and achievement: A survey of Northern Blacks*. New York: Seminar Press, 1972.

Crandall, V. J., Katkovsky, W., & Preston, A. Motivation and ability determinents of young children's intellectual achievement behaviors. *Child Development*, 1962, *33*, 643–661.

Cusick, P. *Inside high school*. New York: Holt, 1973.

Damon, W. *The social world of the child*. San Francisco: Jossey-Bass, 1977.

Davies, M., & Kandel, D. B. Parental and peer influences on adolescents' educational plans: Some further evidence. *American Journal of Sociology*, 1981, *87*, 363–387.

Davis, J. The campus as a "frog pond." *American Journal of Sociology*, 1966, *72*, 17–31.

Davis, J., & Leinhardt, S. The structure of positive interpersonal relations in small groups. In J. Berger (Ed.), *Sociological theories in progress* (Vol. 2). Boston: Houghton, 1972.

Davis, K. *Human Society*. New York: Macmillan, 1949.

Davis, N. The reasons of misrule: Youth groups and charivaris in XVI century France. *Past and present*. Oxford: Baillol, 1971.

Davitz, J. R. Social perception and sociometric choice of children. *Journal of Abnormal and Social Psychology*, 1955, *50*, 173–176.

Deaux, K. Sex differences. In T. Blass (Ed.), *Personality variables in social behavior*. New York: Wiley, 1977.

De Charms, R. *Personal causation*. New York: Academic Press, 1968.

Demos, J. *The little commonwealth*. New York: Oxford Univ. Press, 1970.

Deutsch, H. *The psychology of women*. London: Research Books, 1947.

Deutsch, M. An experimental study of the effects of cooperation and competition upon group process. *Human Relations*, 1949, *2*, 199–231.

Deutsch, M. Education and distributive justice: Some reflections on grading systems. *American Psychologist*, 1979, *34*, 391–401.

Deutsch, M., & Gerard, H. B. A study of normative and informational social influence upon individual judgement. *Journal of Abnormal and Social Psychology*, 1955, *51*, 629–636.

DeVries, D. L., & Edwards, K. Learning games and student teams: Their effects on classroom process. *American Journal of Educational Research*, 1973, *10*, 307–318.

DeVries, D. L., & Edwards, K. J. Student teams and learning games: Their effects on cross-race and cross-sex interaction. *Journal of Educational Psychology*, 1974, *66*, 741–749.

DeVries, D. L., Edwards, K. J., & Slavin, R. E. Biracial learning teams and race relations in the classroom: Four field experiments on Teams-Games-Tournament. *Journal of Educational Psychology*, 1978, *70*, 356–362.

DeVries, D. L., Edwards, K. J., & Wells, E. H. Teams-Games-Tournament in the social studies classroom: Effects on academic achievement, student attitudes, cognitive beliefs, and classroom climate. Report 173. Baltimore: Johns Hopkins University, Center for Social Organization of Schools, 1974.

DeVries, D. L., & Slavin, R. E. Teams-Games-Tournament (TGT): Review of ten classroom experiments. *Journal of Research and Development in Education*, 1978, *12*, 28–38.

DeVries, D. L., Slavin, R. E., Fennessey, G. M., Edwards, K. J., & Lombardo, M. M. *Teams-Games-Tournament: The team learning approach*. Englewood Cliffs, N.J.: Prentice-Hall, 1980.

Dittes, J. E., & Kelley, H. H. Effects of different conditions of acceptance upon conformity to group norms. *Journal of Abnormal and Social Psychology*, 1956, 53, 100–107.

Douvan, E., & Adelson, J. *The adolescent experience.* New York: Wiley, 1966.

Douvan, E., & Gold, M. Modal patterns in American adolescence. In L. Hoffman & M. Hoffman (Eds.), *Review of child development research* (Vol. 2). New York: Russell Sage, 1966.

Dreeben, R. *On what is learned in school.* Reading, Mass.: Addison-Wesley, 1968.

Duck, S. *Personal relationships and personal constructs: A study of friendship formation.* New York: Wiley, 1973.

Duck, S., & Miell, D. Towards a comprehension of friendship development and breakdown. In H. Tajfel (Ed.), *Social identity of intergroup relations.* New York: Cambridge University Press, 1982.

Duck, S., Miell, D., & Gaebler, H. Attraction and communication in children's interactions. In H. C. Foot, A. J. Chapman, & J. Smith (Eds.), *Friendship and social relations in children.* New York: Wiley, 1980.

Duncan, O. D., Featherman, D. L., & Duncan, B. *Socioeconomic background and achievement.* New York: Seminar Press, 1972.

Duncan, O. D., Haller, A. O., & Portes, A. Peer influences on aspirations: A reinterpretation. *American Journal of Sociology*, 1968, 74, 119–137.

Dunphy, D. C. The social structure of urban adolescent peer groups. *Sociometry*, 1963, 26, 230–246.

Dweck, C. Social-cognitive processes in children's friendships. In S. Asher & J. Gottman (Eds.), *The development of children's friendships.* New York: Cambridge Univ. Press, 1981.

Eckstein, H., & Gurr, T. R. *Patterns of authority: A structural basis for political inquiry.* New York: Wiley, 1975.

Eder, D. Ability grouping as a self-fulfilling prophesy: A microanalysis of teacher–student interaction. *Sociology of Education*, 1981, 54, 151–162.

Eder, D., & Hallinan, M. Sex differences in children's friendships. *American Sociological Review*, 1978, 43, 237–250.

Edwards, A. L. *Edwards personal preference schedule.* New York: Psychological Corporation, 1953.

Edwards, K. J., & DeVries, D. L. Learning games and student teams: Their effects on student attitudes and achievement. Report 147. Baltimore: Johns Hopkins University, Center for Social Organization of Schools, 1972.

Edwards, K. J., & DeVries, D. L. The effects of Teams-Games-Tournament and two structural variations on classroom process, student attitudes, and student achievement. Report 172. Baltimore: Johns Hopkins University, Center for Social Organization, 1974.

Edwards, K. J., DeVries, D. L., & Snyder, J. P. Games and teams: A winning combination. *Simulation and Games*, 1972, 3, 247–269.

Eisenstadt, S. *From generation to generation.* New York: Free Press, 1964.

Elder, G. H. *Age groups, status transitions, and socialization.* Washington, D.C.: National Institute of Child Health and Human Development, 1968.

Elder, G. H. Parental power legitimation and its effect of the adolescent. In J. P. Hill & J. Shelton (Eds.), *Readings in adolescent development and behavior.* Englewood Cliffs, N.J.: Prentice-Hall, 1971.

Elder, G. H. Adolescence in historical perspective. In J. Adelson (Ed.), *Handbook of adolescent psychology.* New York: Wiley, 1980.

Elkind, D. Egocentrism in adolescence. In J. P. Hill & J. Shelton (Eds.), *Readings in adolescent development and behavior.* Englewood Cliffs, N.J.: Prentice-Hall, 1971.

Elkind, D. *Children and adolescents: Interpretive essays on Jean Piaget.* New York: Oxford Univ. Press, 1974.

Emerson, R. Power–dependence relations: Two experiments. *Sociometry*, 1964, 27, 282–298.

Epps, E. G. Impact of school desegregation on aspirations, self-concepts and other aspects of personality. *Law and Contemporary Problems*, 1975, 39, 300–313.

Epstein, J. L. A longitudinal study of school and family effects on student development. Report 301. Baltimore: Johns Hopkins University Center for Social Organization of Schools, 1980. (To appear in S. A. Mednick & M. Harway (Eds.), *Longitudinal research in the U.S.*, in preparation.)

Epstein, J. L. *The quality of school life.* Lexington, Mass.: Lexington Books, 1981.

Epstein, J. L. Longitudinal effects of person–family–school interactions on school outcomes. In A. Kerckhoff (Ed.), *Research in sociology of education and socialization* (Vol. 4). Greenwich, Conn.: JAI Press, 1983.

Epstein, J. L., & McPartland, J. M. The effects of open school organization on student outcomes. Report 194. Baltimore: Johns Hopkins University, Center for Social Organization of Schools, 1975.

Epstein, J. L., & McPartland, J. M. *The Quality of School Life Scale, and administrative and technical manual.* Boston: Riverside Press/Houghton Mifflin, 1978.

Epstein, J. L., & McPartland, J. M. Authority structures. In H. Walberg (Ed.), *Educational environments and effects: Evaluation and policy.* Berkeley: McCutchan, 1979.

Erikson, E. *Childhood and society.* New York: Norton, 1950.

Feld, S. The focussed organization of social ties. *American Journal of Sociology,* 1981, 86, 1015–1035.

Feldman, K., & Weiler, J. Changes in initial differences among major field groups: An exploration of the accentuation effect. In W. Sewell, R. Hauser, & D. Featherman (Eds.), *Schooling achievement in American society.* New York: Academic Press, 1976.

Felmlee, D., & Hallinan, M. The effect of classroom interaction on children's friendships. *Journal of Classroom Interaction,* 1979, 14, 1–8.

Festinger, L. A theory of social comparison processes. *Human Relations,* 1954, 7, 117–140.

Fine, G. A. The natural history of preadolescent male friendship groups. In H. Foot, A Chapman, & J. Smith (Eds.), *Friendship and social relations in children.* New York: Wiley, 1980.

Fine, G. A. Friends, impression management, and preadolescent behavior. In S. R. Asher & J. M. Gottman (Eds.), *The development of children's friendships.* New York: Cambridge Univ. Press, 1981.

Fischer, C. S., Jackson, R. M., Stueve, C. A., Gerson, K., Jones, L. M., & Baldassare, M. *Networks and places: Social relations in the urban setting.* New York: Free Press, 1977.

Flavell, J. H. *Cognitive development.* Englewood Cliffs, N.J.: Prentice-Hall, 1977.

Flavell, J. H., Botkin, P. T., Fry, C. L., Wright, J., & Jarns, P. *The development of role taking and communication skills in children.* New York: Wiley, 1968.

Foot, H. C., Chapman, A. J., & Smith, J. R. (Eds.), *Friendship and social relations in children.* New York: Wiley, 1980.

Fraser, R. W. Behavioral and attitudinal differences between teachers in desegregated schools. Unpublished doctoral dissertation, University of California, 1980.

French, D., Brownell, C., Graziano, W., & Hartup, W. Effects of cooperative, competitive and individualistic sets on performance in children's groups. *Journal of Experimental Child Psychology,* 1977, 24, 1–10.

Freiberg, J. The effects of ability grouping on interaction in the classroom. ERIC Document Reproduction Service, No. ED 053 194, 1971.

Furman, W., Rahe, D., & Hartup, W. Rehabilitation of socially withdrawn preschool children through mixed-age and same-age socialization. *Child Development,* 1979, 50, 915–922.

Gans, H. J. *The urban villagers.* New York: Free Press, 1962.

Gerard, H. B., & Hoyt, M. F. Distinctiveness of social categorization and attitude toward ingroup members. *Journal of Personality and Social Psychology,* 1974, 29, 836–842.

Gerard, H. B., Jackson, T. D., & Conolley, E. S. Social contact in the desegregated classroom. In H. B. Gerard & N. Miller, *School desegregation.* New York: Plenum, 1975.

Gerard, H. B., & Miller, N. *School desegregation.* New York: Plenum, 1975.

Gibb, C. Leadership. In G. Lindzey (Ed.), *Handbook of social psychology* (Vol. 2). Reading, Mass.: Addison-Wesley, 1954.

Gilligan, C. In a different voice: Women's conception of self and morality. *Harvard Educational Review,* 1977, 47, 481–517.

Gilligan, C. Moral development in the college years. In A. Chickering (Ed.), *The future American college.* San Francisco: Jossey-Bass, 1980.

Glidewell, J. C., Kantor, M. B., Smith, L. M., & Stringer, L. A. Socialization and social structure in the classroom. In L. W. Hoffman & M. L. Hoffman (Eds.), *Review of child development research* (Vol. 2). New York: Russell Sage, 1966.

Goffman, E. *Behavior in public places*. New York: Free Press, 1963.

Gonzales, A. Classroom cooperation and ethnic balance. Paper presented at the annual meeting of the American Psychological Association, New York, 1979.

Gordon, C. W. *Social system of the high school*. Glencoe, Ill.: Free Press, 1957.

Gottfredson, G. D., & Daiger, D. C. Disruptions in six hundred schools. Report 289. Baltimore: Johns Hopkins University, Center for Social Organization of Schools, 1979.

Gottman, J., Gonso, J., & Rasmussen, B. Social interaction, social competence and friendship in children. *Child Development*, 1975, *46*, 709–718.

Gottman, J., Gonso, J., & Schuler, P. Teaching social skills to isolated children. *Journal of Abnormal Child Psychology*, 1976, *4*, 179–197.

Gottman, J., & Parkhurst, J. A developmental theory of friendship and acquaintanceship processes. In W. A. Collins (Ed.), *Minnesota symposia on child psychology* (Vol. 13). Hillsdale, N.J.: Erlbaum, 1980.

Gouldner, A. Norm of reciprocity: A preliminary statement. *American Sociological Review*, 1960, *25*, 161–178.

Granovetter, M. The strength of weak ties. *American Journal of Sociology*, 1973, *78*, 1360–1380.

Granovetter, M. *Getting a job: A study of contacts and careers*. Cambridge, Mass.: Harvard University Press, 1974.

Granovetter, M. Prospectus for a micro-structural analysis of the school desegregation program. Unpublished paper, State University of New York, Stony Brook, 1982.

Granovetter, M. The strength of weak ties: A network theory revisited. *Sociological Theory*, in press.

Grant, L. Sex roles and statuses in peer interactions in elementary schools. Paper presented at the annual meeting of the American Educational Research Association, New York, 1982.

Graves, N. B. Inclusive versus exclusive interaction styles in Polynesian and European classrooms: In search of an alternative to the cultural deficit model of learning. Paper presented at the biennial meeting of the Society for Research in Child Development, Denver, 1975.

Gronlund, N. *Sociometry in the classroom*. New York: Harper, 1959.

Gunnarsson, L. *Children in day care and family care in Sweden*. Research Bulletin 21 (September), University of Gothenburg, Sweden, Department of Educational Research, 1978.

Gurevich, M. *The social structure of acquaintanceship networks*. Cambridge, Mass.: MIT Press, 1961.

Guttentag, M., & Longfellow, C. Children's social attributions: Development and change. In *Nebraska symposium on motivation* (Vol. 25). Lincoln: Univ. of Nebraska Press, 1977.

Haller, A., & Butterworth, C. E. Peer influences on levels of occupational and educational aspiration. *Social Forces*, 1960, *38*, 289–295.

Hallinan, M. T. Friendship patterns in open and traditional classrooms. *Sociology of Friendship*, 1976, *49*, 254–264. (a)

Hallinan, M. T. *Friendship formation: A continuous time Markov process*. CDE working paper 76-5. Madison: University of Wisconsin Center for Demography and Ecology, 1976. (b)

Hallinan, M. T. *The peer influence process: A reconceptualization*. Paper presented at the National Institute of Education Invitational Conference on School Organization and Effects, San Diego, 1978.

Hallinan, M. T. The process of friendship formation. *Social Networks*, 1978/79, *1*, 193–210.

Hallinan, M. T. Structural effects on children's friendships and cliques. *Social Psychology Quarterly*, 1979, *42*, 43–54.

Hallinan, M. T. Patterns of cliquing among youth. In H. C. Foot, A. J. Chapman, & J.R. Smith (Eds.), *Friendship and social relations in children*. New York: Wiley, 1980.

Hallinan, M. T. Recent advances in sociometry. In S. R. Asher & J. M. Gottman (Eds.), *The development of children's friendships*. New York: Cambridge Univ. Press, 1981.

Hallinan, M. T., & Tuma, N. B. Classroom effects on changes in children's friendships. *Sociology of Education*, 1978, *51*, 270–282.

Hamblin, R. L., & Pitcher, B. L. Modeling collective learning in ongoing conflictual exchange. Paper presented at the annual meeting of the American Sociological Association, Boston, 1979.

Hamilton, S. F. Contexts for adolescent development: The interaction of school, home, peer group and workplace. Paper presented at Conference on Adolescence and Secondary Schooling, Madison, Wisconsin, 1981.

Hansell, S. Ego development and adolescent social networks. Unpublished doctoral dissertation, University of Chicago, 1978.

Hansell, S. Ego development and peer friendship networks. *Sociology of Education*, 1981, *54*, 51–63.

Hansell, S. Cooperative learning and the racial and sexual intergration of peer friendship groups. Paper presented at the Second International Conference on Cooperation in Education, Provo, Utah, 1982.

Hansell, S., & Slavin, R. E. Cooperative learning and the structure of interracial friendships. *Sociology of Education*, 1981, *54*, 98–106.

Hansell, S., Tackaberry, S. N., & Slavin, R. E. Cooperation, competition, and the structure of student peer groups. *Representative Research in Social Psychology*, in press.

Harrison, A. A. *Individuals and groups: Understanding social behavior*. Monterey, Calif.: Brooks/Cole, 1976.

Hartup, W. W. Peer interaction and social organization. In P. Mussen (Ed.), *Carmichael's manual of child psychology* (Vol. 3). New York: Wiley, 1970.

Hartup, W. W. The origins of friendships. In M. Lewis & L. A. Rosenblum (Eds.), *Friendship and peer relations*. New York: Wiley, 1975.

Hartup, W. W. Children and their friends. In H. McGurk (Ed.), *Issues in childhood social development*. London: Methuen, 1978.

Hartup, W. W. Peer relations and the growth of social competence. In M. W. Kent & J. E. Rolf (Eds.), *The primary prevention of psychopathology* (Vol. 3). Hanover, N.H.: Univ. Press of New England, 1979.

Hartup, W. W., Brady, J. E., & Newcomb, A. F. Social cognition and social interaction in childhood. In E. T. Higgens, D. N. Ruble, & W. W. Hartup (Eds.), *Social cognition and social behavior: Developmental issues*. New York: Cambridge Univ. Press, 1982.

Hauser, R. M. Schools and the stratification process. *American Journal of Sociology*, 1969, *74*, 537–611.

Hauser, R. M. Context and consex: A cautionary tale. *American Journal of Sociology*, 1970, *75*, 645–664.

Hauser, R. M. *Socioeconomic background and educational performance*. Rose Monograph. Washington, D.C.: American Sociological Association, 1971.

Hauser, R. M. Disaggregating a social-psychological model of educational attainment. *Social Science Research*, 1972, *1*, 159–188.

Hauser, R. M. Contextual analysis revisited. *Sociological Methods and Research*, 1974, *2*, 365–375.

Hauser, R. M., Sewell, W. H., & Alwin, D. High school effects on achievement. In W. H. Sewell, R. M. Hauser, & D. L. Featherman (Eds.), *Schooling and achievement in American society*. New York: Academic Press, 1976.

Heider, G. *The psychology of interpersonal relations*. New York: Wiley, 1958.

Herriott, R. E. Some determinants of educational aspirations. *Harvard Educational Review*, 1963, *33*, 157–177.

Heyns, B. Social selection and stratification within schools. *American Journal of Sociology*, 1974, *79*, 1434–1451.

High school and beyond, 1980 sophomore and senior data, User's Guide, No. 1. Chicago: National Opinion Research Center, 1980.

Hinkle, S., & Schopler, J. Ethnocentrism in the evaluation of group products. In W. Austin & S. Worchel (Eds.), *The social psychology of intergroup relations*, Monterey, Calif.: Brooks/Cole, 1979.

Hoffman, M. L. Moral development in adolescence. In J. Adelson (Ed.), *Handbook of adolescent psychology*. New York: Wiley, 1980.

Hollingshead, A. *Elmtown's youth*. New York: Wiley, 1949.

Homans, G. C. *Social behavior: Its elementary forms*. New York: Harcourt, 1974.

Horrocks, J. E. *The psychology of adolescence*. Boston: Houghton Mifflin, 1976.

Hurn, C. J. *The limits and possibilities of schooling*. New York: Allyn & Bacon, 1978.

Inhelder, B., & Piaget, J. *The growth of logical thinking*. New York: Basic Books, 1958.

Inkeles, A. Society, social structure and child socialization. In J. A. Clausen (Ed.), *Socialization and society*. Boston: Little, Brown, 1968.

Isherwood, G. B., & Hammah, C. K. Home and school factors and the quality of school life in Canadian high schools. In J. L. Epstein (Ed.), *The quality of school life*. Lexington, Mass.: Lexington Books, 1981.

Jackson, P. *Life in classrooms*. New York: Holt, 1968.

Jencks, C. S. The Coleman report and the conventional wisdom. In F. Mosteller & D. P. Moynihan (Eds.), *On equality of educational opportunity*. New York: Vintage Books, 1972.

Jencks, C. S., Acland, H., Bane, M., Cohen, H., Gintis, H., Heyns, B., Michaelson, S., & Smith, M. *Inequality: A reassessment of the effect of family and schooling in America*. New York: Basic Books, 1972.

Jencks, C. S., & Brown, M. The effects of high schools on their students. *Harvard Educational Review*, 1975, *45*, 273–324.

Johnson, D. W. Student–student interaction: The neglected variable in education. *Educational Researcher*, 1981, *10*, 5–10. (a)

Johnson, D. W. Letter to the editor in response to Slavin's "A policy choice: Cooperative or competitive learning." *Character*, 1981, *2*, 8–9. (b)

Johnson, D. W., & Johnson, R. T. Instructional goal structure: Cooperative, competitive, or individualistic. *Review of Educational Research*, 1974, *44*, 213–240.

Johnson, D. W., & Johnson, R. T. *Learning together and alone*. Englewood Cliffs, N.J.: Prentice-Hall, 1975.

Johnson, D. W., & Johnson, R. T. Effects of cooperative and individualistic learning experiences on interethnic interaction. *Journal of Educational Psychology*, 1981, *73*, 444–449.

Johnson, D. W., Johnson, R. T., & Maruyama, G. Interdependence and personal attraction among heterogeneous and homogeneous individuals. A theoretical formulation and a meta-analysis of the research. Unpublished manuscript, University of Minnesota, 1982.

Johnson, D. W., & Johnson, S. The effects of attitude similarity, expectation of goal facilitation, and actual goal facilitation on interpersonal attraction. *Journal of Experimental Social Psychology*, 1972, *8*, 197–206.

Joreskog, K. G. A general method for estimating a linear structural equation system. In A. S. Goldberger & O. D. Duncan (Eds.), *Structural equation models in the social sciences*. New York: Seminar Press, 1973.

Kahl, J. A. Education and occupational aspirations of 'common man' boys. *Harvard Educational Review*. 1953, *23*, 186–203.

Kandel, D. Homophily, selection and socialization in adolescent friendships. *American Journal of Sociology*, 1978, *84*, 427–436.

Kandel, D., & Lesser, G. S. Educational plans of adolescents. *American Sociological Review*, 1969, *34*, 213–223.

Kandel, D., & Lesser, G. S. Related influences of parents and peers on the educational plans of adolescents in the U.S. and Denmark. In M. Miles & W. W. Charters (Eds.), *Learning in social settings*. Boston: Allyn & Bacon, 1970.

Karweit, N. Student friendship networks as a wtihin-school resource. Unpublished doctoral dissertation, Johns Hopkins University, 1976.

Karweit, N. School size effects on friendships. Unpublished manuscript, Center for Social Organization of Schools, Johns Hopkins University, 1981.

Katz, E., & Lazarsfeld, P. *Personal influence: The part played by people in the flow of mass communications*. New York: Free Press, 1955.

Katz, I. Review of the evidence relating to effects of desegregation on the intellectual performance of Negroes. *American Psychologist,* 1964, *19,* 381–399.

Keats, J. A., Biddle, B. J., Keats, D. M., Bank, B. J., Hauge, R., Rafaei, W., & Valentin, S. Parents, friends, siblings, and adults: Unfolding referent other importance data for adolescents. Unpublished manuscript, National Institute of Alcohol Abuse and Alcoholism, 1981.

Keeves, J. P. *Educational environment and student achievement.* Stockholm: Arngust & Wiksell, 1972.

Kelley, H. H. The two functions of reference groups. In G. E. Swanson, T. M. Newcomb, & E. L. Hartley (Eds.), *Readings in social psychology.* New York: Holt, 1952.

Kelley, H. H., & Volkart, E. The resistance to change of group anchored attitudes. *American Sociological Review,* 1952, *17,* 453–465.

Kelley, G. A. *The psychology of personal constructs.* New York: Norton, 1955.

Kennedy, R. J. R. Single or triple melting pot? Intermarriage trends in New Haven, 1870–1942. *The American Journal of Sociology,* 1944, *49,* 331–339.

Kerckhoff, A. The status attainment process: Socialization or allocation? *Social Forces,* 1976, *55,* 368–381.

Kerckhoff, A., & Davis, K. Value consensus and need complementarity in mate selection. *American Sociological Review,* 1962, *20,* 317–325.

Klineberg, O. *Negro intelligence and selective migration.* New York: Columbia Univ. Press, 1935.

Kohlberg, L. Stage and sequence: The cognitive developmental approach to socialization. In D. A. Goslin (Ed.), *Handbook of socialization theory and research.* Chicago: Rand McNally, 1969.

Kohlberg, L. Continuities in childhood and adult moral development revistied. In P. B. Baltes & L. R. Goulet (Eds.), *Life-span developmental psychology: Research and theory.* New York: Academic Press, 1970.

Kohn, M. L., & Schooler, C. The reciprocal effects of the substantive complexity of work and intellectual flexibility: A longitudinal assessment. *American Journal of Sociology,* 1978, *84,* 24–52.

Kozberg, G. Left out kids in a left out school. *Harvard Graduate School of Education Association Bulletin,* 1980, *25,* 24–26.

Krauss, I. Sources of educational aspirations among working-class youths. *American Sociological Review,* 1964, *29,* 867–879.

Kurth, S. B. Friendship and friendly relations. In O. McCall, M. McCall, N. Donzin, G. Shuttles, & S. Kurth (Eds.), *Social relationships.* Chicago: Aldine, 1970.

La Gaipa, J. A developmental study of the meaning of friendship in adolescence. *Journal of Adolescence,* 1979, *2,* 201–213.

La Gaipa, J. L. Children's friendship. In S. Duck & R. Gilmore (Eds.). *Personal relations 2: Developing personal relations.* New York: Academic Press, 1981.

Langlois, S. Les reseaux personnels et la diffusion des informations sur les emplois. *Recherches Sociographiques,* 1977, *2,* 213–245.

Larkin, R. W. *Suburban youth in cultural crisis.* New York: Oxford Univ, Press, 1979.

Laumann, E. O. *Prestige and association in an urban community.* Indianapolis: Bobbs-Merrill, 1966.

Laumann, E. O. *Bonds of pluralism: The form and structure of urban social networks.* New York: Wiley, 1973.

Lavin, D. E. *The prediction of academic performance.* New York: Wiley, 1965.

Lazarsfeld, P. F., & Merton, R. K. Friendship as a social process: A substantive and methodological analysis. In M. Berger, T. Abel, & C. Page (Eds.), *Freedom and control in modern society.* New York: Van Nostrand, 1954.

Leinhardt, S. Developmental change in the sentiment structure of children's groups. *American Sociological Review.* 1972, *37,* 202–212.

Leventhal, H. Toward a comprehensive theory of emotion. In L. Berkowitz (Ed.), *Advances in experimental social psychology* (Vol. 13). New York: Academic Press, 1980.

Lever, J. Sex differences in the games children play. *Social Problems,* 1976, *23,* 478–487.

Levinger, G. A three-level approach to attraction: Toward understanding pair relatedness. In T. Houston (Ed.), *Foundations of interpersonal attraction.* New York: Academic Press, 1974.

Lewin, K. Environmental forces in child behavior and development. In C. Murchison (Ed.), *Handbook of child psychology.* Worcester, Mass.: Clark Univ. Press, 1931.

Lewin, K. *A dynamic theory of personality.* New York: McGraw-Hill, 1935.

Lewin, K. *Resolving social conflicts.* New York: Harper, 1948.

Lewin, K., Lippitt, R., & White, R. Patterns of aggressive behavior in experimentally created social climates. *Journal of Social Psychology,* 1939, *10,* 271–299.

Lewis, M., & Rosenblum, L. *Friendship and peer relations.* New York: Wiley, 1975.

Lewis, R., & St. John, N. H. Contribution of cross-racial friendship to minority group achievement in desegregated classrooms. *Sociometry,* 1974, *37,* 79–91.

Lin, N., Ensel, W. M., & Vaughn, J. C. Social resources and strength of ties: Structural factors in occupational status attainment. *American Sociological Review,* 1981, *46,* 393–405.

Lindsay, P. The effect of high school size on student participation, satisfaction and attendance. *Educational Evaluation and Policy Analysis,* 1982, *4*(1), 57–66.

Lippitt, R. Improving the socialization process. In J. Clausen (Ed.), *Socialization and society.* Boston: Little, Brown, 1968.

Lippitt, R., Polansky, N., Redl, F., & Rosen, S. The dynamics of power. In D. Cartwright & A. Zander (Eds.), *Group dynamics: Research and theory* (2nd ed.) New York: Harper, 1960.

Lipsitz, J. S. The age group. In M. Johnson (Ed.), *Toward adolescence: The middle school years.* Seventy-ninth Yearbook of the National Society for the Study of Education. Chicago: Univ. of Chicago Press, 1980.

Lott, A. J., & Lott, B. E. Group cohesiveness as interpersonal attraction: A review of relationships with antecedent and consequent variables. *Psychological Bulletin,* 1965, *64,* 259–309.

Lucker, G. W., Rosenfield, D., Sikes, J., & Aronson, E. Performance in the interdependent classroom: A field study. *American Educational Research Journal,* 1976, *13,* 115–123.

Maas, H. S. Preadolescent peer relations and adult intimacy. *Psychiatry,* 1968, *3,* 161–172.

Maccoby, E. E. The development of moral values and behavior in childhood. In J. Clausen (Ed.), *Socialization and Society.* Boston: Little, Brown, 1968.

Maccoby, E., & Jacklin, C. *The psychology of sex differences.* Stanford, Calif.: Stanford Univ. Press, 1974.

Madden, N. A., & Slavin, R. E. Cooperative learning and social acceptance of mainstreamed academically handicapped students. Paper presented at the annual meeting of the American Psychological Association, Montreal, 1980.

Maehr, M. L. Sociocultural origin of achievement motivation. In D. Bar-Tal & L. Saxe (Eds.), *Social psychology of education.* New York: Wiley, 1978.

Magnusson, D., Duner, A., & Zetterblom, G. *Adjustment: A longitudinal study.* New York: Wiley, 1975.

Mannarino, A. P. The development of children's friendships. In H. C. Foot, A. J. Chapman, & J. R. Smith (Eds.), *Friendship and social relations in children.* New York: Wiley, 1980.

Mannheim, K. *Essays on the sociology of knowledge.* London: Routledge & Kegan Paul, 1952.

Martin, E. Reflections on the early adolescent in school. *Daedalus,* 1971, *100,* 1087–1103.

Maruyama, G., & Miller, N. Reexamination of normative influence processes in desegregated classrooms. *American Educational Research Journal,* 1979, *16,* 273–284.

Maruyama, G., & Miller, N. Physical attractiveness and personality. In B. A. Maher & W. B. Maher (Eds.), *Progress in experimental personality research* (Vol. 10). New York: Academic Press, 1981.

Maruyama, G., & Miller, N. Does popularity cause achievement? A longitudinal test of the lateral transmission of values hypothesis. Unpublished manuscript, University of Southern California, 1982.

Mayhew, B., & Levinger, R. Size and the density of interaction in human aggregates. *American Journal of Sociology,* 1976, *82,* 86–110.

McArthur, C. C. Personality differences between middle and upper classes. *Journal of Abnormal Social Psychology,* 1955, *50,* 247–254.

McCall, G. J. The social organization of relationships. In G. J. McCall, M. M. McCall, N. K. Denzin, G. D. Suttles, & B. Kurth (Eds.), *Social relationships.* Chicago: Aldine, 1970.

McClelland, D. C. *Power: The inner experience.* New York: Irvington, 1975.

McClelland, D. C., Atkinson, J. W., Clark, R. A., & Lowell, E. L. *The achievement motive.* New York: Appleton, 1953.

McDill, E., & Coleman, J. High school social status, college plans and interest in academic achievement: A panel analysis. *American Sociological Review,* 1963, *28,* 905–918.

McDill, E., & Coleman, J. Family and peer influences in college plans of high school students. *Sociology of Education,* 1965, *38,* 112–126.

McDill, E., Meyers, D., & Rigsby, L. C. Institutional effects on the academic behavior of high school students. *Sociology of Education,* 1967, *40,* 181–189.

McDill, E. L., & Rigsby, L. *Structure and process in secondary schools: The academic impact of educational climates.* Baltimore: Johns Hopkins Press, 1973.

McDonald, M. *The curriculum and cultural reproduction.* Milton Keynes, Eng.: Open University Press, 1977.

McGarvey, W. *Longitudinal factors in school desegregation.* Unpublished doctoral dissertation, University of California, 1977.

McPartland, J. M. The relative influence of school and classroom desegregation on the academic achievement of ninth grade Negro students. *Journal of Social Issues,* 1968, *25,* 93–102.

McPartland, J. M., & Epstein, J. L. Open schools and achievement: Extended tests of a finding of no relationship. *Sociology of Education,* 1977, *42,* 133–144.

McPartland, J. M., & McDill, E. L. *Violence in schools.* Lexington, Mass.: Lexington Books, 1977.

McPartland, J. M., & York, R. Further analysis of Equality of Educational Opportunity survey. In U.S. Commission on Civil Rights, *Racial Isolation in the Public Schools* (Vol. 2). Washington, D.C.: U.S. Government Printing Office, 1967.

Mead, G. H. *Mind, self and society.* Chicago: Univ. of Chicago Press, 1934.

Mead, G. H. Language and the development of the self. In T. M. Newcomb & E. L. Hartup (Eds.), *Readings in social psychology.* New York: Holt, 1947.

Metz, M. H. *Classrooms and corridors.* Berkeley: Univ. of California Press, 1978.

Meyer, J. H. High school effects on college intentions. *American Journal of Sociology,* 1970, *76,* 59–70.

Meyers, C. E., Dingman, H. F., Orpet, R. E., Sitkei, E. G., & Watts, C. A. Four ability factor hypotheses: Three preliterate levels in normal children. *Monographs of the Society for Research in Child Development,* 1964, *29,* No. 5.

Michael, J. A. High school climates and plans for entering college. *Public Opinion Quarterley,* 1961, *25,* 585–595.

Michael, J. A. On neighborhood context and college plans (II). *American Sociological Review,* 1966, *31,* 702–706.

Miller, N. Summary and conclusions. In H. B. Gerard & N. Miller (Eds.), *School desgregation.* New York: Plenum, 1975.

Miller, N. The social scientist's brief from the perspective of 1979. Paper presented at the annual meeting of the American Psychological Association, New York, 1979.

Minuchin, P. P. *The middle years of childhood.* Monterey, Calif.: Brooks/Cole, 1975.

Minuchin, P., Biber, B., Shapiro, E., & Zimiles, H. *The psychological impact of school experience.* New York: Basic Books, 1969.

Minnesota Law Review. The effects of segregation and the consequences of desegregation: A social science statement. Appendix to appellant's briefs: Brown vs. Board of Education of Topeka, Kansas. 1953, *37,* 427–439.

Mischel, W. Preference for delayed reinforcement: An experimental study of a cultural observation. *Journal of Abnormal and Social Psychology,* 1958, *56,* 57–61.

Montemayor, R., & Van Komen, R. The development of sex differences in friendships and peer group structure during adolescence. Unpublished manuscript, 1982.

Moreno, J. L. *Who shall survive: Foundations of sociometry, group psychiatry and sociodrama* (Rev. ed.). Beacon, N.Y.: Beacon House, 1953. (Originally published, 1934.)

Morgan, D., & Alwin, D. When less is more: School size and student social participation. *Social Psychology Quarterly*, 1980, *43*, 241–252.

Morgan, E. P. *Inequality in classroom learning*. New York: Praeger, 1977.

Mueller, E., & Cooper, C. (Eds.), *Peer relations: Process and outcomes*. New York: Academic Press, forthcoming.

Nelson, J. I. High school context and college plans: The impact of social structure on aspirations. *American Sociological Review*, 1972, *37*, 143–148.

Newcomb, T. *Personality and social change: Attitude formation in a student community*. New York: Holt, 1943.

Newcomb, T. *The acquaintance process*. New York: Holt, 1961.

Newcomb, T., Koenig, K., Flacks, R., & Warwick, D. P. *Persistence and change: Bennington college and its students after 25 years*. New York: Wiley, 1967.

Oakes, J. The reproduction of inequity: The content of secondary school tracking. *The Urban Review*, 1982, *14*, 107–120.

Oden, S., & Asher, S. R. Working children in social skills for friendship making. *Child Development*, 1977, *48*, 495–506.

Parsons, T. The school class as a social system: Some of its functions in American society. *Harvard Educational Review*, 1959, *29*, 297–318.

Parsons, T. On the concept of influence. *Public Opinion Quarterly*, 1963, *27*, 37–62. (a)

Parsons, T. Rejoinder to Bauer and Coleman. *Public Opinion Quarterly*, 1963, *27*, 87–92. (b)

Parsons, T. W. Ethnic cleavage in a California school. Unpublished doctoral dissertation, Stanford University School of Education, 1966.

Patchen, M., Davidson, J. D., Hoffman, G., & Brown, W. R. Determinants of students' interracial behavior and opinion change. *Sociology of Education*, 1977, *50*, 55–75.

Patchen, M., Hoffman, G., & Brown, W. R. Academic performance of black high school students under different conditions of contact with white peers. *Sociology of Education*, 1980, *53*, 33–51.

Peevers, B. H., & Secord, P. Developmental change in attribution of descriptive concepts to persons. *Journal of Personality and Social Psychology*, 1973, *27*, 120–128.

Piaget, J. *The moral judgement of the child*. London: Routledge & Kegan Paul, 1932.

Piaget, J. *Judgement and reasoning in the child*. Patterson, N.J.: Littlefield, Adams, 1959.

Picou, J. S., & Carter, T. M. Significant-other influence and aspiration. *Sociology of Education*, 1976, *49*, 12–22.

Pool, I. deS., & Kochen, M. Contacts and influence. *Social Networks*, 1979, *1*, 5–51.

Pope, B. Socioeconomic contrasts in children's peer culture prestige values. *Genetic Psychology Monographs*, 1953, *48*, 157–220.

Porter, J. D. R., & Washington, R. E. Black identity and self-esteem: A review of studies of black self-concept, 1968–1978. *Annual Review of Sociology*, 1979, *5*, 53–74.

Precker, J. A. Similarity of valuings as a factor in selection of peers and near-authority figures. *Journal of Abnormal and Social Psychology*, 1952, *47*, 406–414.

Putallaz, M., & Gottman, J. M. Social skills and group acceptance. In S. R. Asher & J. M. Gottman (Eds.), *The development of children's friendships*. New York: Cambridge Univ. Press, 1981.

Rabbie, J. M., & Horwitz, M. Arousal of ingroup–outgroup bias by chance win or loss. *Journal of Personality and Social Psychology*, 1969, *13*, 269–277.

Rehberg, R. A., & Rosenthal, E. R. *Class and merit in the American high school*. New York: Longman, 1978.

Reisman, D. *The lonely crowd*. New Haven: Yale Univ. Press, 1950.

Reisman, J., & Shorr, H. Friendship claims and expectations among children and adults. *Child Development*, 1978, *49*, 913–916.

Renshaw, P. D. The roots of peer interaction research: A historical analyses of the 1930's. In S. R. Asher & J. M. Gottman (Eds.), *The development of children's friendships*. New York: Cambridge Univ. Press, 1981.

Rogers, M., & Miller, N. The effect of school setting on cross-racial interaction. Paper presented at the annual meeting of the American Psychological Association, Montreal, 1980.

Rogers, M., & Miller, N. Quantitative and qualitative differences in peer selection in a desegregated school. Paper presented at the annual meeting of the American Psychological Association, Los Angeles, 1981.

Rogers, M., Miller, N., & Hennigan, K. Cooperative games as an intervention to promote cross-racial acceptance. *American Educational Research Journal*, 1980, *18*, 513–516.

Rogoff, N. *Social structure and college recruitment.* New York: Bureau of Applied Social Research, Columbia University, 1962.

Rosenbaum, J. E. *Making inequality: The hidden curriculum of high school tracking.* New York: Wiley, 1976.

Rosenbaum, J. E. Social implications of educational grouping. In D. C. Berliner (Ed.), *Review of Research in Education* (Vol. 8). Washington, D.C.: American Educational Research Association, 1980.

Rosenholtz, S. J., & Wilson, B. The effect of classroom structure on shared perceptions of ability. *American Educational Research Journal*, 1980, *17*, 75–82.

Rubin, Z. *Children's friendships.* Cambridge, Mass.: Harvard Univ. Press, 1980.

Rutter, M., Maughan, B., Mortimore, P., & Ouston, J. *Fifteen thousand hours: Secondary schools and their effects on children.* Cambridge, Mass.: Harvard Univ. Press, 1979.

St. John, N. H. *School desegregation: Outcomes for children.* New York: Wiley, 1975.

St. John, N. H., & Smith, M. S. School racial composition, achievement and aspirations. Unpublished manuscript, Center for Educational Policy Research, Harvard University, 1969.

Sarason, S. B., Davidson, K. S., Lighthall, F. F., Waite, R. R., & Ruebush, B. K. *Anxiety in elementary school children.* New York: Wiley, 1960.

Savin-Williams, R. C. Social interaction of adolescent females in natural groups. In H. C. Foot, A. J. Chapman, & J. R. Smith (Eds.), *Friendship and social relations in children.* New York: Wiley, 1980.

Schaefer, W., & Olexa, C. *Tracking and opportunity.* Scranton, Penn.: Chandler, 1971.

Schlecty, P. C. *Teaching and social behavior.* Boston: Allyn & Bacon, 1976.

Schmuck, R. A. Some relationships of peer liking patterns in the classroom to pupil attitudes and achievements. In M. B. Miles & W. W. Charters (Eds.), *Learning in social settings.* Boston: Allyn & Bacon, 1970.

Schmuck, R. A. Application of social psychology to classroom life. In D. Bar-Tal & L. Saxe (Eds.), *Social psychology of education.* New York: Wiley, 1978.

Schofield, J. W. School desegregation and intergroup relations. In D. Bar-Tal & L. Saxe (Eds.), *Social psychology of education.* New York: Wiley, 1978.

Schofield, J. W. Complementary and conflicting identities: Images and interaction in an interracial school. In S. R. Asher & J. M. Gottman (Eds.), *The development of children's friendships.* New York: Cambridge Univ. Press, 1981.

Schonfeld, W. R. *Youth and authority in France: A study of secondary schools.* Beverly Hills: Sage Professional Papers in Comparative Politics, 1971.

Selman, R. L. Toward a structural analysis of developing interpersonal relations concepts: Research with normal and disturbed adolescents. In A. D. Pick (Ed.), *Minnesota Symposia on Child Psychology* (Vol. 10). Minneapolis: Univ. of Minnesota Press, 1976.

Selman, R. The child as a friendship philosopher. In S. R. Asher & J. M. Gottman (Eds.), *The development of children's friendships.* New York: Cambridge Univ. Press, 1981.

Selman, R. L., & Byrne, D. F. Structural developmental analysis of levels of role taking in middle childhood. *Child Development*, 1974, *45*, 803–806.

Selman, R. L., & Jacquette, D. Stability and oscillation in interpersonal awareness: A clinical developmental analysis. In C. B. Keasey (Ed.), *Nebraska Symposium on Motivation* (Vol. 25). Lincoln: Univ. of Nebraska Press, 1978.

Selman, R. L., Jacquette, D., & Bruss-Sanders, E. Assessing interpersonal understanding: An interview and scoring manual. Harvard–Judge Baker Social Reasoning Project. Cambridge, Mass.: Judge Baker Guidance Clinic, 1979.

Serbin, L., Tonick, I., & Sternglanz, S. Shaping cooperative cross-sex play. *Child Development*, 1977, *48*, 924–929.

Serow, R. C., & Solomon, D. Classroom climate and students' intergroup behavior. *Journal of Educational Psychology*, 1979, *71*, 669–676.

Sewell, W. H., & Armer, M. J. Neighborhood context and college plans. *American Sociological Review*, 1966, *31*, 159–168. (a)

Sewell, W. H., & Armer, M. J. Reply to Turner, Michael & Boyle. *American Sociological Review*, 1966. *31*, 707–712. (b)

Sewell, W. H., & Hauser, R. M. Causes and consequences of higher education: Models of the status attainment process. *American Journal of Agricultural Economics*, 1972, *54*, 851–861.

Sewell, W. H., & Hauser, R. M. *Education, occupation and earnings: Achievement in the early career*. New York: Academic Press, 1975.

Sewell, W. H., & Hauser, R. M. The Wisconsin longitudinal study of social and psychological factors in aspirations and achievements. *Research in Sociology of Education and Socialization*, 1980, *1*, 59–99.

Sharon, S., & Hertz-Lazarowitz, R. A group-investigation method of cooperative learning in the classroom. In S. Sharon, P. Hare, C. Webb, & R. Hertz-Lazarowitz (Eds.), *Cooperation in education*. Provo, Utah: Brigham Young Univ. Press, 1980.

Shellef, L. *Generations apart: Adult hostility to youth*. New York: McGraw-Hill, 1981.

Sherif, M., Harvey, O. J., White, B. J., Hood, W. R., & Sherif, C. W. Intergroup conflict and cooperation: The Robber's Cave experiment. Norman: Institute of Group Relations, University of Oklahoma, 1961.

Sherif, M., & Sherif, C. *Groups in harmony and tension*. New York: Harper, 1953.

Shrauger, J. S., & Osberg, T. M. The relative accuracy of self-predictions and judgments by others in psychological assessment. *Psychological Bulletin*, 1981, *90*, 322–351.

Simmons, R. G., Blyth, D., Van Cleave, E., & Bush, D. M. Entry into early adolescence: The impact of school structure, puberty, and early dating on self-esteem. *American Sociological Review*, 1979, *44*, 948–967.

Simpson, R. L. Parental influence, anticipatory socialization, and social mobility. *American Sociological Review*, 1962, *27*, 517–522.

Singleton, L., & Asher, S. R. Racial integration and children's peer preferences: An investigation of developmental and cohort differences. *Child Development*, 1979, *50*, 936–941.

Slavin, R. E. Student learning team techniques: Narrowing the achievement gap between the races. Report No. 228. Baltimore: Johns Hopkins University, Center for Social Organization of Schools, 1977. (a)

Slavin, R. E. How student learning teams can integrate the desegregated classroom. *Integrated Education*, 1977, *15*(6), 56–58. (b)

Slavin, R. E. Student teams and achievement divisions. *Journal of Research and Development in Education*, 1978, *12*, 39–49.

Slavin, R. E. Effects of biracial learning teams on cross-racial friendships. *Journal of Educational Psychology*, 1979, *71*, 381–387.

Slavin, R. E. Cooperative learning. *Review of Educational Research*, 1980, *50*, 315–342. (a)

Slavin, R. E. Effects of student teams and peer tutoring on academic achievement and time on-task. *Journal of Experimental Education*, 1980, *48*, 252–257. (b)

Slavin, R. E. *Using student team learning* (Rev. ed.). Baltimore: Johns Hopkins University, Center for Social Organization of Schools, 1980. (c)

Slavin, R. E. A policy choice: Cooperative or competitive learning. *Character*, 1981, *2*, 1–6.

Slavin, R. E., & Karweit, N. L. Student teams and mastery: A factorial experiment in urban math-9 classes. Paper presented at the annual meetings of the American Educational Research Association, New York, 1982.

Slavin, R. E., & Madden, N. A. School practices that improve race relations. *American Educational Research Journal*, 1979, *16*(2), 169–180.

Slavin, R. E., Madden, N. A., & Leavey, M. Combining cooperative learning and individualized interaction: Effects on the social acceptance, achievement and behavior of mainstreamed students. Paper presented at the annual meeting of the American Educational Research Association, New York, 1982.

Slavin, R. E., & Oickle, E. Effects of cooperative learning teams on student achievement and race relations: Treatment by race interactions. *Sociology of Education*, 1981, *54*, 174–180.

Slavin, R. E., & Wodarski, J. S. Effects of student teams and peer tutoring on academic achievement, mutual attraction, and student attitudes. Paper presented at the annual meeting of the American Educational Research Association, Toronto, 1978.

Smith, M. Equality of educational opportunity: The basic findings reconsidered. In F. Mosteller & D. P. Moynihan (Eds.), *On equality of educational opportunity.* New York: Vintage Books, 1972.

Smith, R. B. Neighborhood context and college plans: An ordinal path analysis. *Social Forces*, 1972, *51*, 199–217.

Sorensen, A. Talcott Parson's theory of influence. Unpublished paper, Johns Hopkins University, 1968.

Sorensen, A. Organizational differentiation of students and educational opportunity. *Sociology of Education* 1970, *43*, 355–376.

Sorensen, A. The organizational differentiation of students in schools. Paper presented at the National Invitational Conference on School Organization and Effects, San Diego, 1978.

Spady, W. G. Lament for the letterman: Effects of peer status and extra-curricular activities on goals and achievement. *American Journal of Sociology*, 1970, *75*, 680–702. (a)

Spady, W. G. Simple techniques for multivariate analysis. *Interchange*, 1970, *1*, 3–20. (b)

Spady, W. G. The impact of school resources on students. In F. N. Kerlinger (Ed.), *Review of research in education.* Itasca, Ill.: Peacock, 1973.

Stephan, W. G. School desegregation: An evaluation of predictions made in *Brown vs. board of education. Psychological Bulletin*, 1978, *85*, 217–238.

Stephan, W. G., & Rosenfield, D. Black self-rejection: Another look. *Journal of Educational Psychology*, 1979, *71*, 708–716.

Sullivan, H. S. *The interpersonal theory of psychiatry.* New York: Norton, 1953.

Summers, A. A., & Wolfe, B. L. Do schools make a difference? *American Economic Review*, 1977, *67*, 639–652.

Thibaut, J. W., & Kelley, H. H. *The social psychology of groups.* New York: Wiley, 1959.

Tiger, L. *Men in groups.* New York: Random House, 1969.

Tjosvold, D. Alternative organization for schools and classrooms. In D. Bar-Tal & L. Saxe (Eds.), *The social psychology of education: Theory and research.* Washington, D.C.: Hemisphere Press, 1978.

Tuma, N. B., & Hallinan, M. T. The effects of sex, race, and achievement in school children's friendships. *Social Forces*, 1979, *57*, 1265–1285.

Turner, R. *The social context of ambition.* San Francisco: Chandler, 1964.

Turner, R. On neighborhood context and college plans (I). *American Sociological Review*, 1966, *31*, 698–702.

U.S. Commission on Civil Rights. *Racial isolation in the public schools.* Washington, D.C.: U.S. Government Printing Office, 1967.

Verbrugge, L. M. The structure of adult friendship choices. *Social Forces*, 1977, *56*, 576–597.

Verbrugge, L. M. Multiplexity in adult friendships. *Social Forces*, 1979, *57*, 1286–1309.

Walberg, H., & Thomas, S. C. Open education: An operational definition and validation in Great Britain and the United States. *American Educational Research Journal*, 1972, *9*, 197–207.

Waldrop, M. F., & Halverson, C. F., Jr. Intensive and extensive peer behavior: Longitudinal and cross section analysis. *Child Development*, 1975, *46*, 19–26.

Wallace, W. *Student culture: Social structure and continuity in a liberal arts college.* Chicago: Aldine, 1966.

Waller, W. *The family: A dynamic interpretation.* New York: Dryden, 1938.

Walster, E., Aronson, V., Abrams, D., & Rottman, L. Importance of physical attractiveness in dating behavior. *Journal of Personality and Social Psychology*, 1966, *46*, 19–26.

Wang, M. C., & Stiles, B. An investigation of children's concept of self-responsibility for school learning. *American Educational Research Journal*, 1976, *13*, 159–179.

Weigel, R., Wiser, P., & Cook, S. The impact of cooperative learning experiences on cross-ethnic relations and attitudes. *Journal of Social Issues*, 1975, *31*, 219–243.

Weiss, L., & Lowenthal, M. F. Life course perspectives on friendship. In M. F. Lowenthal, M. Turner, & D. Chiriboga (Eds.), *Four stages of life*. San Francisco: Jossey-Bass, 1975.

Weiss, R. S. *Marital separation*. New York: Basic Books, 1975.

Werner, H. The concept of development from a comparative and organistic point of view. In D. B. Harris (Ed.), *The concept of development*. Minneapolis: Univ. of Minnesota Press, 1957.

Westman, G., & Miller, N. Concomitants of outgroup prejudice in desegregated elementary school children. SSRI Research Report, Social Science Research Institute, University of Southern California, 1978.

Wheeler, L., & Nezlek, J. Sex differences in social participation. *Journal of Personality and Social Psychology*, 1977, *35*, 742–754.

Whyte, W. *Street corner society*. Chicago: Univ. of Chicago Press, 1967.

Wicker, A. *An introduction to ecological psychology*. Monterey, Calif.: Brooks/Cole, 1971.

Wilder, D. A. Reduction of intergroup discrimination through individuation of the outgroup. *Journal of Personality and Social Psychology*, 1976, *36*, 1361–1374.

Williams, R. A. *Peer influence vs. peer selection: An attempted separation*. Unpublished master's thesis, University of Wisconsin, Madison, 1981.

Wilson, A. B. Residential segregation of social classes and aspirations of high school boys. *American Sociological Review*, 1959, *24*, 836–845.

Wilson, A. B. Social stratification and academic achievement. In A. H. Passow (Ed.), *Education in depressed areas*. New York: Columbia Univ. Press, 1963.

Wilson, A. B. Educational consequences of segregation in a California community. In U.S. Commission on Civil Rights, *Racial isolation in the public schools* (Vol. 2). Washington, D.C.: U.S. Government Printing Office, 1967.

Witkin, H., Lewis, H., Machover, K., Meisner, P., & Wagner, S. *Personality through perception*. New York: Harper, 1954.

Woelfel, J., & Haller, A. O. Significant others, the self-reflexive art and the attitude formation process. *American Sociological Review*, 1971, *36*, 74–78.

Wylie, R. C. *The self-concept: Theory and research on selected topics* (Rev. ed.) (Vol. 2). Lincoln: Univ. of Nebraska Press, 1979.

Youniss, J. *Parents and peers in social development*. Chicago: University of Chicago Press, 1980.

Ziegler, S. The effectiveness of cooperative learning teams for increasing cross-ethnic friendship: Additional evidence. *Human Organization*, 1981, *40*, 264–268.

Author Index

Numbers in italics refer to the pages on which complete references are listed.

273

M

Maas, H. S., 239, 266
Maccoby, E. E., 43, 61, 119, 182, 266
Machover, K., 207, 272
Madden, N. A., 95, 99, 107, 213, 217, 250, 266, 270, 271
Maehr, M. L., 242, 266
Magnusson, D., 5, 190, 238, 266
Mannarino, A. P., 10, 16, 44, 266
Mannheim, K., 66, 266
Martin, E., 117, 266
Maruyama, G., 209, 213, 214, 264, 266
Maughan, B., 10, 269
Mayhew, B., 31, 266
McArthur, C. C., 68, 266
McCall, G. J., 238, 266
McClelland, D. C., 124, 207, 267
McDill, E. L., 10, 14, 31, 74, 118, 120, 126, 132, 141, 143, 152, 156, 159, 165, 196, 220, 221, 222, 255, 267
McDonald, M., 144, 267
McGarvey, W., 209, 267
McPartland, J. M., 7, 10, 31, 45, 75, 78, 85, 87, 92, 93, 164, 178, 204, 220, 221, 258, 261, 267
Mead, G. H., 44, 199, 267
Meisner, P., 207, 272
Merton, R. K., 242, 265
Metz, M. H., 146, 267
Meyer, J. H., 165, 221, 267
Meyers, C. E., 206, 267
Meyers, D., 14, 165, 267
Michael, J. A., 165, 267
Michaelson, S., 142, 164, 264
Miell, D., 42, 198, 242, 260
Miller, N., 93, 103, 203, 205, 206, 208, 209, 211, 212, 213, 261, 266, 267, 268, 272
Minuchin, P. P., 10, 13, 16, 78, 86, 267
Mischel, W., 207, 267
Montemayor, R., 118, 119, 120, 267
Mood, A., 93, 164, 204, 258
Moreno, J. L., 9, 101, 250, 267
Morgan, D., 31, 138, 268
Morgan, E. P., 37, 142, 145, 268
Mortimore, P., 10, 269
Mueller, E., 10, 268

N

Nelson, J. I., 165, 220, 268
Newcomb, A., 13, 263

Newcomb, T., 15, 122, 164, 166, 168, 169, 170, 171, 172, 173, 193, 223, 268
Nezlek, J., 118, 272

O

Oakes, J., 21, 74, 146, 268
Oden, S. L., 11, 77, 238, 249, 256, 268
Oickle, E., 98, 99, 100, 108, 271
Olexa, C., 35, 134, 138, 269
Orpet, R. E., 206, 267
Osberg, T. M., 203, 270
Otto, L., 165, 196, 255
Ouston, J., 10, 269

P

Padilla, A. M., 202, 257
Parkhurst, J., 16, 39, 44, 262
Parsons, T. W., 6, 40, 116, 224, 228, 268
Patchen, M., 23, 210, 240, 268
Peevers, B. H., 43, 44, 268
Pettigrew, T., 220, 258
Piaget, J., 43, 44, 45, 55, 64, 264, 268
Picou, J. S., 74, 165, 196, 224, 268
Pitcher, B. L., 53, 263
Polansky, N., 173, 266
Pool, I. deS., 91, 147, 268
Pope, B., 51, 268
Porter, J. D. R., 202, 203, 268
Portes, A., 165, 173, 177, 222, 260
Precker, J. A., 169, 268
Preston, A., 207, 259
Putallaz, M., 239, 249, 268

R

Rabbie, J. M., 106, 268
Rafaei, W., 190, 265
Rahe, D., 249, 251, 261
Ramussen, B., 249, 262
Redl, F., 173, 266
Rehberg, R. A., 34, 141, 268
Reisman, D., 239, 268
Reisman, J., 39, 268
Renshaw, P. D., 10, 11, 238, 249, 256, 268
Rigsby, L. C., 10, 14, 118, 120, 126, 132, 143, 152, 159, 165, 221, 267
Riley, R., 220, 258
Rogers, M., 209, 211, 212, 213, 268, 269
Rogoff, N., 165, 269

Subject Index

A

Achievement, influence, 179–182, 183, 185–187, 189, 190–192, 194–195, 198, 202–205

Activity structure, *see* Task structure

Adolescence, 9, 13–14, 16, 39–62, 63–67, 115–130, 196, 198
and loyalty, 64–65

Age, *see also* Developmental patterns
and expanding boundaries, 82–83
and selection patterns, 33, 76–77
and size of group, 119–120

Age-grading, 32–33

Attitudes toward school, influence, 179–182, 183, 185–187, 189, 194–195, 198

Authority structure, 7, 74–92
and adult behaviors, 144
and patterns of friendship, 19

B

Balance theory, 40–41, 58, 59
and reciprocation, 47–50
and stress, 50

C

Classroom organization, 7, 36, *see also* Authority structure; Participation; Reward structure; School organization; Task structure
and cross-race acceptance, 210
and cross-sex choices, 117, 118
versus extracurricular organization, 131–132
and influence process, 229
and peer association, 247–248
and selection, 12, 77–92
and sex differences in reciprocity, 121, 122
and sex differences in selection, 120
and tracking, 145–146
and visibility, 37

Clique structure
and sex differences, 121–122
and similarity, 223

Coaching
effects, 249–250
social skills, 248–250

Cognitive development
and other-perspective-taking, 44, 56–58
and restructuring perspectives, 55–56
and selection, 60–61
theoretical perspectives, 43–44, 64–66

Tracking, *see also* Differentiation; Grouping
  practices
  and adult attainment, 141–144, 147, 161
  and association, 6, 21
  and extracurricular activities, 21, 134–138
  and school organization, 33–35, 141–161,
    169
  scope, 34
  and selection, 134–137, 145, 153–156, 160

and size of friendship group, 120
and socialization, 141–143, 145–146
and student status, 35

V

Visibility
  of student abilities, 37, 93, 131, 137
  and vulnerability to influence, 227